Columbus

Celebrates The Millennium

AN INTERNATIONAL QUEST

Best wishes to
our new friends at
the Well House!,
Frank and Jay Brown
5 August 2001

Produced in cooperation with
The Commission on International Relations & Cultural Liaison Encounters (C.I.R.C.L.E.)
and the Greater Columbus Chamber of Commerce.

Photo by Jim Cawthorne.

Columbus
Celebrates The Millennium
AN INTERNATIONAL QUEST

By Pam Baker
Corporate Profiles by Delane Chappell
Featuring the Photography of Jim Cawthorne and Herb Cawthorne

Columbus Celebrates the Millennium
An International Quest

Produced in cooperation with:
Commission on International Relations & Cultural Liaison Encounters
(C.I.R.C.L.E.)
1200 Brookstone Centre Parkway, Suite 105
Columbus, Georgia 31904
Phone: 706-660-1160/Fax: 706-660-1215

Greater Columbus Chamber of Commerce
901 Front Street
P.O. Box 1200
Columbus, Georgia 31904
Phone: 706-327-1566/Fax: 706-327-7512

By Pam Baker
Corporate Profiles by Delane Chappell
Featuring the Photography of Jim Cawthorne and Herb Cawthorne
Contributing Photographer Steven Duffey

Community Communications, Inc.
Publishers: Ronald P. Beers and James E. Turner
Publisher's Sales Associates: John Lorenzo, Dick Hadley and Dahlia Davis
Acquisitions: Henry S. Beers
Executive Editor: James E. Turner
Senior Editor: Mary Shaw Hughes
Managing Editor: Bonnie Ashley Harris
Profile Editor: Lenita Gilreath
Design Director: Scott Phillips
Designer: Rebecca Hockman Carlisle
Photo Editors: Rebecca Hockman Carlisle and Bonnie Ashley Harris
Production Manager: Jarrod Stiff
Contract Manager: Katrina Williams
Sales Assistant: Annette Lozier
Proofer: Angela Mann
Accounting Services: Sara Ann Turner
Pre-press and Separations: Artcraft Graphic Productions

Community Communications, Inc.
Montgomery, Alabama
James E. Turner, Chairman of the Board
Ronald P. Beers, President
Daniel S. Chambliss, Vice President

Photo by Jim Cawthorne.

Columbus Celebrates The Millennium

Table of Contents

FOREWORD, 9 • PREFACE, 11

CHAPTER 1
~
A Snapshot Perspective - Columbus Today, 12

CHAPTER 2
~
Beginnnings and Endings, 26

*Indian Civilization to the city's founding (52 years after the birth of America)
to its early days through the Civil War and Recovery*

Columbus Regional Healthcare, 46-49
Greater Columbus Chamber of Commerce, 50-51
Synovus Financial Corp./1888, 52-53
Columbus Foundry, 54
Willcox-Lumpkin Co., 55
Swift Textiles, Inc. d.b.a. Swift Denim, 56
David Rothschild Company, Inc., 57
The Hardaway Company, Inc., 58
SunTrust Bank, 59

CHAPTER 3
~
A New Century - A World At War, 60

*1900-1040, post Civil War, WWI, Ft. Benning, the Great Depression,
WWII & Recovery*

Columbus Water Works, 80-81
The Jordan Company/Prudential Jordan Real Estate, 82-83
Royal Crown Cola Company, 84-85
Blue Cross and Blue Shield of Georgia, 86-87
Page, Scrantom, Sprouse, Tucker & Ford, P.C., 88
Tom's Foods Inc., 90
Georgia Power Company, 91
Robinson, Grimes & Company, P.C., 92
Litho-Krome, 93
Columbus Paper Company, 94
Reaves Wrecking Company, Inc., 95

Photos by Jim Cawthorne.

An International Quest

CHAPTER 4

The Modern Era, 96

1950s, 1960s, 1970s, 1980s

St. Francis Hospital, 116-119
The Hughston Clinic, P.C., 120
Rehabilitation Services of Columbus, Inc., 121
Hughston Sports Medicine Hospital, 122
Hughston Sports Medicine Foundation, 123
AFLAC Incorporated, 124-125
Mead Coated Board, 126-127
Johnston Industries, Inc., 128-129
West Chattahoochee Development Council, 130-131
Matsushita Battery Industrial Corp. of America, 132-133
Kodak Polychrome Graphics, 134-135
Industrial Metal Fabricators, 136
TIC Federal Credit Union, 137
Columbus State University, 138
Dolly Madison-Interstate Baking Co., 139
Regions Bank, 140
The Pastoral Institute, 141
Peachtree Mall, 142
J. H. Williams-A division of Snap-on, 143
Weyerhaeuser, 144
Phillips Construction Company, Inc., 145
Cessna Columbus, 146
Columbus Convention & Visitors Bureau, 147
Historic Columbus Hilton, 148
Freeman & Associates Inc., 149
Kysor/Warren, 150
Meacham, Earley & Jones, P.C., 151
SouthTrust Bank, 152

CHAPTER 5

The Millennium Milieu, 154

1990s and Beyond...

Diaz-Verson Capital Investments, Inc., 176
Miramar Securities, Inc., 177
Commission on International Relations and Cultural Liaison Encounters
(C.I.R.C.L.E.), 178-179
Beacon College, 180
Holiday Inn-Center City, 181
Dougherty McKinnon & Luby, 182
River City Orthopaedics, 183
RiverCenter for the Performing Arts, 184

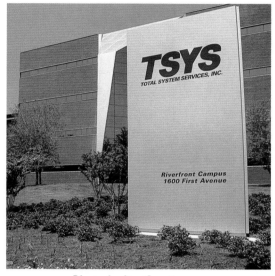

Photo by Jim Cawthorne.

Photo by Herb Cawthorne.

Photo by Steven Duffey.

Foreword

Columbus is a city with much to celebrate, a city with a proud past and a dynamic future. In this beautiful book Columbus indeed celebrates the millennium and the many elements that cluster around this historic point in time. Our spirits are high as we approach the new millennium; we believe the dynamism that has moved the city so positively during recent years will enable us to meet the challenges and opportunities of the twenty-first century.

We celebrate the diversity that constitutes a fantastic pool of skills, talents, and cultural traditions. We celebrate Columbus' unique quality of life that includes excellent facilities for entertainment, recreation, and education. We celebrate the spectacular economic development that provides a firm footing for our roadway to the future. We celebrate the international relationships that connect Columbus, Georgia, to the world. We celebrate the friendship that characterizes life in this city and makes it truly a great place to live, a place where *people* come first.

The Commission on International Relations and Cultural Liaison Encounters, commonly known as CIRCLE, is the primary sponsor of this book, and it is co-sponsored by the Greater Columbus Chamber of Commerce. Both organizations are dedicated to the best interests of Columbus, and it is most appropriate that they should sponsor a publication that tells the remarkable story of this city. The story is one of a textile town on the Chattahoochee riverbank and its transformation over the years into a thriving cosmopolitan city with a diversified business/industrial base where fiber optics and cotton fibers are interwoven in industry and commerce.

The following pages will show that Columbus today is an international city with a highly attractive quality of life. The marks of success are everywhere in this city—from the RiverCenter for the Performing Arts to the high-tech campus of Total System Services; from the Chattahoochee Riverwalk linking the city with its good neighbor, Fort Benning, to Columbus State University; from the South Commons Softball Complex to the Woodruff Farm Soccer Complex; from the hockey arena in the Columbus Civic Center to the Hollywood Connection theater and entertainment complex.

We thank the writers, photographers, editors, and publishers who did such fine work producing *Columbus Celebrates the Millennium, An International Quest*. In it you will find the open secrets of Columbus' success, which are the belief of the citizens in their city—they voted a special sales tax to produce $170,000,000 for many of the recent projects; public/private partnerships in quest of community goals; and leaders willing to do and dare for those same goals. May these pages give the reader not only a look at Columbus, Georgia, but a feel for the motivating spirit that makes this place the great place that it is, one of the very best places on earth!

Bobby G. Peters
Mayor of Columbus

Photos by Jim Cawthorne.

Preface

Having written an earlier book, *Columbus, The Spirit, The People, The Promise*, I was honored to be asked to write another some seven years later. However, this book is not a rehashing of the earlier one, nor is it merely an update. Rather, these pages explore the upcoming millennium as though the passage of time were only one long, continuous story with elements routinely arcing from past to present, and past to future. There are also several references to contemporary and historic world views to lend our story a perspective beyond our own.

Numerous little-known facts about Columbus are included in the history portion of this work that are not found, as far as I am aware, in earlier books written about the city. In fact, the book is so very different from its predecessors, that I asked Billy Winn, noted author and historian and Editorial Page Editor at the *Columbus Ledger-Enquirer*, to examine the piece for accuracy. I also asked several other noted historians to do the same. I am grateful to them all, but to Billy, I send a very special thanks. Without Billy's constant efforts in charting the fullness of our history, and without his personal perusal of this manuscript, this work would be a far more myopic view of the past.

Another special thanks is in order to my faithful brother and diligent researcher, Steven Duffey. Without his help, the information contained herein on world views and millennial fevers, plus a thousand other details would be woefully short on accuracy and color, two elements essential to a good read.

Although this is not an authoritative work, it is a largely accurate popular telling. If there are errors or omissions, such are totally accidental and the reader should blame only me as Billy and Steven are without a doubt two of the most diligent and intelligent professionals in their fields, as are the dozens of others who contributed to this book. Bonnie Harris, the editor, is by far one of the best and most talented editors I have ever known, and I thank her from the bottom of my heart for her wisdom and encouragement! To my mother, Nana Duffey, I am forever in your debt! To my husband, Donnie and our two children, Stephanie and Ben, thanks for your understanding and patience during this—and every other-writing marathon. Thanks to all of you. And, to all of you...

Chattahoochee Falls.

Happy Millennium!!!
Pam Baker

Left: This beautiful bronze sculpture along the Columbus Riverwalk is so lifelike that people often slow down upon seeing it, not wanting to interrupt the concentration of the young artist as she sketches the Chattahoochee Falls. Photo by Jim Cawthorne.

Chapter One

A Snapshot Perspective

Columbus Today

The Columbus Civic Center is an integral part of the city's planned Riverwalk. The beautiful structure sits majestically between Columbus city proper and Ft. Benning. National and international acts regularly appear at the Civic Center, as well as numerous local special events and Cottonmouth hockey games. Photo by Herb Cawthorne.

It is the nature of man to perceive time only in the context of here and now, as though this moment alone is real and permanent. But today is fleeting, and though it may demand our total attention at the moment, it slips into obscurity almost as soon as day slips into night. Here is a glimpse of Columbus on one today out of thousands, suspended in time somewhere in the middle of what once was and what will be. As this was written, all that is in this chapter existed in the now; as it is read, all is past. And so it is with the nature of man and his time.

But know that in this place, in this time… hope did, indeed, spring eternal. It is, or rather was, extraordinary times couched in ordinary days. People got up every morning and headed out to school or work, or church or play, and they moved about with an air of expectation and a lightness of step that comes from hearts secure in their journeys. The economy boomed and labor shortages led to better quality of life for workers from janitor to executive stations. The city appeared in chaotic rubble from the constant building of new public buildings, homes for the various arts, historic preservation sites, and ultra-new office campuses and complexes. Downtown, always referred to with the optimistic term "uptown," went crazy with the fevered frenzy of revitalization and Columbus burst forth as the state's Masters of the Renaissance.

New bridges were built across the Chattahoochee in more ways than one. The much awaited 13th street bridge finally got underway and the old 14th street and Dillingham bridges began to evolve into pedestrian bridges. Phenix City began a massive revitalization effort as well, so the bridges connect two revitalized downtown districts and the connecting spirits rejuvenated hopes for regional economic wins of historic proportions.

The river became a time-loop of its own, morphing from its relatively recent status as a backdoor embarrassment to its former glory of frontdoor beckoner. A flotilla was formed to carry dignitaries and media types down river to remind all of the Chattahoochee's splendor and fragility. The "Hootch" became our pride and joy; the flotilla a modern version of the riverboat trips of old. Columbus looked once again to become the premier stop for water-vessels

Like Christopher Columbus of old discovered new worlds, the city of Columbus today is exploring and creating new horizons, blending its rich heritage with a strong and balanced mix of culture, the arts, and high technology. Photo courtesy of the Columbus Convention and Visitors Bureau.

Columbus is filled with unique architecture and lots of local character as seen here in the Rankin Courtyard. Behind this mysterious door lies a majestic garden that tempts the soul to partake of nature in harmony with city life. Photo by Steven Duffey.

on their way to the Gulf of Mexico and began to plan a new marina to berth the water-bound visitors.

The Riverwalk began creeping north from Ft. Benning up beyond the new Civic Center and around the border of Uptown Columbus and the new Total System Services office campus. The plans are to also border Green Island and perhaps even further north. Public parks are springing from the ground all over the city and major sports are played on the South Commons and the Woodruff Farm Soccer Complex. Regional and national tennis championships were held at Cooper Creek Park and the Cottonmouth hockey team won the Central Hockey League Championship.

Columbus State University (CSU) celebrated its 40th anniversary. It used to be a community college but today it reaches far into the community by operating Oxbow Meadows Environmental Learning Center, the Coca-Cola Space Science Center, and the Columbus Regional Mathematics Collaborative with 26 area school systems among other endeavors. The University is also a prime factor in the RiverCenter, a performing arts center that will house the University's Schwob Department of Music as well. The Intellectual Capital Partnership Program (ICAPP) trained approximately 1200 computer professionals by the end of 1998 and was one of the largest reasons Total System Services

stayed in Columbus. Today CSU is seen as education in action rather than a place for passive study.

The South did rise again… that is to say, South Columbus rose again. Beautification efforts, new parks, a new golf course, Oxbow Meadows Environmental Learning Center, new retail developments, plans for a new Enterprise Zone, and other activities and developments designed to better living standards in the area were well underway and pride among the residents soared again.

City Manager Carmen Cavazza of Olympic fame held town meetings to sort out what kind of city was most desired by the year 2010; mostly he gathered gripes about potholes, potsherds, and ponderings. But, in the end, a plan was drawn up depicting our collective hopes and dreams and there wasn't a doomsayer in sight.

Mayor Bobby Peters became the first two-term mayor in the city's history since consolidation. Peters, a peacemaker and diplomat, provided a steady hand on a city infected with euphoria.

But, it is in the depths of the shadows of the past that the greatest lessons are learned and so the city worked hard to preserve the historic reminders and balance those with the fruits of progress. Heritage and hope, experience and expectation, exist together on brick streets and concrete highways. The cityscape reflects both old and

Mayor Bobby Peters is the first mayor since consolidation to hold two terms. His popularity was so high that he ran for his second term uncontested. Peters is renowned as a consensus-builder and as the main force behind Columbus' renaissance and race cohesion. Photo by Herb Cawthorne.

Columbus Consolidated City Government is people-friendly. Mayor Peters, City Manager Carmen Cavazza, City Council, and all the others keep an open-door policy that has led to unprecedented confidence in government and rapport with the people. Photo by Steven Duffey.

Each year, the Springer Opera House, a National Historic Landmark, reaches over 100,000 people through its innovative arts, education, and historic tourism programs. Over 1800 season ticket holders routinely drive from Atlanta, Macon, Americus, and other Georgia cities to catch a production at the official State Theater of Georgia. The Columbus Challenge and other substantial donations provided the funding for the complete restoration of the Springer at a total cost of $11.3 million. Photo by Jim Cawthorne.

new in its architecture giving the present a sort of crossroads look.

And so this story of Columbus begins in the middle as a place in time where we might anchor our perspective in order to spin time backwards to see where we have been and from whence we came. Then, and only then, are we sufficiently equipped to dare to return to this particular day to watch time spin forward to the millennium and beyond.

Back we go to a time before times, long ago on another day before time took the shape of the written word.... ☞

Columbus State University is seen as education in action rather than a place for passive study. Photo by Brady Rogers.

The Coca-Cola Space Science Center is operated by Columbus State University, a perfect example of CSU's active role in the community. Photo courtesy of the Columbus Convention and Visitors Bureau.

The new Total System Services Campus. Photo by Jim Cawthorne.

Birds eye views of the new Oxbow Creek Golf Course and Columbus State University's Oxbow Meadows Environmental Learning Center, a "natural" learning place for people of all ages. Photos by Jim Cawthorne.

Columbus Celebrates...

Bo Didley performing for an enthusiastic Uptown Jam crowd. Photo by Jim Cawthorne.

The Riverwalk Grand Staircase provides a beautiful setting for the Riverfest fireworks. Photos by Jim Cawthorne.

(Left) Riverfest attracts artists of all types—from potters to painters. Photo by Jim Cawthorne.

J. Alden Weir

Chapter Two

Beginnings and Endings

Each new "end"—whether a sad or a triumphant end—brings about a new beginning. Photo of Julian Alden Weir's painting, Pelham Lane, ca. 1902. Gift of the A. and M.L. Illges Memorial Foundation to The Columbus Museum. Courtesy of The Columbus Museum.

Columbus, Georgia, has always attracted foreigners. The city is like the Holy Grail long sought by the knights of the round table in King Arthur's court; it is a place where no man-group started but where they all stayed at the end of their quests. So the story of the city was, and is, and probably forever will be.

In the beginning… long before Christopher Columbus sailed the sea and even millenniums before that, early man stalked a giant and deadly prey across the Bering Strait some 12,000 years ago or more and ambled over ice and rock for another 2,000 years before their descendants finally arrived here. The future Columbus, Georgia, was then simply a raw and cold chunk of land poised at the rim of the fall line with only a raging Chattahoochee River pointing the way.

The way was treacherous and so was the hunt as the Paleo Indians clung to the high ground and made their way traveling light and fast over the river ridges. It was cold, the kind of cold that seeps to the marrow of one's bones, the kind of cold no one has seen in 10,000 years. As if that were not

bad enough, the cold was wrapped with a wetness in the air that never eased. This was life for early man and it was primal and savage and unforgiving of even the slightest mistake.

The Paleo Indians were highly skilled in the way of the hunt, the lay of the land and the secrets of working wood and stone. They were experts at creating deadly points using crude tools; their precision a matter of life and death… both their own and that of their prey. The resulting workmanship was both beautiful and lasting for the spear points still exist today. A Clovis-type flint point was found by an archaeologist in the Columbus area, in a 1936 excavation at Bull Creek.

It is believed that Paleo Indians did not throw their spears, rather they thrust them into the animal with the combined body weights of multiple men. Killing the giant prey was an extremely risky enterprise. Dealing up close and personal with a raging and wounded wooly mammoth is a task few modern hunters could endure, much less survive.

These prehistoric hunters and their

This dog effigy vase was excavated under the supervision of Mrs. Isabel Patterson in 1936 from a prehistoric Indian site in Columbus. It is on display at The Columbus Museum. Courtesy of The Columbus Museum.

(Right) Early 1700s English bronze sword hilt found by The Columbus Museum at the Creek Indian town site of Coweta Tallassee. Courtesy of The Columbus Museum.

(Opposite) From the time of the Paleo Indians through the centuries to the current space age of today, Providence Canyon, Georgia's "Little Grand Canyon", has been a sight to behold. Photo by Brady Rogers.

Early 1600s Spanish glass trade beads found by the Columbus Museum at an Indian site near Columbus. Courtesy of The Columbus Museum.

The reconstructed interior of a prehistoric Indian house is part of the Chattahoochee Legacy exhibit at The Columbus Museum. Courtesy of The Columbus Museum.

families knew only the dangers of terrain and animal, the fear of cold and night, the endless rumblings of hunger gnawing the gut. Still, for thousands of years, these tough and courageous people followed the trail of the behemoths: mammoth, mastodon, ground sloth, and giant bison. For all those years they survived, all the while molding a primitive beginning for a people yet to come.

Around 8,000 B.C., ice lost ground as the Pleistocene Epoch came to an end and a gradual warming trend began to grace the land. Ice melted, the air warmed and by 6,000 B.C. the air became less humid, the

waters calmer, and the ground drier. The massive beasts of old were replaced by the white-tailed deer, black bear, rabbit, raccoon, fox, and all the other creatures we are familiar with today. Plant life changed from the fodder of prehistoric giants to pines, oaks, hickories, and a variety of gums that are the dominant trees in the forests of now.

The descendants of early man became known as Archaic Indians. The major changes in man are marked by technological advancement in the form of newer projectile point styles and ground stone tools among others. Although the climate had

Flatrock Park has surely witnessed centuries of "Beginnings & Endings." Much of Columbus offers park and greenspace for the enjoyment of residents and visitors alike. Photo by Brady Rogers.

Lithograph portrait of Neamathla, leader of the Creek Indian War of 1836. Neamathla was marched westward in chains from Fort Mitchell on the infamous Creek Trail of Tears. Columbus Museum collection. Courtesy of The Columbus Museum.

common mound-building practice. Their towns stretched across and down both sides of the Chattahoochee River for a hundred miles below the falls. These immigrants/early-Americans were known as the Yuchi, Apalachicola, Muskogulgi, and the Hitchiti when it was necessary to identify them by ethnic grouping.

During the 14th century another group migrated to the area; they were the Muskogean-speakers. According to their own history detailed on buffalo skin, they crossed into Georgia at Coweta Falls and destroyed the inhabitants on the east side of the river. Only two survived the attack and they were followed to the Apalachicola town. The peaceful Apalachicolas struck a deal by offering to share medicines, knowledge, goods, and their king to one group of the invaders called the Cussetas. The remaining half of the invaders, the Cowetas, retreated back across the river: their home would later become known as the "war town" of the middle Chattahoochee confederation and the people known as the Lower Creeks.

In the year of our Lord 1513, Ponce De Leon established the Spanish claim over the region they called Florida. The area was vaguely defined but extended into Georgia's coastal towns and islands. By the 17th century, the Spaniards and the Brits were competing to expand their territories and Georgia was part of the prize. Because the Creeks preferred the guns of the English to the religion of the Spanish, the British held the largest market share in Indian trade from 1702 to 1713. But gaining market share came at a cost of blood and human lives.

Henry Woodward, the most aggressive of English traders from Charleston, eluded the Spanish time and time again as he set about constructing trading posts in Indian-Spanish territory all the way to Coweta Town itself. Governor Don Juan de Cabrera was determined to capture the offending Englishman and end the threat to the Apalachicola province posthaste. He sent all the soldiers he could spare from St. Augustine to join those under the command of Lieutenant Antonio Matheos at San Luis.

Matheos never captured the elusive Woodward even after the brutal torture and interrogation of a captive Coweta. The town of Coweta was deserted when Matheos and his troops descended upon it

stabilized and was similar to what we know today, life was still brutal, harsh, and unrelenting. The first evidence of Archaic Indians found by archaeologists in the original Columbus site was discovered by Southern Research on the site of the new Total System Services, Inc. campus in 1998.

Time churned on and the immigrants, now several generations deep, saw the land as their own and began to gather in larger groups. They built early civilizations, developed social customs from religion to recipes, gathered nuts and plants, and hunted the smaller game with bow and arrow. Around 1000 A.D. there was a booming township below the Coweta Falls. There were hereditary kings, a priesthood, and huge governmental buildings built around and on top of gigantic pyramidal earth mounds. They were called the Mound Builder civilization because their populace was a mix of several ethnic groups united in a confederation by a common religion that was expressed through a and he was furious. That very day Matheos ordered all the chiefs of the Creek confederation to meet with him and reveal the whereabouts of the troublesome English. The Indians refused to tell and so Matheos made good his threat. On January 30, 1686, he burned the towns of Tuskegee, Coweta, and Cusseta. The Indians were left homeless and hungry in the jowls of winter.

The English and the Creeks remained on good terms, a relationship essential to the well-being of the English. So much so that General James Edward Oglethorpe, founder of the colony of Georgia and commander of the British forces in the colony, traveled to Coweta at great personal risk to ensure the friendship with the Creeks would not be weakened by French incursions from Mobile. If the French were to become too chummy with the Indians, the English would be left exposed to the powerful Spaniards. The journey took ten days and Oglethorpe, accompanied by only 20 soldiers, had to survive a fever and the passage through territory frequently terrorized by unfriendly bands of Choctaw Indians and Spanish patrols. He arrived in the area just south of present-day Columbus on August 8, 1739, signed a treaty with the Creeks, and returned to Savannah. The Creeks had not promised in the treaty to fight to defend the English; rather, they promised not to fight against the English in any future wars.

Before Oglethorpe could finish his return trip, war broke out and hundreds of Indian warriors came to the aid of the English even though they were under no obligation to do so. Without Indian assistance, the fledgling colony of Georgia would not have survived the three-year War of Jenkin's Ear.

Though the Indians and the English continued as friends for many years, it was not an easy, trusting relationship. By the time of the American Revolution, the Americans were ready to end the alliance. It all began when the Creeks, who remained officially neutral in the war, played roles on both sides thereby permanently angering the Georgia frontiersmen, many of whom became political leaders in the new state. Another major factor in the break-up was that the Americans had discovered the profits of cotton and openly coveted the very ground on which the Indians lived.

In 1802 Georgia and the federal government came to an agreement whereby the state would relinquish all claims to the northern territories of Alabama and Mississippi. In return, the U.S. would remove all Indians from the remaining state territory and move the state's boundary to include the western banks of the Chattahoochee River.

The federal government built a road west from Milledgeville along the old Lower Creek Path to Cusseta Town, which today is Lawson Airfield at Ft. Benning. Later extended, the road crossed the river near the spot where Oglethorpe crossed in 1739 and where the esteemed naturalist, William Bartram, crossed in the opposite direction in 1775. General John Floyd built a fort on the high ground west of this crossing and named it for Governor David Mitchell. The fort was abandoned soon

General James Edward Oglethorpe, founder of the colony of Georgia. Courtesy of Georgia Department of Archives and History.

Engraving showing the site of Columbus before the sale of lots in 1828. Photo courtesy of the Columbus Museum.

(Opposite) Creek descendant and educator, Jim Sawgrass, travels throughout the Southeast with his informative program and interesting exhibits and displays. Photo by Jim Cawthorne.

after the War of 1812. The facility was revived in 1824 and became the headquarters for a U.S. garrison and Indian agency. It kept the name Fort Mitchell.

In March 1825, a distinguished foreign visitor set out on the Federal Road bound for Cusseta as a guest of the Creek nation. His name was Marquis de Lafayette, the French hero of the American Revolution. The elderly Frenchman was on a grand tour of all the American states. He was met with much fanfare from Americans and Indians alike, but the most touching welcome was delivered by the aged Creek, Chief Little Prince, on the parade ground of Fort Mitchell. The chief delivered an emotional and eloquent speech extolling his happiness to meet Lafayette in person. Little Prince then explained the ancient substitute for war—the stick ball game and a game was played as a special honor for the distinguished guest.

Unbeknownst to the men, women, and children who were there, this would be the last time the Creeks would entertain a foreign visitor on their ancient homeland. Even as the ball sped across the ground and the players positioned their sticks hoping to take control and score the point, the Second Treaty of Indian Springs was ratified by the

United States Senate. Within three weeks from the game's final score, events would unfold at Milledgeville, expelling the Creeks and Yuchis from the domain of their ancestors forevermore. The Indians were eventually driven from Georgia and many would die from exposure and hunger on the infamous Trail of Tears.

As all the eons before have witnessed, each new end, no matter how tragic, brings about a new beginning. It is not whether one is better than the other, for time does not know of justice, only of change. The old cannot help but give way to the new, the new cannot help but to become old. History is born in terms of now and recorded as days long gone. But whatever is written, it cannot be finished until time itself stops.

It was a dramatic birth, this town called Columbus. The year was 1828. The air crackled with excitement, children noisily ran and played, and the sound of hammers thumped the air as people built buildings on wheels in preparation of moving them to whatever lot they would win at auction. It was only a path on a side of a river with precious few existing buildings (there primarily because of trade with the Indians), yet all the onlookers could see were acres

A Jim Sawgrass exhibit of the European items sought and traded for by the Native Americans. Photo by Jim Cawthorne.

went on to accomplish great things. He is best known as the president of the Republic of Texas, a position he would hold much later. But here he was in Columbus at the town's unveiling, documenting an event he thought nothing less than monumental. The town and its birth affected him, and he affected it.

The first manufacturing facility was built and operated within the city's first year of existence. The City Mills, built by Seaborn Jones, marked the first use of Chattahoochee water-power by Columbus industry. Steamboats arrived even earlier. The *Fannie*, the *Steubenville*, the *Robert Emmett,* and the *Virginia* all made their way via New Orleans, steaming along the Gulf Coast to the port at Apalachicola, Florida, and from there upstream. From the beginning, Columbus attracted permanent residents of sufficient wealth to cause builders, craftsmen, doctors, entrepreneurs, lawyers, statesmen, and others to follow. The city was never a primitive settlement in the typical frontier tradition. Still, the city had a certain frontier mentality situated as it was on the state's western frontier, directly across the river from Indian territory and an utter absence of white man's law.

The trading town formed by the Georgia legislature and dubbed Columbus hit the ground running. From the founding of the city until shortly after the turn of the 20th century, many American records were set in thoroughbred horse racing at the track where the South Commons softball fields are today. George Odum, one of the most famous jockeys in American racing history, was from Columbus and rode to fame at the turn of the century.

When it came to exploding growth, all bets were on and the odds were in favor of Columbus. By 1833 Columbus' first bridge across the Chattahoochee was built by John Godwin. It connected the city with Girard, now called Phenix City, Alabama. From the time it was opened, Columbus collected tolls from users… a profitable venture since there was pleasure to be had on one side of the bridge and booming commerce and respectability… sort of… on the other.

There were hangings, shootings, and plundering befitting the wild west on both sides of the river. It was, however, a rough and tumble time, in which a lot was taken, little given, and law was pretty much a joke. The city stood as a monument of civility but its people had some catching up

and acres of hope. Stagecoaches, travelling wagons, carts, gigs, the whole line of wheeled vehicles, moved about in an endless, disorderly array of arriving townspeople to a place that didn't even have a name yet. Bakers, grocers, doctors, and lawyers were all in line for a place to call home. Speculators evaluated the land prior to auction, seeking fortune over farmland.

In the latter part of May of the same year, Mirabeau Buonaparte Lamar began publishing a one-page weekly newspaper called the *Columbus Enquirer*. Lamar had come to resume his journalism career when his employer, Governor Troup, lost reelection. Lamar, like many who would hail from Columbus at some point in their life,

(Above) Mirabeau Buonaparte Lamar, founder of the Columbus Enquirer who later became the President of the Republic of Texas. Many Columbusites have had a lasting impact on the development of the nation and on the contemporary international scene. Photo courtesy of the Ledger Enquirer.

(Left) Modern day Columbus Ledger-Enquirer building retains all the charm of its early days as the town's one-page weekly, the Columbus Enquirer. A Knight-Ridder paper, it has captured two of the six Pulitzer Prizes earned by Georgia newspapers, one in 1926 and the other in 1955. Photo by Steven Duffey.

to do. A full scale war with the Creeks refocused the residents on a common threat. Tension had built for years among the Creeks, but their more recent hardships from displacement had brought the situation to a hard boil.

In 1836 the Indians raided Georgia and slaughtered families that had settled on former tribal lands in Alabama. By May, hundreds of refugees fled from Alabama to Columbus. Forty-four Georgia militia companies, totaling 950 troops, marched into town to subdue the Indian threat. Federal troops supported by Alabama units converged at Ft. Mitchell and, under the command of General Winfield Scott, rounded up the hostiles. Creeks, Yuchis, and Hitchitis were chained and either walked or were transported by steamboat from Montgomery to Fort Smith, Arkansas.

They died by the hundreds on the crowded vessels and the cruel march. By July 1836, the Indian problem had been terminated and life resumed the pattern of former days until constant rain brought about a flood that carried away the bridge in 1841. John Godwin built its replacement, and trade across the river and down the river continued undisturbed for years.

By 1853, Columbus was a bustling commercial and manufacturing center with a population of 6,000. The first railroad was completed and three fabric and yarn mills operated on the waterfront, Coweta Falls Factory, Howard Manufacturing Company, and the Eagle Mill. Inside the city was another mill, The Variety Works, which had two sawmills and machinery for making wooden tubs, buckets, and churns as well as producing 7,000 feet of dressed

Teen skaters enjoy a fruitful history at Heritage Park, which connects the Historic District to the Coca-Cola Space Science Center. The centerpiece of the new park is a miniature replica of the Chattahoochee River complete with a waterfall. The falling water turns a turbine, and below the falls floats a mini-replica of the W.C. Bradley steamboat. Photo by Steven Duffey.

was of many minds regarding the conflict. Some agreed with the South's desire for economic freedom; others agreed with the North; still others simply hated state government and wanted to be left to their frontier ways. Columbus was not terribly unusual in this regard; after all, the Civil War is well-known as the war between brothers, a phrase intended literally more than figuratively.

A good example of how the Civil War tore both the city and families apart was the experience of a prominent family named Mott. Colonel R.L. Mott was a successful businessman and a Union supporter through and through. He flew the Union flag throughout the War, yet he was well-liked and well-respected by the townspeople. He certainly was not the only openly known Union sympathizer. His home still stands today and is part of the Total System Services, Inc.'s new campus. Mott's son, however, was a distinguished Confederate soldier who served the cause with passion and fortitude. Such was the way of the war throughout the South.

Columbus was home to Martin J. Crawford, Raphael Moses, Alfred Iverson, Henry Benning, and numerous other persons prominent in the Confederate government and/or its army. The city was also the most important manufacturing center in the Confederacy south of Richmond, Virginia. Columbus supplied the rebels with everything from shoes to rifles. The Confederate Naval Yard was also here and it produced both a gunboat and an ironclad. There were, then, many good reasons for General James Wilson and his Union troops to take the city of Columbus on Easter Sunday in 1865. But, the timing of the offense is thought to have more to do with the suspicion of federal intelligence officers that Jefferson Davis and the Confederate Cabinet were on their way to Columbus after the fall of Richmond.

Many have ventured a guess as to why Davis may have been headed to Columbus but no one seems to know for sure. If he was intending to escape to South America, the city, with its access to the Gulf of Mexico via the Chattahoochee and Apalachicola Rivers and its gunboat and ironclad supplied to the hilt with munitions, would seem to be a good choice for such a maneuver. Then again, perhaps Davis and the Cabinet were simply trying to buy time.

lumber daily. The E.T. Taylor & Company was a steam-operated manufacturer of 1,000 cotton gins each year. And, the Rock Island Paper Company turned out 2500 pounds of writing, printing and wrapping paper per day, consuming 3000 pounds of rags in the process. The Washington and New Orleans Telegraph Company reached Columbus from Macon in 1848, opening the city to the rest of the nation. The census of 1850 reflected the immigrant status of the residents; there were natives of Ireland, Scotland, England, France, Germany, Denmark, Switzerland, Italy, and most of the seaside states as well as from Ohio, Tennessee, and Louisiana, and 44 free blacks presumed from Africa. All was well in the land of cotton for the song "Dixie" had not yet been written to the tune of war.

Cotton was the catalyst for much of the tension that brewed in Columbus. It was a principal reason for initial white settlement, one of the main reasons Indians were driven out of the area, and it was the bottom-line of the Civil War. Cotton meant money and money meant war . . . .

January 21, 1861, Georgia officially withdrew from the Union and several Columbusites played a major role. The city

How the feds found out about Davis' alleged plans is a much easier guess: The Peace Society. This seditious underground movement was a group of Southern men, several of whom were men from Columbus and the surrounding area, dedicated to ending the war.

The Peace Society included traitors and spies who infiltrated the rebel army and sought to disrupt and destroy the Southern war effort by any means possible. Members swore a bloody oath and used secret signs to identify themselves one to another. A special handshake was used in most encounters. A soldier on the battlefield gave a sign by carrying his gun with the muzzle pointed to the right. A mounted officer would tip his sword to the right. If there were no sword or gun at hand, a man would hold a stick with both hands and then throw it away to the right. An answering member would then touch a lock of hair on the right side of his head and then pretend to pull something from it and throw it away to the right.

The society was in full operation in Columbus and the surrounding area. Its members openly bragged of causing, at least

in part, the surrender of Vicksburg and the Confederate defeat at Missionary Ridge. Both were battles heavily manned by Columbus soldiers. The society was also discovered to be extremely active in encouraging desertion from the Confederate army and in promoting resistance to conscription among the populace. Its members may have also been responsible for the fall of Columbus.

On that Easter Sunday of 1865, no one knew that President Lincoln had been fatally shot on Good Friday by a man well-known in Columbus as John Wilkes Booth who had performed as an actor in Columbus, or that the Civil War had officially ended. A few days earlier the overcrowded city had been flooded with additional refugees, black and white, from the fall of Montgomery. There was much confusion and debate as to where Wilson's troops were headed next. By April 15 they knew for certain that the massive calvary was headed toward Columbus. A feeling of dread consumed them because the federal forces seemed undefeatable. Still the city defenders plotted and planned and erected additional defenses as best they could in

The City Mills, built by Seaborn Jones, marked the first use of Chattahoochee water-power by Columbus industry. Photo by Brady Rogers.

Westville, a living history village representing daily life in the 1850s, is just a short drive from Columbus in Lumpkin, GA. Photo by Jim Cawthorne.

Downtown Columbus in the 1860s. Courtesy of Columbus State University Archives.

the time that they had. Little did they know that someone was going to reveal their secrets-down to the last-minute details-to the Union army before the battle would actually begin.

Most able-bodied men from Columbus were away serving on other fronts leaving the defense of the city to the very young, the old, the wounded here to recover, and the inexperienced. The shortage of manpower was beyond desperate. There is a telegram on record written by the Confederate field commander here requesting authority from Richmond to allow the enlistment of free blacks and slaves who had volunteered. It was sent just eight days before the battle. Ironically, while the city did everything in its power to muster every man it could find, the war was over and Columbus men were walking home from every direction. They knew nothing of the impending danger to their kinfolk and homes. And... they would not arrive in time to do anything about it.

So it was that the great city of Columbus fell a week after the South's surrender after a brief but bloody skirmish. General James Wilson was given command of the city and he ordered the burning of any and all properties that may be of service to the Confederate Army. Fires raged as citizens looked on in horror. The gunboat Jackson was set afire and left to float downstream like an ancient funeral pyre. In quick succession, the flames licked the Haiman Factory, the Navy Yard, the Iron Works, the Eagle Mill, the Quartermaster Depot, the paper mill, and an estimated 100,000 bales of cotton. The industrial area of the city lay in total ruin. Smoldering embers glowed through the night punctuated randomly by the occasional shell exploding in either the ruined arsenal or the smoking Naval yard. As lost as the Confederate cause itself, the city was reduced to rubble and the people wondered if recovery would ever truly be possible.

Reconstruction did follow. For all practical purposes, it was completed by

A familiar sight in mid-nineteenth century Columbus. Photo courtesy of Columbus State University Archives.

The end of an era... Photo by Herb Cawthorne.

1871. While things did get better, the getting there hurt. Terrible racial incidents marked the period, including the shooting of Major John Warner by black troops and the mysterious murders and disappearances of many black men. The murder of a white Republican, George W. Ashburn, who was shot by a mob of whites, brought national attention to the town. The anger, hurt, and frustration birthed by a hateful war spilled over in a dozen dastardly ways. The city struggled to survive its own revival. In true Southern style, sheer tenacity restored the city and carried it beyond its former glory.

Once an agricultural and textile king in the U.S., Columbus evolved into a modern city brimming with intellectual capital. Still, cotton was responsible for much of the city's early wealth and the rise of many influential families in Columbus.

SWIFT MANUFACTURING CO.
MANUFACTURE CHECKS, PLAIDS, COTTONADES AND THE CELEBRATED MITCHELINE BED SPREADS.

THE GEORGIA HOME INSURANCE CO.
THE NATIONAL BANK OF COLUMBUS.

G.J. PEACOCK.
CLOTHING MANUFACTORY.

M. JOSEPH
WHOLESALE DRY GOODS.

CHATTAHOOCHEE BANK

COLUMBUS
ICE & REFRIGERATING CO.
ARTIFICIAL ICE. KANSAS CITY DRESSED MEATS.

THE LARGEST COTTON & WOOLEN MILLS IN THE SOUTH.

EAGLE & PHENIX MANUFACTURING CO.

WHOLESALE & RETAIL DEALERS IN
STEAM GAS & WATER PIPE AND FITTINGS.
GEORGIA STEAM & GAS PIPE CO.
1005 BROAD STREET.

COLUMBUS IRON WORKS CO.
FOUNDERS & MACHINISTS.
STRATTON'S ABSORPTION ICE MACHINE.

GARRETT & SONS,
IMPORTERS, JOBBERS & MANUFACTURERS OF
CIGARS & TOBACCO.
SHIELD CIGAR FACTORY.

COLUMBUS STEAM BAGGING CO.

PERSPECTIVE MAP OF
OLUMBUS, GA.
COUNTY SEAT OF MUSCOGEE COUNTY.
1886.
POPULATION: 25000.

30 Joel Bush, Hardware.
31 Mulford & Epping, Insurance Agents.
32 Frank McArdle's Residence.
33 Chancellor & Pearce, Clothiers and Merchant Tailors.
44 J. L. Pollard, Grocer.
45 Wells & Curtis, Boots and Shoes.
46 G. W. Dillingham's Residence.
47 Wm. Beach & Co., Hardware.
48 C. A. Redd & Co., Wholesale Grocers.

49 Soule, Redd & Co., Brokers and Real Estate Agents.
30 Mayor C. Grimes Residence.
31 Hunt Bros., Wholesale Grocer.
32 Frazer & Dozier, Hardware.
33 Merchant's and Mechanic's Bank.
34 B. T. Hatcher's Residence.
35 J. J. Slade, Slades School for Boys.
36 A. M. Elledge, Proprietor, Monumental Marble Works.

37 Springer Opera House, Thos. M. Foley, Manager.
38 O. S. Jordan's Residence.
39 Frazer & Dozier, Hardware.
40 T. S. Young & Co., Grocers.
41 W. B. Slade, Attorney and Counsellor at Law.
42 J. S. Garrett's Residence.
43 G. Gunby Jordan's Residence.
44 C. Schomburg Jeweler.

47 Cooper & Newsome, Wholesale Grocers.
46 H. P. Everett, Stoves and Tin Ware.
47 Thos. Gilbert, Printer, Binder and Paper Box Manufacturer.
40 O. C. Johnson, Red Star Stores.
49 J. A. Kirven & Co., Dry Goods.
50 J. C. Ready, Real Estate Agent.
51 Swift & Hamburger.
52 Planter's Ware House.
52 C. A. Lovelace & Co., Merchant Tailors and Gent's Furnishers.

53 T. S. Spear, Watches and Jewelry.
54 Ville Reich.
55 Thos. Chaffin, Books and Music.
56 A. A. Williams, Photograph Gallery.
57 Wittich & Kinsel, Watches and Jewelry.
58 Chas. Phillips, Residence and Grounds: Rose Hill.
59 G. E. Thomas, Jr., Attorney at Law.
60 R. P. Sommerkamp, will be with Loeb & Kaufman.

These vestiges of the Civil War play their part in keeping us ever-mindful of the time in history when our young nation endured and survived an internal battle that threatened its very existence. Photos by Jim Cawthorne.

The Chattahoochee has been a wellspring of hope and prosperity for the people of Columbus from the early Indians to modern-day riverfront developers. Its glistening waters have flooded many a mind with dreams, and many a heart with peace and calm—and hope. Photo by Steven Duffey.

When Columbus erected its first "hospital" in 1841 near the Chattahoochee River's lower steamboat wharf, it was little more than a place of respite for the critically ill. From these modest beginnings has come one of the most comprehensive and

Columbus Regional Healthcare System

sophisticated networks of health and medical care in the Southeast: Columbus Regional Healthcare System. Columbus Regional stands poised to meet the challenges of the twenty-first century with an unprecedented array of health, medical, and educational services for citizens throughout west Georgia, east Alabama, and beyond.

Established in 1986 as a not-for-profit diversified health services holding company with The Medical Center as its flagship, Columbus Regional has evolved into a comprehensive health services network providing over 700 inpatient hospital beds in two states, more than 300 long-term care beds, retail community pharmacies, a mobile health unit serving rural and medically underserved areas, a thriving network of home health care services, cancer care and specialized women's health care,

The Medical Center offers highly specialized services available nowhere else in the region.

physician practices in Georgia and Alabama, an ambulatory care center that houses the Southeast's oldest and largest family practice residency program, and a health plan meeting the business needs of west Georgia.

Columbus Regional has earned the pinnacle of recognition in health care: Accreditation with Commendation from the Joint Commission on Accreditation of Healthcare Organizations. It was the first Joint Commission-accredited health network in Georgia outside Atlanta. In addition, all of Columbus Regional's eligible facilities and services hold full Joint Commission accreditation.

From yesterday's place of respite to today's thriving network of advanced service and care, Columbus Regional is here, planning and working for a safer, healthier community for us all—today and tomorrow.

Hospital Services
The Medical Center

The Medical Center has spanned the better part of two centuries to become the region's most comprehensive acute care facility. The Medical Center's comprehensive offerings include many services that are available nowhere else in the region. As the region's trauma center, The Medical Center provides life-saving emergency care and response for the 13-county west Georgia area. The Medical Center is the region's leading provider of intensive care services, and with its Level III neonatal intensive care unit and specialized neonatal transport team, offers the hope of life to critically ill newborns throughout 21 counties in southwest Georgia and Russell and Lee Counties in Alabama.

The hospital's family-based service offering begins in Your Family Birth Place, where every day, families welcome their tiny new

additions in a comfortable, like-home setting where labor, delivery, and recovery take place together in a single room. The region's only high-risk nursery stands ready nearby, with support for infants who need intensive care. The Medical Center continues its long-standing tradition of service to families and children with the area's only dedicated inpatient pediatric program and pediatric intensive care unit.

The Amos Cancer Center at The Medical Center offers the most advanced diagnostic and treatment capabilities in the region. A testament to AFLAC founder John B. Amos, the Amos Cancer Center provides complete chemotherapy and radiotherapy services and a dedicated inpatient hospital unit just steps away. Services include precise external beam radiotherapy, and advanced internal radiation therapies, such as brachytherapy, iodine "seed" implants, and a high-dose afterloader that targets cancers of the prostate, lung, uterus, and other areas. The Center also is home to the region's only gynecologic oncology program, specializing in diagnosis and treatment of cancers of the female reproductive system.

A skilled team of professionals in more than a dozen advanced medical disciplines works in concert to carry out each patient's custom treatment protocols and provide compassionate support to patients and their families.

The Center's credentials include certification as a Comprehensive Community Cancer Center by the American College of Surgeons and membership in the National Association of Community Cancer Centers. In addition to services at The Medical Center, the Amos Cancer Center offers chemotherapy and oncology services at the Phenix Regional Cancer Clinic at Phenix Regional Hospital.

Recognizing the special health care needs shared by women, The Medical Center provides a complete program of diagnostic care and information at the Breast Care Center, offering a cadre of mammographic imaging and breast health counseling services, risk evaluation, and preventive education in a private, relaxed setting. The Breast Care Center is the sole area provider of leading-edge nonsurgical stereotactic biopsy, a less invasive biopsy technique.

As an active participant in the advancement of medical education, The Medical

Center is home to one of the oldest and most respected family practice physician training programs in the Southeast. The Medical Center also serves as a hub of continuing education to hundreds of practicing physicians. As the area's only teaching hospital, The Medical Center also is home to the School of Radiologic Technology and a Pharmacy Doctoral Residency program, and serves as a clinical training site for nurses, respiratory therapists, emergency medical technicians, and other allied health professionals.

Phenix Regional Hospital

Phenix Regional Hospital provides vital medical and surgical care to residents of Russell County and portions of Lee County in Alabama. The only hospital in Russell County, Phenix Regional Hospital provides acute care services, 24-hour emergency care, outpatient surgery, and a growing program of maternal and pediatric services. Through Phenix Regional Hospital, Alabama neighbors enjoy quality medical care through the dedication and support of the entire Columbus Regional family of services.

Unmatched Pediatric Care for Children

In addition to inpatient care, Columbus Regional provides an array of outpatient care and support for children from the Columbus Regional Pediatrics Center, a thoughtfully planned facility designed to provide general pediatric care, speech and language therapy, X-ray, laboratory, and pharmacy services in a vibrant setting designed to make "going to the doctor" a little less frightening. After-hours care is available for minor pediatric emergencies.

Respected and Accomplished Physicians

Every family needs a relationship with a trusted, hometown physician. Through Columbus Regional's alliances with talented physicians, area residents can enjoy the advantages of a "group practice without walls" through Regional Physicians Group, which represents a broad spectrum of medical disciplines. All physician members are board-certified or board-eligible in their respective disciplines and gain added strength through affiliation with Columbus

Phenix Regional Hospital has served Russell County, Alabama, for more than 50 years.

Regional's Joint Commission-accredited health network. Area citizens also can receive care in a unique teaching environment at The Family Practice Center, where resident physicians in The Family Practice Residency Program deliver quality primary care services alongside skilled faculty physicians and build upon their skills in a modern practice environment.

Cost-Effective Services for Business and Industry

Managing health care costs is critical to business success. Columbus Regional continues its tradition of response through Evergreen Medical Group LLC, a partnership between Columbus Regional, area physicians, and other health providers designed to help businesses of all sizes provide top-quality care to employees and contain health care costs with preventive, primary, and specialty care, as well as extended and home care services, billing and claims processing, wellness education, and work-site safety programs. Local ownership gives Evergreen Medical Group added effectiveness and flexibility in meeting employers' needs,

Columbus Regional offers the region's only pediatric center dedicated to the health and medical needs of children.

from the practice setting to the workplace. As an added enhancement, Regional Occupational Medicine offers businesses a comprehensive program of health and safety services, such as physical and disability examinations, drug and alcohol screenings, workers' compensation injury treatment, audiometric and pulmonary function testing, occupational health and corporate medical consultations, immunizations, and job surveillance.

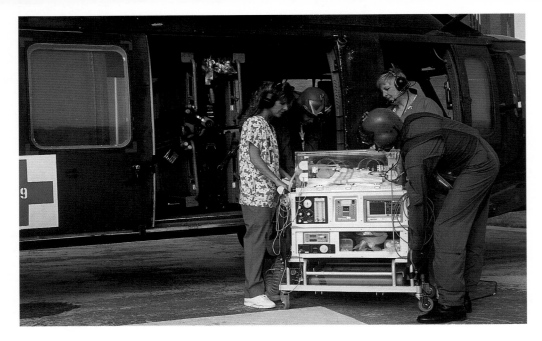

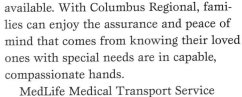

The Medical Center provides the region's only advanced obstetric service, high-risk nursery, and neonatal transport program.

A Continuum of Extended and Home Care

The elderly or disabled can benefit from the wide range of care available through Columbus Regional, at a level just right for their needs. Columbus Regional's specialized transitional care unit at Hamilton House and Rehabilitation Center helps patients in making a healthy transition home with rehabilitative services following discharge from the hospital.

A complete spectrum of medical and home care, including diagnostic and health maintenance testing, nursing and assistant care, home delivery and intravenous medication administration, and physical, speech, and occupational therapy, is designed to help patients stay healthy and at home, where they want to be. When living at home is no longer an option, families can turn to extended care provided through Hamilton House Nursing and Rehabilitation Center and Azalea Trace Nursing Center located in Columbus, within minutes of The Medical Center, and Marion Memorial Nursing Home in Buena Vista, serving Marion and Talbot Counties. These facilities also offer outpatient physical, speech, and occupational therapy. Hospice services also are available. With Columbus Regional, families can enjoy the assurance and peace of mind that comes from knowing their loved ones with special needs are in capable, compassionate hands.

MedLife Medical Transport Service offers emergency and nonemergency medical transport to patients in west Georgia. Phenix Ambulance Service provides emergency medical transportation in east Alabama.

Extending Health to the Community

People need quality health care no matter where they live. Columbus Regional is answering the need through a variety of unique, collaborative efforts with community officials and area health providers designed to extend care and improve health status in underserved areas. Residents in outlying counties receive vital primary care and health education services at local medical clinics through the Community Healthcare Network. The CommunityCare mobile health unit reaches thousands in the region with basic health services. And in a unique local partnership with the Columbus Consolidated Government, public health, and family service providers, Columbus Regional has helped create the Health and Human Services Center to afford access to essential public health, mental health, medical and family services, outpatient care, and ancillary services to those in need.

Reaching out through health and wellness education remains a priority, as thousands are touched each year with programs that include prenatal education classes, convenient "Lunch & Learn" sessions, disease prevention and management programs, senior adult programming, and a variety of ongoing support groups for patients, families, and friends. In addition, thousands throughout the region can get access to the latest health news and information through "Health Connections," Columbus Regional's free telephone-based information system, and the bimonthly *Health Connections* publication, along with television and Internet programming.

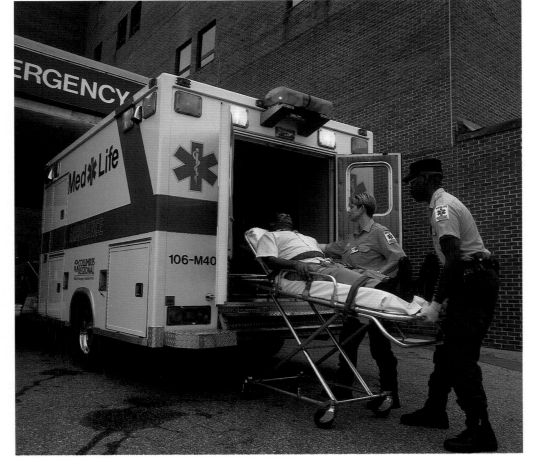

MedLife Medical Transport Service offers emergency and nonemergency medical transport to patients in west Georgia. Phenix Ambulance Service provides emergency medical transportation in east Alabama.

Strength Through Stewardship

The Columbus Regional family puts its belief in community stewardship to action, giving thousands of volunteer hours and financial support in an untold number of ways. The Columbus Regional Medical Foundation supports scholarships for students in nursing and radiologic technology and generates regional support for the Amos Cancer Center, the Ronald McDonald House of West Georgia, and the Children's Miracle Network. Members of The Medical Center Auxiliary continue the philanthropic spirit, giving generously of time and money in support of clinical, patient care, and educational programs.

As one of the largest private employers in the region and the provider of nearly 96 percent of all indigent and charity care delivered by Columbus's acute care hospitals, Columbus Regional not only has a significant impact on the area's economic base, but also serves as a wellspring of hope and well-being for all area citizens.

The Twenty-first Century and Beyond

"The twenty-first century holds revolutionary change for health care and Columbus Regional," said Larry Sanders, FACHE, chairman and chief executive officer.

"But what will not change are our core-value commitments to compassion and community stewardship. Since our founding nearly two centuries ago, we have served this region well by focusing on

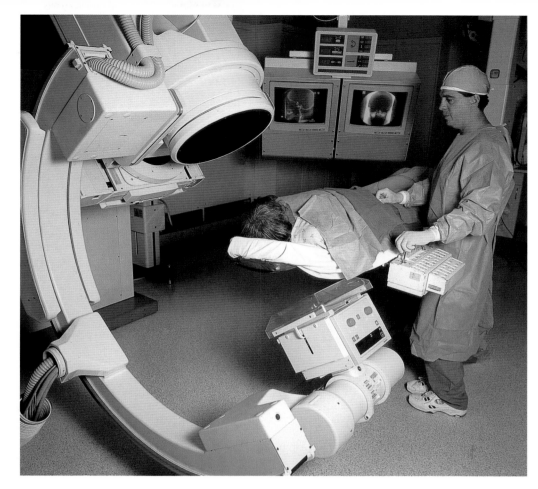

our core values; they've stood the test of time and will continue to guide us in the twenty-first century.

"The days of autonomy for hospitals and health systems are over," said Sanders. "In the days ahead, the consumers of health services will be increasingly involved in maintaining health and in treating their diseases.

"As technology and research reduce the need for large inpatient facilities, we will need each other to survive and prosper, and to return benefit to the community.

"As always, we will vigorously pursue

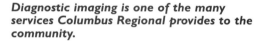

Diagnostic imaging is one of the many services Columbus Regional provides to the community.

ways to enhance our facilities to make health care more accessible, more convenient, and ever higher in quality. We'll continue to seek out innovative, mutually beneficial partnerships with physicians, other providers, and the business community.

"Above all, we'll continue in our quest to improve the manner and spirit in which we deliver our services, always remembering the real reason we're here—service excellence and the delivery of quality, compassionate care." ⟡

The CommunityCare mobile health unit provides health, medical, and educational services to medically underserved communities in the region.

One of a business's measurements of success is the numbers on the bottom line. The Greater Columbus Chamber of Commerce measures success by other sets of numbers. It looks at the number of volunteers who support its programs, at the

Greater Columbus Chamber of Commerce

capital investment of new and existing industries, at the number of new jobs created, and at the number of prospective companies that look at the community. The Columbus Chamber also looks at the number of public/private partnerships that improve the quality of life in the region.

Whatever the measure, the Greater Columbus Chamber of Commerce hit the jackpot in the last decade of the twentieth century. Since 1988, the Columbus region has experienced unprecedented growth, adding in excess of $1.5 billion in capital investments and more than 31,084 new jobs. As a result, the region's economic base, industry mix, quality of life, and even its attitude have been enhanced as businesses such as Pratt and Whitney, Matsushita Battery Industrial, and Kodak Polychrome Graphics located here, and other companies, such as Total System Services, Char-Broil, and AFLAC Inc., expanded, providing new jobs for local

More than 200 community leaders, school administrators, parents, and students joined the Greater Columbus Chamber of Commerce to celebrate the success of the Partners In Education program. Students performed several instrumental pieces to thank their business partners for their contributions to the program and area schools.

Governor Roy Barnes signed HB 177, better known as the "Taxpayers' Bill of Rights," during his visit to Columbus April 29, 1999. HB 177 will require a rollback of property taxes when higher reassessments occur. Pictured are (front, left to right) Governor Roy Barnes, Senator Ed Harbison, Representative Maretta Mitchell Taylor, Representative Carolyn Hugley, and Representative Tom Buck.

employees and attracting employees from around the country and the world.

It is the spirit of a community that sets it apart, and nothing exemplifies the spirit of Columbus better than the number of new public/private partnerships. The list of collaborative projects is long, beginning with the city's procurement of the Super Ball Classic games in 1995 that drew athletes and spectators from around the world and its winning the Women's Fast Pitch Softball venue in the 1996 Summer Olympic games. The Olympic flame fueled other community enhancements, including the Coca-Cola Space Science Center, the South Commons Sports Complex, Oxbow Meadows Environmental Learning Center, the Chattahoochee Riverwalk, and the RiverCenter for the Performing Arts.

The spirit of cooperation extends beyond the boundaries of Muscogee County. In 1997, the Chamber took a proactive role in helping create the Valley Partnership, a public/private economic development initiative of Chattahoochee, Harris, Marion, Muscogee, Talbot, and Taylor Counties. Designed to promote the region and recognizing the value of cooperation, the partnership assisted with the building of speculative buildings, created a joint development authority, and marketed itself as a regional entity throughout the state.

The Chamber, through its staff and

volunteers, is a major player in making things happen in the community. Thousands of volunteers—the heart and soul of the organization—have logged countless hours supporting the programs and initiatives of the Chamber, including a series of campaigns such as "Columbus on the Move" and "M-Power Columbus." Through the generous donation of their skills, talents, and financial support, volunteers make it possible for the Chamber to conduct its mission of promoting a probusiness and procommunity environment for Columbus and the region.

The Chamber staff provides leadership to the community by focusing on economic development strategies, providing support to education, addressing the needs of small and minority businesses, reinforcing relationships with the military, and enhancing marketing approaches.

Among a multitude of tasks, the Economic Development Division of the Chamber promotes the region to

Chamber representatives discuss Columbus's progress with state leaders at a luncheon in Atlanta.

prospective companies, puts together company-specific incentives to encourage companies to locate in the region, and helps meet the expansion, training, and labor needs of existing industries. It also works with existing businesses with special needs.

The Economic Development Committees include the Commercial Development Committee, which works with commercial prospects and assists in expansions and relocations of commercial and retail enterprises; the Property Development Committee, which oversees the construction and sale of speculative buildings and helps in the leasing and sale of sites; and Corporate Office Development, which works with existing and new white-collar industries, tracks office space availability, and assists in infrastructure development for office projects and labor training for high-technology environments. Economic Development also includes the Industrial Recruitment and Retention Committee, which focuses on strategies to provide a positive business climate for new and existing businesses; the Labor Committee, whose job it is to monitor training, wages, labor/management issues, and education, and to conduct an annual labor forum; the Quality Council, which provides insight into team building and empowerment, process improvement, and customer satisfaction; and the Riverfront Development Committee, which focuses on the development along the river.

The Governmental Affairs Committee works on issues between the public and private sectors, tracks and aggressively supports the passage or defeat of local, state, or national government issues affecting business, and hosts the annual "Courtyard Campfire," an event that honors elected officials.

The Military Affairs Committee serves as a liaison between Columbus and Fort Benning as well as supports the military in various undertakings. It was, for instance, involved in a land exchange between the city and the post and was instrumental in helping the post win numerous awards. The relationship that exists between the post and the community is so viable that it was one of the deciding factors in the U.S. Army's naming Fort Benning the "Best Army Installation in the World" numerous times.

The Community Relations Committee coordinates Leadership Columbus, Leadership Columbus Alumni, the Inter-City Leadership Conference, the Intra-City Study Groups, and the Chamber Foundation.

The Workforce Education Literacy Development Committee supports the Columbus Literate Community Program; the Manufacturing Industry Academy; the Partners In Education partnerships; the Service Industry Academy, the first in Georgia; and the West Georgia School-to-Work apprenticeship program.

Recognizing that small businesses create more than 80 percent of the jobs in the community, the Chamber is committed to an active program focusing on the needs of businesses with less than 50 employees. Of special interest to small businesses are the Professional Consultants Program, the Small Business Trade Show, and an annual regional procurement conference. On the drawing board is a one-stop shop for small businesses that is designed to take some of the hassle out of start-up. Recognition of small business is provided by the Small Business Giant award.

The Chamber also provides educational and networking programs related to workplace issues, develops marketing materials, and sponsors Eye Opener Breakfasts, Fun Lunches, Business After Hours, and Crime Stoppers.

It also coordinates the Business Against Drugs (BAD) Program, the first such program in the state and the model for a drug-free workplace program statewide. The Minority Mentoring Program pairs a minority business owner with a recognized business leader for purposes of learning and mentoring.

The Chamber has a long history of community service. Its lineage dates back to 1845, when a coalition of businesses created the Columbus Board of Trade to look after the city's business interests. It was incorporated in 1890 and changed its name to the Columbus Chamber of Commerce in 1914. The name was changed to the Greater Columbus Chamber of Commerce in 1997, when it broadened its scope to include a regional perspective.

As the clock ticks off one millennium and another begins, numbers will continue to tell the story of the Columbus Chamber. "In the future, I see a more finely tuned focus on who we are and what we are all about," F. Michael Gaymon, Chamber president said. "We'll be bolder in staking out that claim with an increased intensity on the measurement of where we can make the biggest impact, and then, go about doing it." ➔

TheChamber's Business Against Drugs program, together with Muscogee County School District and McDonald's, encouraged more than 3,000 area seventh graders to say no to drugs during the "Drug Free . . . You and Me" conference.

S Synovus Financial Corp. takes seriously its stewardship of the rich legacy of integrity, character, and business philosophy set by its founders more than 100 years ago. By guarding those ideals, this multifinancial services company with $10.5

Synovus Financial Corp.

billion in assets has experienced a history of financial stability and growth that placed it on the *Standard & Poor's 500 Index* of the best-performing companies in 1997. And its unwavering dedication to its team members prompted *Fortune* magazine in 1999 to name Synovus the "Best Company to work for in America."

Synovus began its banking tradition in 1888 with the formation of two state-chartered banks in Columbus—Third National Bank and Columbus Savings Bank. The two banks merged in 1930 to form Columbus Bank and Trust Co. Known for its innovative spirit, CB&T has often led innovations in the financial industry. It offered a charge card in 1959, before other charge cards came on the scene. CB&T recognized the need for computer operations in 1965, and in the 1970s became the first bank in Columbus to offer automated teller machines and electronic

Knowing the value of hometown connections and people-to-people banking, Synovus Financial leaders decided that all banks in its corporate family would be decentralized and run by leaders in their own communities.

fund transfer system services.

In 1972, CB&T leaders created CB&T Bancshares, now called Synovus Financial Corp., as a one-bank holding company, with plans to add more companies as soon as banking regulations allowed. It didn't take long. In 1976, the Georgia Legislature passed the multibank holding company bill, and CB&T Bancshares became the first holding company to act by filing an application to acquire the LaGrange Banking Co. in LaGrange, Georgia, and Commercial Bank in Thomasville. Today, Synovus has 36 banking affiliates in Georgia, Alabama, Florida, and South Carolina. Columbus Bank and Trust remains its flagship bank with deposits of $1.5 billion.

Knowing the value of hometown connections and people-to-people banking, CB&T Bancshares policymakers decided that all banks in its corporate family would be decentralized and run by leaders in their own communities. Despite trends to the contrary, Synovus stood by its philosophy of decentralization and local leadership and reaped the benefits provided through this personal touch to banking.

Synovus Technologies, Inc. facilitates and accelerates the use of technology in the company, assists in the development of new banking products and services, and oversees bank data-processing services.

As consumer needs have changed, so has the company. There is perhaps no better example than Total System Services, Inc. (TSYS), a CB&T spin-off that is now one of the world's largest credit, debit, commercial, and private-label card-processing companies. Total System started as a backroom data-processing operation for credit cards issued by CB&T. It did such a good job that Landmark Bank of St. Petersburg, Florida, asked CB&T to provide it the same service. Recognizing that there might be a market for credit card data-processing services, CB&T wrote THE TOTAL SYSTEM®, the first bank software that allowed credit card operations to handle both MasterCharge and Bank Americard transactions. By 1975, TSYS was processing card transactions for banks in five states. Business exploded and Total System Services went public in 1983.

TSYS provides card-processing services to organizations in the United States, Puerto Rico, Canada, and Mexico, representing more than 110 million cardholder accounts.

Synovus still owns 80.8 percent of the company. Headquartered in a new $100-million campus on the Columbus riverfront, Total System provides card-processing services to organizations in the United States, Puerto Rico, Canada, and Mexico, representing more than 110 million cardholder accounts.

Total System has ranked among *Forbes* magazine's "200 Best Small Companies in America" for more than 10 years straight. Now Total System is on the Forbes' Honor Roll, a distinction held by only one other company.

As barriers that limited banking services crumbled, CB&T Bancshares was ready. In 1985, it entered the broker/dealer and investment services industry with the acquisition of Calumet Financial, a full-service brokerage firm that is now Synovus Securities, Inc.

The year 1989 was a milestone for the holding company. First, its name changed from CB&T Bancshares to Synovus Financial Corp., a name that represented a regional focus. Synovus is derived from *synergy,* meaning the interaction of separate components such that the total is greater than the sum of its parts, and *novus,* meaning usually of superior quality and different from the others. That year Synovus stock was first publicly offered for trade on the New York Stock Exchange. Synovus Data Corp. was formed to provide banking technology support for Synovus

companies. This company merged with Synovus Technologies in 1998 and now facilitates and accelerates the use of technology in the company, assists in the development of new banking products and services, and oversees bank data-processing services.

Even more diversification occurred in the 1990s, as the holding company formed

other divisions: Synovus Mortgage Corp., to offer mortgage services throughout the Southeast; Synovus Trust Company, to offer trust, risk management, and other service products; and Synovus Service Corp., to provide consistent administrative services to Synovus companies.

The key to Synovus's success in the age of megabanks is a focus on creating value—for shareholders, for customers, for team members, and for the community. As the financial services industry evolves to meet changing consumer needs, Synovus has responded with new services and products designed for its customers' changing lifestyles. To meet demands of the next century, Synovus has created The New Bank, a one-stop shop that focuses on all the bank's core operations—from automation to retail sales, customer marketing, training, and small business services. It has invested in its team members by providing training opportunities, including the new Leadership Institute at Synovus, a series of initiatives designed to encourage growth and personal development and prepare Synovus team members to become leaders in the new millennium. ✦

Synovus Financial Corp. takes seriously its stewardship of the rich legacy of integrity, character, and business philosophy set by its founders more than 100 years ago.

Millions of Americans cast their lot with Columbus Foundry every time they get behind the wheel of their automobiles. But few people know about this unsung hero of automotive safety. The foundry designs and manufactures automobile safety parts such

Columbus Foundry, L.P.

as steering mechanisms, brakes, and suspension systems that are found on vehicles manufactured by Chrysler, Ford, Honda, General Motors, Mercedes, BMW, and others. The company manufactures 100,000 tons of ductile iron castings each year.

One of the largest foundries in the United States, Columbus Foundry employs 700 at its 250,000-square-foot facility located on 26 acres on Northside Industrial Boulevard. An extensive research and development program, along with a committed workforce and state-of-the-art technology, has made the company a leader in

Columbus Foundry designs and manufactures automobile safety parts such as steering mechanisms, brakes, and suspension systems that are found on vehicles manufactured by Chrysler, Ford, Honda, General Motors, Mercedes, BMW, and others.

its industry. Its contributions to the industry include developing the commercial ductile iron process, building the first shell foundry in the United States, developing the modern water-cooled cupola melting furnace, and installing the country's first impact molding line.

The foundry, a heavy metal industry in what was formerly a textile mill town, has a rich and colorful history. The company is descended from the Columbus Iron Works, which was founded in 1853. During its early years, it manufactured cast iron goods, agricultural implements, and industrial and building supplies. During the War Between the States, the company manufactured primarily boilers and steam engines for Confederate gunboats. In 1862, the government leased the facility, converting it to the C. S. Naval Iron Works. From 1880 to the 1920s, the Iron Works manufactured Stratton ammonia-absorption ice machines. After the turn of the century, the Columbus Iron Works manufactured the iron water pipes used on Manhattan Island. In 1925, the W. C. Bradley Co. acquired the Iron Works and began manufacturing circulating heaters, pot-bellied stoves, and horse-drawn farm implements. In 1949, it made its first cast iron outdoor grill.

In 1965, the Iron Works was closed and a new facility was built in north Columbus to manufacture gray and ductile iron castings. George W. Mathews Jr. and other investors bought the foundry in 1971, changed its name to Columbus Foundries Inc., and converted its operations exclusively to the production of ductile iron castings. Its name was changed to Columbus Foundry, L.P. in 1997.

In 1984, Columbus Foundry formed Intermet Corporation, a holding company that was to become its parent company. Intermet Corp., the world's largest independent foundry company, manufactures and machines

One of the largest foundries in the United States, Columbus Foundry employs 700 at its 250,000-square-foot facility located on 26 acres on Northside Industrial Boulevard.

iron and aluminum castings for the automotive and industrial markets. A publicly traded company with revenues of $814 million, Intermet has 23 locations in North America and Europe.

Columbus Foundry, which adds $30 million to the local economy, works diligently to be a good corporate citizen, spending millions each year on environmental collection systems that comply with EPA and OSHA regulations. Its employees are active in the community and support many worthwhile charitable organizations. The company is involved in the Partners-in-Education Program, providing worthwhile learning activities and support to Carver High School.

The melting furnaces at Columbus Foundry will be bright and hot as the company forges into the future with a $30- to 50-million investment, said General Manager Robert Bridges. "We have plans to expand by 50 percent our production capability as we approach the new millennium. The work is there."

Though its name isn't stamped on its products, Columbus Foundry will continue in its role as an innovator in the ductile iron casting business to ensure the company's continued growth and success. ➛

When it comes to the saga of American insurance history, a Columbus company helped write the book. For four generations, the Willcox-Lumpkin Co., a family-owned independent insurance agency, has provided insurance coverage for the citizens of the community for everything from ferrying cotton down the Chattahoochee River to natural disasters to fender benders.

The company, founded by DeWitt Fisk Willcox in 1848, is the oldest insurance agency in Georgia and one of the oldest in the country that has been continuously owned by the same family. It specializes in property and casualty insurance. Willcox, born in 1820 and educated at Yale University, was one of the South's insurance pioneers. Known first as D. F. Willcox, Agent, the firm later became D. F. Willcox & Son, D. F. Willcox & Co., and since 1924 it has been called the Willcox-Lumpkin Co. Today, Frank Lumpkin III, the great-great-grandson of DeWitt Willcox, is president of the company, carrying on the traditions and high principles which guided his ancestors.

Willcox's daughter Katherine married Frank Gilmore Lumpkin. On the night their son was born, Lumpkin died at age 36 of injuries sustained in the War Between the States. Frank Grieve Lumpkin grew up under his grandfather's tutelage and began working in his insurance office at age 15. On his grandfather's death, Frank, age 23,

Willcox-Lumpkin Co., founded by DeWitt Fisk Willcox in 1848, is the oldest insurance agency in Georgia and one of the oldest in the country that has been continuously owned by the same family.

assured him, "Grandpa, I'll take care of everything."

The young man had his work cut out for him. Selling a Yankee product in the heart of the Confederacy was hard enough, but Lumpkin also found the company had been mismanaged by someone his grandfather had brought in as a partner. Not only did he have to put the firm back on sound financial footing but he also had to take over its day-to-day operations. In those days everything—the policy, the forms, the daily reports, the registry, and the monthly and annual reports—was handwritten. It was a long, slow process, but Frank Lumpkin, with a handful of committed employees, built Willcox-Lumpkin into one of the most important agencies in the South.

Lumpkin's son, Frank Lumpkin Jr., graduated from the University of Georgia and was a veteran of World War II. A major in the 709th Tank Battalion, he served from the invasion of Normandy to the battle of Huertgen Forest. Returning to the insurance business, he became president on his father's retirement.

From its horse-and-buggy days to the twenty-first century, the company has partnered with some of the most reputable insurance companies in the country, including in earlier years the Hartford Fire Insurance Co. and Travelers Insurance Co. More recently, because of changes in the industry, it has focused on providing insurance coverage for its clients from regional and national companies such as Commercial Union, Southern Mutual Insurance Co., Unisun Insurance, Auto Owners Insurance Co., and Progressive Insurance Co.

Today, Frank Lumpkin III follows in the footsteps of his forefathers at the firm located at 200 Thirteenth Street. But he works in an office they wouldn't recognize, except for old framed handwritten contracts and a wall of ancient filing cabinets. Computers replaced handwritten ledgers.

Electricity did away with gas lights. But Lumpkin has kept the hallmark of the company—personalized service provided by caring employees. And they'd recognize his commitment, "Grandpa, I'll take care of everything." ❖

Willcox-Lumpkin Co.

Frank Lumpkin III follows in the footsteps of his forefathers at the firm located at 200 Thirteenth Street.

From blue jeans to designer apparel, Swift Denim is known throughout the textile industry as the premier denim manufacturer. Basic denim. Stone-washed denim. "Peach-finished" denim. Black denim. White denim. All kinds of denim.

Swift Denim Inc.

Swift's history of innovation has made it the world's leading manufacturer of denim. In October 1990, an advertisement for Swift appeared on the cover of *America's Textiles International (ATI),* a trade magazine for the textile industry. The ad wasn't there to sell denim; it was there to make a point. The ad is a picture of East Berliners on the Berlin Wall, tasting independence for the first time, all wearing denim. The caption reads: "Denim . . . with freedom of

The diversity and innovation of Swift's fabric is represented by the colors available, as well as the numerous denim products in the marketplace.

choice, it's the fabric of choice." The photograph represents a country expressing its desire to be better. That is a key reason why Swift bought the photograph; not only does the photograph demonstrate the wide recognition of denim, but it also represents Swift's posture as a player in the global marketplace.

Swift appeared on the cover of *ATI* again in February 1998, this time as the winner of ATI's 1998 Award for Innovation. Swift's innovations include developing Soda Pop Denim, an environmentally friendly denim made from recycled two-liter soda bottles and cotton fibers; increasing the focus on the top-of-the-line ring-spun fabrics; developing a blacker black denim, one that stays black, retaining its fabric color; and establishing a methodology for matching customer color needs as well as delivering a quality product without delay.

Swift's product development and marketing groups have been instrumental in placing denim in new and unique markets, such as in dog beds, nuns' habits, automobiles, apparel, home fashions, umbrellas, and endless more.

The threads that make up Swift's history are richly hued. The company was founded in 1882 as Excelsior Mill at a plant on First Avenue. A year later it moved into a new plant on Sixth Avenue and changed its name to Swift Manufacturing Co. for three of its five founders, who were Swifts. In 1967, the name was changed to Swift Textiles Inc. to better reflect its product line in a more global economy. It was bought by Montreal, Canada-based Dominion Textile in 1975 and operated as Dominion's largest business unit. In 1996, the name changed again, this time to Swift Denim. In 1997, Dominion,

Swift maintains a high degree of visibility in the market.

including the Columbus plants, was bought by Polymer Group Inc. of Charleston, South Carolina. The company changed hands again in 1998, when it was acquired by Galey & Lord Inc., a Greensboro, North Carolina, manufacturer of fabrics for casual and work wear.

With customers including leading merchandisers such as Levi Strauss, Calvin Klein, Tommy Hilfiger, Ethan Allen, Wrangler, Eddie Bauer Home, The Gap, Ralph Lauren, JCPenney, and Land's End, Swift operates manufacturing and distribution facilities in Columbus; Erwin, North Carolina; Drummondville, Quebec, Canada; North Africa; and a joint venture with J. G. Summit in the Philippines. It has sales offices throughout most of the world.

In Columbus, Swift operates two plants employing 1,400. The Sixth Avenue plant, in operation since 1883, manufactures and dyes yarn and houses administrative offices. The Boland plant, built in 1980 and named for former Swift Chairman John A. Boland Jr., produces thousands of yards of denim each day from yarn made at the Sixth Avenue plant.

The company's spirit of innovation, commitment to continuous improvement, and responsiveness to customers' needs positions Swift to remain a leader in denim manufacturing well into the millennium. Swift's world-class manufacturing technology, product development, and people will ensure that it stays there. ➷

For four generations, the Rothschild family and textiles have been woven intricately together like a fine Jacquard pattern. Today, the company manufactures and markets upholstery fabrics to major furniture manufacturers and decorative fabric distributors in this country and overseas with showrooms in High Point, North Carolina, and Los Angeles, California. The home office of this 112-year-old business is located in Columbus, Georgia, and the mill in North Carolina. Rothschild fabrics can be seen on furniture in homes and hotels all over this country.

The family legacy started with David Rothschild, a German immigrant who, in 1886, founded the original wholesale dry goods and notion business in Columbus. Traveling on dusty dirt roads by horse and cart, its sales force sold to the small town stores within a limited radius of Columbus.

David's sons, Irwin, Maurice, and Jac Rothschild, continued the business. The advent of the automobile brought paved roads, which made larger towns more accessible and rang the death knell for many crossroad country stores. With these stores gone, so was much of their market. To face this twist of fate, Irwin Rothschild found a new product and a new focus for the company in the 1930s—contract weaving of popularly priced upholstery fabrics. The company contracted with local textile mills to weave its upholstery fabrics and later bought Cherokee Mills in Acworth, Georgia, to weave its own tapestries.

The family tradition continued into the third generation. After serving in World

War II, Irwin's sons Norman, David II, Irwin Jr., and Jac's son, Benno, joined the business and opened sales offices and warehouses across the country. Showrooms were opened in all major furniture markets managed by Irwin Jr. in California, David II in North Carolina, Benno in Chicago, and Norman in Texas.

In 1980, the family sold its weaving mill to Reigel Textile Corporation of Greenville, South Carolina. However, David II, who had worked in the family business since he was a boy, bought the print converting part of the company and kept the David Rothschild Company alive.

After college two of David II's sons, Walter and David III, representing the fourth generation, came into the business. Walter moved to North Carolina and, in 1991, started a new upholstery mill in Reidsville to put the company back into manufacturing. As the business grows, the mill continues to expand, and now the company weaves all of its own upholstery fabrics.

Today, David II is chairman of the board; Walter is president and manages the mill. Irwin Rothschild Jr. is vice president of West Coast sales, and David III is in charge of the decorative fabrics outlet store in Columbus.

The future looks bright for the company, Rothschild says. Technology that allows computers to generate designs and run the looms has provided a major breakthrough in textiles. Today, the mill has the most modern machinery, which permits the company to compete in the world marketplace. In an industry of giants, the company is a niche player with its original designs and tradition of personalized service.

The company's best assets are not found on its balance sheets. They are its people: their dedication, their willingness to adapt

to meet changing business conditions, their talent to design fabrics that world markets want, and the family's commitment to keep the family business intact for future generations. ❧

David Rothschild Company, Inc.

The David Rothschild mill is located in North Carolina, producing Rothschild fabrics that can be seen on furniture in homes and hotels all over the country.

The David Rothschild Company, located on Broad Street in Columbus, is shown here sometime before 1895.

The new 18-mile Chesapeake Bay Bridge expansion does more than span the mouth of the bay, linking Norfolk to Virginia's Eastern Shore. For The Hardaway Company, it bridges an illustrious past and a promising future.

The Hardaway Company

Shown here is the construction of the Thompson S. Baker Cement Plant in Newberry, Florida, for Florida Rock Industries, Inc.

The $200-million project is the last bridge the company built, the grand finale to more than 100 years of building public sector bridges and highways. The Hardaway Company, headquartered in Columbus, historically takes on projects ranging from $5 million to $100 million. The company is one of the "Top 400 Contractors" in the country on *Engineers News-Record's* annual list.

The company, under the leadership of President Mason H. Lampton, is redirecting its focus toward private sector industrial construction. The move allows the company to do what it does best—manage projects that require the unusual. Using the design-build model, where a design and construction team work together on projects from concept to completion, The Hardaway Company's new focus includes projects like the $40-million Florida Rock Industries, Inc. cement plant in Newberry, Florida.

Founded in 1886 by Benjamin Hurt Hardaway Sr., The Hardaway Company has been one of the Southeast's leading construction companies since its inception. The family-owned company, which employs 500, holds a reputation for excellence. Among its most remarkable projects were the Sunshine Skyway Bridge across Tampa Bay, the Oroville Dam in California, Georgia Power Company's first nuclear power plant, and the International Concourse at Hartsfield International Airport.

Standard Concrete Products, Inc.

A changing marketplace led The Hardaway Company in 1996 to divest itself of a portion of its internationally known construction business and allowed it to expand into a growing market—the manufacture of concrete products such as pilings, girders, and beams.

The Hardaway Company bought Gary Concrete Company in Augusta, Georgia, and two other plants in Savannah and Atlanta, and created a new company called Standard Concrete Products, Inc. The management team of The Hardaway Company also manages Standard Concrete, which employs 350.

In 1997, Standard Concrete Products bought the Tampa Prestress Division from The Hardaway Company, giving the new company the capability of manufacturing structural products that are the concrete equivalent to steel. The prestressed concrete products, which The Hardaway Company has manufactured since 1952, are used in parking garages, on bridges, and on structures.

Standard Concrete Products' Atlanta plant, which sits on 14 acres in northwest Atlanta, produces more prestressed concrete girders for Georgia, Alabama, North Carolina, South Carolina, and Tennessee than any other supplier.

The Savannah plant, located on 32 acres with access to deep water for barge transportation, produces prestressed concrete products for projects in Georgia, South Carolina, and North Carolina.

The Tampa plant is located on 33 acres surrounded on three sides by deep water for barge transportation. The plant produced rails for the Venetian Causeway in Miami; beams for the new National Football League Tampa Stadium for the Tampa Bay Buccaneers; and inverted tee-beams for the Universal Studios Parking Garage, the largest parking garage in the world.

A construction boom in the Southeast bodes well for Standard Concrete as it approaches the millennium, Lampton said. "We're looking to acquire more plants in the concrete product area, and we're looking to develop new products through research that will utilize the high strength concrete."

Pictured is the first girder being swung into place on the Craven County, North Carolina, Neuse River Bridge Project in New Bern, North Carolina. All prestressed concrete products for this project were produced in the Savannah, Georgia, plant of Standard Concrete Products, Inc.

Vision and service are indispensable qualities of the SunTrust Bank organization. They define its purpose and give it meaning. Although some aspects of the vision may change as times change, the core beliefs on which it is built do not change—they are timeless. More than anything else, customers care about the quality of service they receive. SunTrust's commitment is to be accessible and responsive at all times. For more than a century, SunTrust Bank, West Georgia has remained true to its vision—growth through service.

SunTrust is the oldest national bank chartered in Columbus. Founded as Fourth National Bank in 1892, it has served the financial needs of families and businesses for generations. The parent company, SunTrust Banks, Inc., believes in decentralized management, which means it operates under a local board of directors with local decision-making authority. This allows SunTrust to offer both its personal and commercial customers the best of everything—access to the resources of one of the nation's premier financial service companies and the ease of working with hometown folks whom you know and have trusted for years. It's simply how SunTrust has done business in the past and how it will continue to do business in the future, because it works.

Although it's important to see where SunTrust has been, growth and forward thinking are the keys to its vision. SunTrust's merger with Crestar Financial Corporation has created the tenth largest banking company in the United States, with assets of more than $88 billion. This continued growth has enabled it to provide the very best in products and services to customers.

Locally, through SunTrust's branch network, Publix In-Store Banking Centers, and over 40 SunTrust ATMs throughout the west Georgia and east Alabama areas, it has increased the level of service to its customers. Nationally, through 1,094 branches in Georgia, Alabama, Florida, Tennessee, Virginia, Maryland, and the District of Columbia, SunTrust serves over 3.3 million customers—one at a time, of course.

Growth through service—the way in which SunTrust accomplishes this continues to evolve—but its commitment does not waiver. Through the development of new products, assertive marketing, expanded avenues for customers to access services, and a commitment to an old-fashioned hometown smile, SunTrust is poised for success into the next millennium. ◆

SunTrust Bank

Vision and service are indispensable qualities of the SunTrust Bank organization.

Chapter Three

A New Century

A World at War

Fort Benning's "Iron Mike." Photo by Jim Cawthorne.

Arrival of the 20th century in Columbus was greeted by the familiar optimism characteristic of the city's founders and the folks then living on the banks of the Chattahoochee. The city had far outgrown the ambitious 1200-acre rectangle laid out by surveyor Edward Lloyd Thomas into its first streets, commons, and 614 half-acre lots. In less than 75 years the city had spread like a forest fire to the north and to the east.

The city seemed to defy any label of the day. One could just as easily call it a river town as a mill town, but even if you were to use both names, much of the city would be left undefined. Columbus was a bustling mix of a diverse people engaged in numerous activities that sometimes appeared, quite comically, in contrast rather than in harmony. For example, the ears of a traveler in the lower downtown area were often assaulted by the discordant tunes played simultaneously on the one end by steamboat whistles and on the other by mill whistles. The cosmopolitan nature of the city came from a distinctive character bred

of people of all races and kinds whose mix of cultures, cuisines, and ideas led to a happy chaos of progress. The cacophony of sounds, smells, and flavors bounced and reflected from the constant building to the hallowed halls of churches. The scene would have made even Norman Rockwell chuckle in childlike delight.

The city was very neat and orderly from its wood-frame row tenements to its sprawling mansions to its perfectly square town blocks and incredibly straight streets. Everywhere you looked, the city was clean . . . much as is the practice in present-day Europe. There were shops and small mercantile and service establishments of every kind. Many were in two-story buildings where the shop was on the ground floor and the proprietor lived above on the second floor. Several had porches that covered the sidewalk and were decorated with potted flowers and shaded by vines or awnings—also reminiscent of the southern European cities from which many had recently come.

Hints of Europe were not the only

The car was a true symbol of the new century, not just in Columbus but all over the United States.

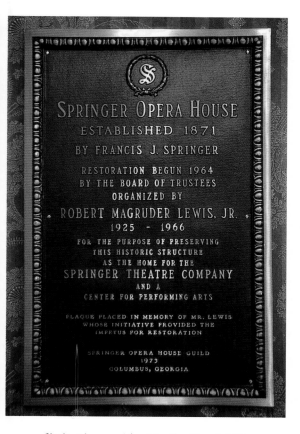

The Springer Opera House, built in 1871 by Frances Joseph Springer, a native of Alsace, France, has a celebrated and colorful history. Photos by Jim Cawthorne.

distinctions evident in the blend. F.X. Profumo, a confectioner, was famous for his Italian ice cream. Sang Sing, a Chinese grocer, stocked goods from everywhere while Ben Lee worked magic on the fashions of the day in his Chinese laundry. Dr. E.H. Mayer and Dr. C.S. Swan, both black physicians, enjoyed booming practices. A.B. Daniel's fish and oyster shop sat not far from Angelo Spano's fruit and oyster shop. Mrs. Dreyspool's clothing and dry-goods store sat between the two. The Springer Opera House routinely presented national and international acts and the Chase Conservatory music school enjoyed wide repute. Even major league baseball came to town when the Cincinnati Reds set up their spring training camp in Columbus in 1912.

The monumental Temple B'nai served as the center of religious and social activities for the city's large and well-established Jewish community in the midst of beautifully built churches of other faiths engaged in similar activities. But, the busiest places in town were the City Market and the Meat Market. These were the days before the invention of an efficient refrigerator so shopping for fresh farm produce and meats was a near-daily experience.

The city was in constant pursuit of improvement from the new Muscogee County Courthouse to the installation of granite blocks as street curbing, the paving of the main streets, the planting of trees downtown, and the establishment of a new water system. Several fire stations, public schools and a Carnegie Library were built in rapid succession.

The school system rose to national attention as the city implemented the nation's first public kindergarten and executed a new concept called the Industrial High School. A group of closely associated local industrialists and financiers like G. Gunby Jordan, William Clark Bradley, Edward W. Smith, Rhodes Browne, Frederick B. Gordon, James P. Kyle, A. Illges, Henry L.

The old Muscogee County Courthouse shadowed by the new twentieth century building. Photo by Herb Cawthorne.

This reconstructed interior of an early 1900s one-room school house can be viewed in the Chattahoochee Legacy gallery of The Columbus Museum. Courtesy of The Columbus Museum.

Woodruff, Ezra Frank Lummus, and J. Homer Dimon added to the fame and fortunes of the entire city and generated personal wealth that would last for generations. The automobile became part of the local daily scene and three moving-picture houses sprang into being. It was a time when values and traditions were the cornerstone of social life.

Alas, nothing lasts forever especially not peace. In the final months of 1916 and through the early spring of 1917, war invaded life in Columbus. The Columbus Guard had been called into federal service the previous June and sent to join the hunt for the infamous Mexican guerrilla, General Pancho Villa. The young men back home were busy volunteering for the army or navy and would soon be in hot pursuit of German submarines.

The day following President Woodrow Wilson's request to Congress for a declaration of war against the Central Powers, Columbus began a campaign to build a military training facility right outside the city. Two days later, on April 6, the country was officially at war. At the same time the city saw the opportunity in economic growth via a new military installation and while the townspeople were deep in the throes of manic patriotism, fear blanketed the town and tucked its corners in the nightmares of children.

Local transportation and power facilities were thought to be under threat of German attack. So on the very day war became official, the city's own guard unit, Company D, arrived back in Columbus, having been summoned specifically to guard the installations. Their train was met by more than 3,000 people who cheered their return. The company was then led in a parade down city streets, amidst thousands upon thousands of clapping and cheering admirers, to the Armory. The day after Company D's arrival, a tent city, complete with flooring and showers, was constructed on Mott's Green to house the soldiers. The Guard commenced patrolling the city the next day and marched on until summoned for overseas duty in mid-June. By the end of the year, they were in France as part of the 121st Infantry of the 31st Division. But, the company was not kept together as a unit. The men were dispersed as needed and the homeboys never again fell rank and file in the Guard Unit known as Company D.

On April 28, 1917, the Selective Services Act passed in Congress and by June all 21- to 31-year-old men in the area were registered and many were already called to duty. Everyone participated in that war. It became fashionable to carry one's knitting to public gatherings as example of one's patriotism. Women all over town knitted sweaters, helmet liners, scarves, and socks for the troops locked in the cold overseas.

Two new local guard companies were formed from the men left behind, one under the lead of Captain W.E. Heard and the other under Captain John P. Illges. The Iron Works labored again under the government's control. The state's first local chapter of the American Red Cross organized in Columbus and built a volunteer base 5,000 strong. Women gathered daily to make bandages and other supplies for overseas hospitals and front-line medics. But perhaps the most noticeable division of the local Red Cross was the Women's Motor Corps wherein local women learned to drive government trucks and tractors in order to transport supplies for the Red Cross, the army, and numerous civic organizations. The Red Cross Volunteers were especially useful during the outbreak of the Spanish flu epidemic of 1918. The service of the Women's Motor Corps was not limited to the city's boundaries. Mrs. Marshall Morton headed the organization and called for women truck drivers to go to France but there is no record of anyone locally accepting.

The YMCA gathered volunteers to man its overseas stations. Mrs. Frank G. Lumpkin, president of the Conservation Kitchen on 12th Street, organized a group to teach people how to raise "victory gardens" and successfully can and preserve their harvests to add to the nation's food supply. James B. Key, Judge C.F. McLaughlin, G. Gunby Jordan, T. Hicks Fort, J. Homer Dimon, and Miss Edwina Wood worked successfully on five Liberty Bond drives promoting U.S. Bonds and War Savings Stamps. On one occasion, more than one million dollars was raised locally.

Attempts to obtain a military training camp had been abandoned as hopeless. The Encampment Committee of the Columbus Chamber of Commerce had given their all in several months of vigorous effort but to no avail. The original committee consisted of Albert F. Kunze, Homer R. McClatchey, Marshall Morton, John A. Betjeman,

Utility lines being laid in downtown Columbus, ca 1920. Photo courtesy Camera 1 Archival Collection.

Many steamboats like this were part of the Chattahoochee River traffic during the first half of the twentieth century. Photo courtesy of Columbus State University Archives.

These historic homes—the Rankin house (above) and the Carter house (right) are very fine examples of the gracious lifestyles lived by some of the prominent Columbus families. Photos by Jim Cawthorne.

Henry B. Crawford, J. Albert Kirven, Frank U. Garrard, J.T. Miller, and J. Ralston Cargill, all of whom had traveled to Washington to promote Columbus. Several members remained in the capital, repeatedly calling on the War Department officials and members of congress. Betjeman, Morton, and Kirven continued to push for the project until the end of February 1918. In the end, even they thought the whole idea a lost cause. Seventy-year-old Kirven, who founded the city's largest department store in 1876 and who had been a stalwart in education and civic affairs, fell ill on the way home from Washington and died of pneumonia.

Events in Washington were unfolding at an unprecedented rate even for wartime. These events would affect Columbus and the dreamed-of training camp in ways that would echo all the way past the new millennium.

Enter General John J. Pershing, commander of the American Expeditionary Force in France. He sent an urgent cablegram to the War Department urging better training for soldiers. Reports from other high-ranking field officers told of alarmingly

high numbers of battlefield casualties… blood shed needlessly in the name of ignorance. The weight of the combined communiques led the War Department to create a special board to determine the type of instruction needed and select a site for such a school. Because of the earlier work of the Encampment Committee, Columbus was one of the four prospective sites considered by the board headed by Colonel Henry E. Eames, commander of the training facility at Ft. Sill.

As soon as the Columbus Chamber of Commerce got wind of the news, John Betjeman was released from his responsibilities as an engineer for the Jordan Company and was sent right away to Washington to see the deal through. He telegraphed his colleagues on August 17, 1918, that the General Staff of the U.S. Army had accepted and approved the recommendation of the special board that the Infantry School of Arms be located near Columbus. The dream suddenly turned into a nightmare.

Major J. Paul Jones was assigned as construction quartermaster for the project. He was misinformed that the infantry school

Ft. Benning Chapel. Photo by Jim Cawthorne.

and Jones didn't have possession of a dime nor even the means to render purchase orders guaranteeing payment. The locals came to his aid and materials and workers of every kind flooded in, all agreeing to wait for payment until the proper authorization was in place.

A site was chosen by Major Jones, Colonel Eames, commander of the new school, and Reynolds Flournoy, representing the Chamber. The 84-acre farm owned by Alex Reid on Macon Road was to become the school's home. It was only about three miles from downtown Columbus, a mile from the city's water supply, and the nearest point of streetcar service. A few days after the soldiers arrived, the new facility was named Camp Benning in honor of long-time Columbus resident and confederate general, Henry Lewis Benning. Before they could expel a sigh of relief, it became obvious the site wasn't going to be large enough nor was the terrain suitable for rifle ranges.

They finally settled on a new site; the 1800 acre plantation of Arthur Bussey called Riverside, nine miles south of Columbus. A huge public celebration was held at the Ralston Hotel as everyone cheered the successful conclusion to the efforts to obtain the installation and to build it. The celebration proved premature.

Just a few days later, on January 7, 1919, the War Department's director of operations ordered the abandonment of all new construction and lease options and to "salvage" all work already completed. Peacetime had delivered what appeared to be the fatal blow. The order effectively doomed the camp to be extinguished before it could turn on the lights, even though it had been clearly demonstrated during the war that a permanent camp for peacetime training was badly needed.

Determined that Columbus should keep Camp Benning, John Betjeman returned to Washington. When the senate hearings began in early January, Betjeman and a delegation from Columbus were there to argue the point. Meanwhile the boys back home, military and civilian, chose to interpret the word "salvage" in the War Department's order to mean repair or save, rather than dismantle and disperse. So they continued to build and paint in the hopes that the Camp would be saved.

While the argument waxed and waned in D.C., the Boston Braves major league

staff and trainees from Fort Sill would arrive on October 1; instead they were already en route. No funds had been allocated yet, the project was still short of formal approval from the Secretary of War, no site had been selected, nothing built, yet hundreds of troops were already on their way.

Jones high-tailed it out of Washington to Atlanta where he missed his train. Knowing he didn't have a moment to lose, he wired in every direction for plumbing, electrical supplies, lumber, everything he could think of that would be needed to throw together temporary mess halls, tent frames, bath houses, and a water supply. Even that meager construction would take at least $100,000, a fortune in those days, baseball team arrived in Columbus for spring training in 1919. They would return in 1920 to train as well. After that, the team moved on to Galveston and never came back. Camp Benning, however, stayed until this very day but the game was won in overtime with two outs, two strikes, and no runs at hand.

In 1920, despite the Columbus delegation's best efforts, a bill to establish a permanent infantry school in Georgia was defeated by a vote of eight to six in the Senate Committee on Military Affairs. Shortly thereafter, Chamber of Commerce President Kunze and Director Homer McClatchey joined Betjeman in Washington and descended on the War Department. There they found sympathizers who in turn persuaded Georgia Senator Hoke Smith, a member of the Committee on Military Affairs, to reopen the matter. It came to vote again; this time a Democratic senator changed his mind in favor of the bill and a Republican member who had previously voted no withdrew from the committee. Fort Benning was finally permanently established by a vote of seven to six.

Peacetime proved to be anything but peaceful. Social, political, and economic forces hit the country like a cyclone. Headlines in early 1919 spoke of the increased use of the automobile and the insufficient roadways, the widespread efforts to evade Prohibition and the advent of gangsters and mobs, the demands for women's suffrage, and the worldwide threat of Russian communism. Jobs, too, were a source of concern. There were far too few of them for the returning soldiers now unemployed. And so the country and the city struggled for answers and fought to survive the ravages of the Great Depression between the first war and the second.

Although the city had been paving roads since the turn of the century, the roads were all in the city proper and it was difficult to travel in the outskirts or to other cities, even to Ft. Benning. The U.S. Secretary of Labor made a national appeal to cities to build and to pave roads in order to employ the returning war heroes. Columbus tried to respond to both the need and the appeal. The work continued slowly for the next 20 years.

The city's Municipal Airport opened in 1930 replacing an earlier fledgling airport that, despite the existence of the area's first airplane hanger, resembled little more than

This painting of long-time Columbus resident and confederate general, Henry Lewis Benning, (for whom Ft. Benning was named) hangs in the National Infantry Museum, Ft. Benning. Photo by Jim Cawthorne.

an open field. The new airfield created quite a commotion not the least of which surrounded the arrival of Amelia Earhart in November 1931. The city's first airmail arrived in 1938.

Industry and business suffered in the face of employees angered over lack of work and the loss of revenue induced by the end of the war. Eagle and Phenix mill workers went on strike for two weeks closing the mills at a loss of $100,000 per week in payroll dollars that usually found their way into the general economy. The mills reopened on February 19 with nearly 2000 employees back at work, but the uneasiness continued as neither side had any room to give.

Steamboats disappeared from the scene. The last of the riverboats operating on a regular schedule, the *W.C. Bradley*, had operated longer than any of its 200 predecessors. As though a signal from the heavens marking a permanent change in the lifestyles of post-war Americans, the Pershing flood ripped the old vessel from its mooring at the city wharf and sank the

ship five miles downriver. A few steamboats sporadically cruised the river after that, but none held on for very long. The tides had changed... permanently.

Prior to the Great Depression, construction was underway even with scarce financing. A concrete bridge was built at 14th Street connecting Columbus to Phenix City. Roads were paved and a new Columbus High School was built. Several subdivisions were developed and the city limit moved steadily outward.

The popularity of motion pictures and the advent of radio replaced the old ways of live entertainment. Even the historic Springer Opera House eventually succumbed and became a movie theater. Roy E. Martin, a long-time Columbusite, began acquiring movie theaters in the early 1920s, and by the 1950s he owned a chain of 140 theaters in four states. In Columbus he built the Bonita, the Grand, and the Pastime. The following year he built the Liberty Theater in the 800 block of Eighth Avenue exclusively for black clientele. It contained both a stage and a screen allowing for both live entertainment and movies.

The Liberty became host to a distinguished list of nationally famous black entertainers including Louis Armstrong, Fats Walker, Duke Ellington, Cab Callaway, Bill "Bojangles" Robinson, and Lena Horne.

Much of the theater popularity in black entertainment circles was due to its association with Gertrude "Ma" Rainey. A Columbus native, Ma Rainey was nationally known as the "Mother of the Blues" and was the first black woman to have her own traveling band and a major recording contract.

Martin also built a 2700 seat theater called the Royal Theater on Talbotton Road, which was spectacular. In the back of the theater in a tiny dressing room, WRBL, the city's first radio station began broadcasting on May 10, 1928. The station eventually moved to Second Avenue in 1935 but it remained the city's only radio station until the end of World War II.

The 1920s were the most active years of residential construction the city had ever known. The Great Depression drastically slowed private construction after 1930. The Ledger-Enquirer building and the

Riverside, the 1800 acre plantation of Arthur Bussey, was chosen for the site of Fort Benning. Photo by Jim Cawthorne.

(Left) Ft. Benning is one of the largest military training facilities in the world. Photo by Jim Cawthorne.

An early 1900s view of the 14th Street bridge. Courtesy of Columbus State University.

Southern Bell regional office were the last privately financed buildings to be built in Columbus until the late 1940s. Fort Benning would prove to be the saving grace; its construction providing much-needed work to residents who otherwise would have been left with nothing.

Despite the millions of dollars poured into the city's economy by this construction and by the Fort Benning payroll, the effects of the Depression were felt severely in Columbus. Beggars went door to door crying out for even meager scraps of food. People slept on the ground, under bridges, wherever they could find a spot of warmth and comfort. It was a time that ate at the very soul and dignity of man. Public relief efforts and private donations came no where close to preventing starvation and deaths from exposure. The federal government stepped in with a series of programs

that offered some relief. President Roosevelt and the New Deal "alphabet" programs became the mainstay and the city struggled to maintain status quo, or some semblance of it, until time could do its magic and things improved.

The fix for the problem turned out to be another World War. Suddenly industries could not produce enough goods to meet the demand and everyone had plenty of work. Thousands of additional military personnel poured into Fort Benning for training in 1940 doubling and tripling the need for health services and housing and severely straining existing transportation. Still, the extra dollars helped end the economic drought.

The need for improved health services led to the 1940 consolidation of the city and county health departments. It was the first in a series of such mergers that would end in the merger of the governments themselves. The reason for the merger of the two health departments was to better administer a federal program. The program brought several large grants to the area that provided for new test procedures for disease control. The results carried the city to the national forefront. Columbus was the second city in the country to have a venereal disease and tuberculosis case-finding program and one of the first to have a chest X-ray program. It was the first city in the world to have a program responsible for spraying every business establishment, residence, barn, and outhouse for fly and mosquito control. Shortly thereafter, in 1947, Columbus became the first city in the nation to be selected by the U.S. Health Service for citywide vaccination against tuberculosis.

When the United States formally entered World War II, there was one significant change in how the residents proceeded to the front. For the first time in history, war had lost its romantic aura. In years past, men marched off to war together with their neighbors to the cheers of the townsfolk and the beat of a marching band. The volunteers and draftees of this war left without ceremony and without company, headed for foreign lands to join a group of strangers in a nightmarish bloodfest. It was the beginning of the estrangement of the military man from his hometown and the initiation of a deep and scared loneliness among American fighting men that would finally be driven home in the protests of the Vietnam War.

Many of the townsfolk recognized the change and organized activities to support the soldiers and their efforts. The local chapter of the American Red Cross once again gathered volunteers and reinstated their war time supply efforts. The USO and the YMCA worked to alleviate loneliness among soldiers as did a myriad of other local organizations. Numerous local drives and campaigns promoted Liberty Bonds and Savings Stamps. And all of this took place under rather severe limits in the name of conservation.

Coffee, sugar, meats, and gasoline had to be conserved to supply the armed forces. Residents good-naturedly bore the hardships of rationing, tire shortages, a lack of new automobiles and parts, and the imposition of daylight saving time. Scrap metal drives were also initiated to retrieve metal

for war time use.

A metal scrap drive conducted by the Muscogee Salvage Committee evoked strong memories of earlier drives for other wars and debate over the importance of memorabilia from an old war versus the needs of a new war. The August 3, 1943, edition of the *Columbus Ledger's* headline read: "Historic Cannon Going to War's Cause." The story told readers that the two, seven-ton Confederate Naval cannons that had rested at the entrance to Waverly Terrace at Hamilton Avenue and 29th Street could yield enough metal to construct a medium-sized, 27-ton tank. How this was ascertained is unknown for it is difficult to believe 14 tons of cannon could be stretched into a 27 ton tank.

A Columbus native, Ma Rainey was nationally known as the "Mother of the Blues" and was the first black woman to have her own traveling band and a major recording contract. Photo by Brady Rogers.

The City Hospital in the late 1920s.

Nonetheless, the cannons were hauled off to the Knight Scrap Metal Company.

A few days later, a similar incident involving a World War I Austrian 200mm field gun slated for meltdown hit the news. Oddly, citizens were not the least disturbed over the loss of the WWI gun but they were panicked over the impending loss of the Civil War cannons. Whether the armed forces needed the metal in the current war or not, the citizens were determined to retain the rebel guns. Strong words were exchanged and pleas made to the War Department for the return of these important relics from the city's past. The pleas fell on deaf ears while the cannons laid on the scrap heap. Finally, more than a year later, on September 11, 1943, a picture of the restored cannons was in the newspaper. Apparently the damage to the guns amounted to little more than some rust.

Columbus continued to boom during the war, most notably because of the population explosion at Fort Benning with its never-ending stream of incoming troops. On February 28, 1941, Columbus got a dial system and new telephone exchange by virtue of hard-won approval from the Federal Communications Commission (FCC) given because "the city's abnormal growth makes the change necessary." The FCC also granted a license for a second radio station in Columbus, WDAK, for much the same reason.

Federal regulations blocked construction of a new airport however. The War Production Board (WPB) would not approve airports other than those under total control of the military. There was a tiny loophole in the law regulating the WPB's jurisdiction, however, that allowed Columbus to build the new airport anyway. All the city had to do was build it for less than $1000 dollars. By using second-hand materials and fixtures and considerable free labor, the new airport opened on August 1, 1944, at a cost of a few pennies less than the limit.

The end of the war was celebrated in Columbus by a large public gathering at the Memorial Stadium. Soldiers were welcomed home over the next several months,

their pictures and bios faithfully printed in the paper as each arrived. The mood was generally upbeat and the townspeople gathered to determine how to continue the growth of the city in spite of the loss of wartime revenues. It was then that the Columbus Chamber formed a long-standing committee called the Greater Columbus Committee to actively seek growth and thus prevent the economic backslides that followed previous wars.

The results of the Committee were successful and far-reaching. One notable example: a sub-committee's first recommendation called for the consolidation of the city and county school systems and the establishment of a junior college. The city and county learned to work together and soon established another joint venture in the W. C. Bradley Memorial Library that was to be operated by the new consolidated school system. Business boomed in the private sector as citizens, long deprived of goods during the war, placed orders in record num-

bers. Southern Bell Telephone Company was hit with a backlog when 3,707 people, who had been denied phone service earlier due to wartime restrictions, suddenly demanded service. And so it went, the city dreamed of its ideal future and planned the way to get there. The soldiers joined the ranks of everyday citizens. The schools enlarged their holdings and the minds of their students. Business broke sales records. All in all, it wasn't a bad place… or time… to just be. ✒

The Columbus chapter of the American Red Cross was an active and integral force in the WWII effort. Photo courtesy of the American Red Cross.

This historic building was once part of the original Columbus Iron Works. It now houses several corporate offices—the Greater Columbus Chamber of Commerce, Total Systems Services, Synovus Financial Corp., and Blue Cross and Blue Shield of Georgia. Photo by Jim Cawthorne.

(Right) The 11th Airborne Memorial, Ft. Benning. Ga. Photo by Jim Cawthorne.

The Seasons in Columbus...

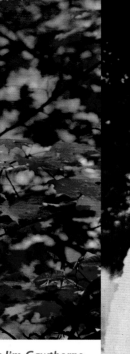

Photos by Jim Cawthorne.

Photo by Jim Cawthorne.

Photo courtesy of Callaway Gardens.

At the Columbus Water Works, word has trickled down from the top. President Billy Turner wants this utility to be the best water resource facility in the country by the year 2000. With the company's 215 employees tapping into the dream, it's

Columbus Water Works

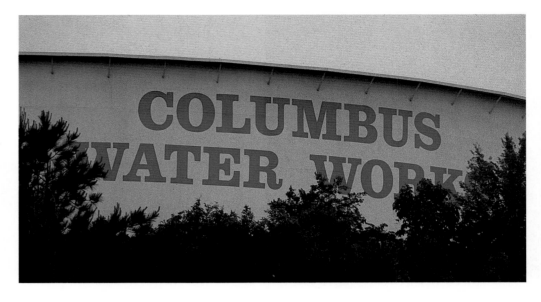

bound to happen.

Already, the Water Works has won numerous awards for every phase of its operation, among them the Environmental Protection Agency's Safe Drinking Water Act Excellence Award, which recognizes it as the best large surface water treatment system in the 10-state Southeast region; the Georgia Water and Pollution Control Association awards for outstanding wastewater collection and water distribution; and the American Academy of Environmental Engineers' grand prize for project design of the Riverwalk and the combined sewer overflow control program.

The function of the Water Works is simple—the implementation complex. The Water Works takes in water from the Chattahoochee River, separates out the particles in its water filtration facility, and kills the bacteria and other organisms to make the water consumable. After water has been used, it flows through the sewer system to the wastewater treatment plants, where it is cleaned via a biological process

In addition to maintaining the infrastructure, the Water Works is under continued pressure to demonstrate that the city's water quality meets ever increasingly tougher standards.

that copies nature before it is funneled back into the river.

Rigorous testing and constant monitoring assure the utility's 65,092 residential and business customers that the 32 million gallons of water they use daily is of high quality and safe to use.

In Columbus, water is plentiful and cheap. By state permit, the Water Works has the capacity to draw as much as 67 million gallons of water a day from the Chattahoochee. The average Columbus water customer uses 15,000 gallons of water per month and pays $31.30 for water and sewer service. In Macon, that same customer pays $33.87; in Atlanta, $78.80; in Charleston, $93.73; and in Nashville, $120.

As the city has changed, so have the methods of obtaining its water. In 1839, residents got their water from cisterns in the streets where rainwater collected. In 1844, they took their buckets to the intersections downtown to buy water that flowed from Leonard Spring, on what is now Country Club Drive, downhill via Randolph Street (now 12th Street) to Broad Street through pipes made from hollowed-out pine trees. People paid a nickel for a bucket of water, far more than the $.001 cents Water Works customers pay for a bucket of it today delivered to the house.

In 1882, a private company, the Columbus Water Supply Co., signed a 30-year agreement with the city to deliver water from creeks in Phenix City. The water, which was piped under the Chattahoochee River, was often muddy when it reached Columbus. Water to fight fires also became a problem as the city's

The Columbus Water Works has won numerous awards for every phase of its operation, among them the Environmental Protection Agency's Safe Drinking Water Act Excellence Award.

population grew. After a rash of complaints from residents about muddy water and lack of fire protection, the city terminated the contract with the private company and hired an engineer to find a suitable water source. Interestingly, in his report in 1898, he recommended the Chattahoochee River because of its ample supply and its high quality, but noted his concerns about pollution flowing downstream from Atlanta.

For eight years, residents got their water from artesian wells, but were constantly confronting problems with contamination. In 1902, state legislation created a Board of Water Commissioners to manage a water system controlled by the City of Columbus. But during its first 10 years, it was involved in a breach-of-contract lawsuit filed by the private water company. The case made its way to the Supreme Court and was one of the test cases about water systems in the United States. The court found in favor of the city, and in 1913, the Board, using funds from a bond referendum, began construction of a new water plant on River Road with the capacity to generate 5 million gallons of water a day. By 1916, the city had a new pumping station, a 20-million-gallon raw water reservoir, a filter plant, a 2.5-million-gallon clear water reservoir, and a 24-inch cast-iron main running down Third Avenue. The Chattahoochee River and plant site on River Road continues to serve the city, having been constantly upgraded and

Columbus Water Works is a national leader in water management and one of the city's most important liquid assets.

modernized to today's capacity of 67 million gallons per day. This gives the city excess capacity, which is a selling point for new industry and residents alike.

Many things have happened since then to impact the quantity and quality of water in Columbus. In 1956, the Board of Water Commissioners assumed responsibility for the city's sanitary sewer system. In 1964, it built the city's first wastewater treatment plant in South Columbus to protect the water quality for its downstream neighbors. The plant has been upgraded several times and a secondary treatment plant added. The wastewater plant has received numerous awards for its operation, including being named the best operated plant in the state for several years.

The Columbus Water Works is nationally known for its innovative ideas. An important part of the wastewater treatment process is handling the solids that are removed. In 1981, it began a program that takes solid wastes from the treatment process and plows them into the soil to grow millet and wheat to be used by the city for landscaping.

This process was taken a step further in 1993, when the city bought additional land on which to continue the process and create a wetlands using inert waste. The area, named Oxbow Meadows, is the site of a science center for educational programs;

natural and man-made wetlands for studying aquatic organisms; and trails for observing wildlife. A golf course and a marina are planned for the area.

In 1990, the Georgia Legislature passed Combined Sewer Overflow legislation that required cities with combined sanitary and storm sewers that overflowed during heavy rains to fix the problems to avoid further pollution of the river. The Water Works responded with a creative solution that not only fixed the overflow problems but also helped revitalize the downtown. It embedded storm sewers along the riverbank behind a retaining wall and created on top of the pipeline a Riverwalk, a 10-mile-long walking, jogging, biking trail that has been the impetus for further development along the riverfront and in downtown Columbus.

A $20-million federal grant, part of the CSO's $90-million price tag, paid for an advance research project at Uptown Park, a site that tests and demonstrates alternative technologies to waste treatment, including the use of dissolved air flotation and ultraviolet light disinfection. Projects such as this one give the Columbus Water Works national visibility and credibility.

"We're prepared to meet the test of the millennium," Turner said. "We have the capacity, the technology, and good people, so I think we are prepared to charge into it full force."

In addition to maintaining the infrastructure, the Water Works will be under continued pressure to demonstrate that the city's water quality meets ever increasing

standards, Turner said. He also predicts that the Water Works will become a regional entity, providing water and technical support to surrounding counties.

The Water Works will continue its involvement as the region's representative in development of the multistate compact, which addresses the utilization of the river for hydropower, recreation, navigation, water supply, and wastewater discharge.

Projects such as these make the Columbus Water Works a national leader in water management and one of the city's most important liquid assets. ◈

Founded at the turn of the century as a full-service real estate development company, The Jordan Company is a Columbus tradition that promises to remain a vital part of the community's future. As one of the area's premier real estate developers,

The Jordan Company

the company has developed over 3,500 homesites and numerous commercial properties at some of the area's most prestigious addresses.

In the early years, The Jordan Company's primary focus was construction, having constructed some of the city's most well-known facilities. Noteworthy projects include St. Francis Hospital, The Waverly Hotel, the Infantry Center at Fort Benning, the Columbus Metropolitan Airport Terminal, and the 17-story Columbus Consolidated Government Center.

The company is well-known for its development of Green Island Hills, a premier master-planned community. Although the master plan was developed in the 1920s, creating the concept of luxury homes near the Chattahoochee River, it was not until the 1970s that the primary focus of the organization shifted to development. While offering spectacular views of

Green Island Hills, a Jordan development, is strategically located along the River Road corridor, offering spectacular views of Lake Oliver.

Lake Oliver, this residential masterpiece epitomizes the company's commitment to design homesites in a superior natural setting, preserving wooded areas, and protecting the essential environment qualities of the land. The Green Island Hills Country Club and neighboring shopping village provide vital elements of the total planned community.

River Crest, another Jordan development, is strategically located along the River Road corridor, and destined to become one of north Columbus's most sought-after neighborhoods. Positioned along the banks of the Heifferhorn Creek, the natural neighbors, wild turkey and deer, seem content to coexist with their newfound human neighbors.

Capitalizing on east Alabama's impressive double-digit growth rate, in 1998 the company expanded into a regional market when it entered into a joint venture with Warr Development, Inc. of Phenix City to develop McIntosh Creek. This 200-acre, upper-end residential and commercial community, with estate homesites as well as garden homes, offers a variety of lifestyle choices. Nearby retail shopping and office facilities will provide the conveniences of working, dining, and shopping within minutes of home.

Commercial developments, such as The Terraces of Green Island, Jordan's headquarters, speak to the standards of

The Terraces of Green Island serve as corporate headquarters for The Jordan Company.

excellence the company seeks in its commercial endeavors. The company offers full-service property and asset management to multiple owners throughout the region. Over 700,000 square feet of office, retail, and multifamily developments are managed to achieve value for the owner and the highest quality level for tenants.

With a thorough knowledge of the marketplace, the company provides development, market research and analysis, and property and asset management. Complete residential and commercial brokerage services are offered through Prudential Jordan Real Estate.

A tradition of excellence built on a century of corporate integrity, an ethical code of conduct, and dedication to the client will serve as the foundation of the company's future growth. With a proud history that began at the turn of the twentieth century, The Jordan Company promises to remain an industry leader throughout the twenty-first century. ❧

Founded in 1998, Prudential Jordan Real Estate builds on the long-standing traditions of two rock solid companies—Prudential Real Estate Associates Inc. and The Jordan Company.

With compatible visions and progressive, growth-oriented operating styles, the affiliation of the companies was a natural fit and created one of the largest real estate companies in the city. Even Prudential's motto of "Satisfaction and Then Some" reflects The Jordan Company's own customer-oriented service philosophy, a tradition that has endured since the company was founded.

Prudential Real Estate Associates, a nationwide network of independently owned and operated brokerage franchisees, is a subsidiary of The Prudential Insurance Company of America, the company with the renowned rock logo. Started in 1988, the Prudential Real Estate Network has grown to more than 1,400 offices with 37,000 sales associates in the United States and Canada.

The Jordan Company is a Columbus-based full-service real estate development company that has served the Columbus market since 1903, when it was founded by G. Gunby Jordan. Originally focused on construction, The Jordan Company has, through the years, expanded its offerings

With a thorough knowledge of the regional marketplace, the innovative use of state-of-the-art technology, and a tradition of integrity and exceptional customer service, the real estate professionals at Prudential Jordan are committed to making the company the area's leading real estate firm.

with primary emphasis on residential and commercial development, property and asset management, and commercial and residential real estate.

Prudential Jordan Real Estate's primary focuses are residential, commercial, and land sales in a regional market. Its goal is to provide simplified, cost-effective real estate transactions based on understanding its customers' needs and exceeding their expectations.

Through the Prudential network, Prudential Jordan agents have access to one of the most sophisticated home marketing systems in the country and one that provides the simplest and most effective system for real estate transactions in the industry. Prudential Jordan agents, who receive training and support services from Prudential Real Estate, are dedicated to using up-to-the-minute technology to provide better and more efficient ways to serve their clients.

As a charter affiliate, Prudential Jordan is a member of the Prudential Referral Services, a national relocation network that provides detailed market information on more than 5,000 communities across the United States and Canada to its members. The services also provide other real estate information and assistance to families moving into or out of

Prudential's motto of "Satisfaction and Then Some" reflects The Jordan Company's own customer-oriented service philosophy, a tradition that has endured since the company was founded.

an area and the names of qualified real estate agents who specialize in transfers and relocations.

Home buyers or sellers who list through Prudential Jordan have the advantage of a program called the PRS Van Line Express,

Prudential Jordan Real Estate

which provides special services and savings from North America's leading van line companies. Included in the package are moving insurance, discounted storage, key account status, and free moving counseling services.

With a thorough knowledge of the regional marketplace, the innovative use of state-of-the-art technology, and a tradition of integrity and exceptional customer service, the real estate professionals at Prudential Jordan, headquartered at The Terraces of Green Island at 6001 River Road, are committed to making the company the area's leading real estate company well into the millennium. ➔

*R*oyal Crown Cola Company's roots run deep in Columbus, but its branches spread all over the world. In addition to the United States, the beverage company sells its soft drink concentrates in 63 foreign countries, with major markets

Royal Crown Cola Company

in Argentina, Australia, Brazil, Israel, Mexico, the Philippines, Russia, Tunisia, and the Ukraine.

Royal Crown produces and sells concentrates used in the production of soft drinks which are sold domestically and internationally to independent, licensed bottlers who manufacture and distribute finished beverage products. All of RC's concentrates are formulated at its Tenth Avenue plant. Brand names include RC Cola®, Diet RC Cola®, Diet Rite Cola®, Diet Rite flavors, Nehi®, and Kick®.

The Royal Crown legacy began in 1905, when a young pharmacist by the name of Claud A. Hatcher set his sights on

Royal Crown Cola Company's roots run deep in Columbus, but its branches spread all over the world.

concocting a good-tasting beverage for his family's wholesale grocery business to sell. Working quietly in the basement of the Hatcher Grocery Co., his efforts were successful, and he and his father founded the Union Bottling Works, later to become the Royal Crown Cola Company.

Hatcher's first beverage, Royal Crown Ginger Ale, was the first in a line of other Royal Crown products, including Chero-Cola, Royal Crown Strawberry, and Royal Crown Root Beer, which emerged in 1912. In 1924, Royal Crown introduced the Nehi line of fruit-flavored beverages that became so popular that the company changed its name to the Nehi Corporation. It retained that name until the 1960s, when it became the Royal Crown Cola Company, in honor of its best-selling beverage. By 1927, Royal Crown had 463 plants in 14 Southern states.

It wasn't until 1934 that Royal Crown actually started making a cola-flavored beverage to challenge the existing cola products. The new Royal Crown Cola quickly became known as RC to the millions who enjoyed its sweet cola flavor. For many Southerners, an "RC Cola and a Moon Pie" was a favored treat. Songwriter Vic McAlpin wrote a song about it called "Give me an RC and a Moon Pie," which was recorded by Lonzo and Oscar in 1951.

When it came to introducing new products, new packaging, and new marketing strategies, Royal Crown was the most innovative of the country's soft drink companies. It was Royal Crown that introduced the first 16-ounce bottle in 1955.

When it came to introducing new products, new packaging, and new marketing strategies, Royal Crown was the most innovative of the country's soft drink companies. It was Columbus-based Royal Crown Cola Co. that distributed the first soft drinks in cans nationally in 1951. It was Royal Crown that introduced the first 16-ounce bottle in 1955.

By the 1960s, Royal Crown was one of the top three soft drink companies in the country and was known throughout the industry for its innovative beverages and marketing strategies. The real coup occurred in 1962, when Royal Crown introduced Diet Rite Cola to an industry that claimed diet soft drinks would never sell. In 18 months, Diet Rite became the fourth best-selling cola in the United States, prompting industry leaders to proclaim the new product "the most amazing breakthrough in soft drink technological history." In 1964, it was Royal Crown that introduced the all-aluminum beverage can.

RC's marketing strategies were also recognized for their creativity. At a time when

In 1962 Royal Crown introduced Diet Rite Cola to an industry that claimed diet soft drinks would never sell. In 18 months, Diet Rite became the fourth best-selling cola in the United States.

it was unusual for a small company to sponsor a radio show, Royal Crown went straight to the top as a sponsor of *Robert Ripley's Believe It or Not.* In 1946, the Nehi Corporation used entertainment celebrities, including Bing Crosby, Joan Crawford, Elizabeth Scott, and Hedy Lamarr, to promote its soft drinks with taste tests. The company was the first to use the designation "best by taste test."

In 1975, as the "Me and My RC" slogan swept the nation, Royal Crown moved its corporate headquarters from Columbus to Atlanta. Also during the 1970s, the company started marketing its products overseas, quickly establishing a viable base in the world market and setting the stage for additional international growth.

Through the years, Royal Crown has continued to lead changes in the industry. In 1980, it introduced the first caffeine-free cola called RC 100 and reintroduced Diet Rite as a salt/sodium-free, caffeine-free, sugar-free cola using NutraSweet™. RC really made headlines in 1984, when the company introduced Cherry RC, Diet RC, and eight flavors of Diet Rite. It was at this time that the corporate headquarters was moved from Atlanta to Fort Lauderdale, Florida.

When the Royal Crown Cola Company was bought by Triarc Companies, Inc. in 1993, the soft drink was once again revamped, this time with a new taste, packaging, and additional flavors. Under this new ownership, Diet RC became the first diet cola in the United States to be sweetened with Splenda, the only no-calorie sweetener made from real sugar.

Though Columbus is no longer the company's corporate headquarters, it is the site of the organization's research and development laboratories and concentrate production facilities. Employing 85 locally, these facilities remain an important contributor to the multibillion-dollar New York-based Triarc Companies, Inc. Royal Crown is a significant component of the Triarc Beverage Group, which also includes Snapple, Mistic, and Cable Car.

In 1998, the RC Cola and Diet Rite brands held a small but profitable niche in the domestic cola market, and Royal Crown was the exclusive worldwide supplier of cola concentrates to Cott Corporation, the world's largest private-label soft drink company. With the world's per capita cola consumption on the rise, the company plans in the new millennium to concentrate on underdeveloped countries where the potential for growth is greatest.

With its eye on increased international sales and invigorated domestic efforts, Royal Crown has positioned itself for a successful entry into the new millennium. ➔

Royal Crown is a significant component of the Triarc Beverage Group, which also includes Snapple, Mistic, and Cable Car.

Blue Cross and Blue Shield of Georgia

Blue Cross and Blue Shield of Georgia, the state's largest health insurer, insures 1.6 million Georgians and has been a leader in Columbus's business community since the mid-1940s.

Prior to the 1940s, Georgians who became sick paid the physician and hospital with cash, if they had it, or in eggs and produce if they didn't. Many never sought medical help because they couldn't afford it. The problem became so acute that hospitals in Georgia, as well as several other states, began offering a new method of payment—paying a small amount on a regular basis in advance of need. The product became known as insurance, and Blue Cross in 1933 became one of the first insurance companies to provide this hospital prepayment plan.

Prepayment plans to cover the cost of physician care first appeared in lumber and mining camps in the 1890s in the United States. This led to the organization of service bureaus of doctors who contracted with employers to provide health care. The first Blue Shield plan was formed in 1939 in California.

After World War II, prepaid medical plans became so popular that national coordination was required. As a result, the Blue Cross and Blue Shield Association was created as an association of independent Blue Cross and Blue Shield plans.

In 1946, Blue Cross had two prepayment hospital plans in Georgia—one in Atlanta and the other in Savannah. Residents of Columbus weren't covered by the plans because state law allowed coverage only within a 50-mile radius of the cities.

That changed when the Muscogee County Medical Association determined that there was a need for a hospital prepayment program in this area, and the local Merchants' Association agreed to organize it using an initial loan of $5,000 from businessman J. D. Kirven. The plan went into effect in October 1947, when it opened its Columbus operations in the Swift Building downtown. With a president, Sam Butler, and a secretary, the company served 5,975 members the first year. Its first salesperson, John Moye, joined Blue Cross in 1948.

Although Blue Cross paid hospital bills, there was no coverage for doctors' bills until 1950, when enabling legislation eliminated the 50-mile-radius limitation, and a Blue Shield plan covering doctors' visits was implemented. With three Blue Cross and Blue Shield plans in existence statewide, the Georgia Commissioner of Insurance divided the state into three districts, each to be served by one of the plans. In 1966, the Savannah plan merged with the Columbus plan, giving Columbus

From its four-story facility on Warm Springs Road, employees serve subscribers by providing fast, efficient service, a hallmark of Blue Cross and Blue Shield of Georgia.

a coverage area of 131 of the state's 159 counties.

Today, Blue Cross and Blue Shield of Georgia, an operating company of Cerulean Companies, Inc., remains affiliated with the Chicago-based Blue Cross and Blue Shield Association, which provides health benefits to more than 70 million Americans. Blue Cross and Blue Shield of Georgia, headquartered in Atlanta, is the state's largest health insurer, providing benefits to more than 1.6 million Georgians, including 25,000 Columbus residents.

The Columbus operation has evolved from a two-employee office into an operation of nearly 1,400 employees and one of 12 Blue Cross and Blue Shield of Georgia operations centers in the state. From its four-story facility on Warm Springs Road, employees serve subscribers by providing fast, efficient service, a hallmark of Blue Cross and Blue Shield of Georgia.

Always on the cutting edge of health care benefits, Blue Cross and Blue Shield has added to its health insurance coverage benefits that help cover the costs of nursing homes, clinics, dentists, optometrists, podiatrists, chiropractors, home health care, and some forms of alternative treatments. It expanded its benefits in 1979 to

include life insurance through Greater Georgia Life Company. It is also the administrative intermediary between the government and voluntary hospitals for Medicare Part A and Part B, providing communications, claims processing, utilization review, and audits.

Ever mindful of the rising costs of health care, Blue Cross and Blue Shield of Georgia has been innovative in establishing effective cost containment and health education programs. In 1986, Blue Cross and Blue Shield created the organization's first managed care organization, called HMO Georgia, Inc. This independent license of the Blue Cross and Blue Shield Association covers more than 420,000 Georgians with its BlueChoice Healthcare Plan (HMO) BlueChoice Option (point of service plan), and BlueChoice Platinum (Medicare HMO) products and has an affiliated network of more than 4,355 physicians and 566 hospitals, giving Georgians a wide choice of medical providers.

As it looks to the future, Blue Cross and Blue Shield will build on its distinguished history. When the plans were first founded in 1947, the nation's primary concern was simply how to pay for medical services. In the new millennium, the major concern is

Always on the cutting edge of health care benefits, Blue Cross and Blue Shield has added to its health insurance coverage benefits that help cover the costs of nursing homes, clinics, dentists, optometrists, podiatrists, chiropractors, home health care, and some forms of alternative treatments.

not just enabling a payment mechanism for health care, but to provide access to affordable health care for as many Georgians as possible.

To that end, Blue Cross and Blue Shield of Georgia will continue to explore, develop, and implement new and expanded health care strategies, expand its health education and cost containment programs, and work to provide the best health care benefits to the greatest number of people at the most economical costs. ✦

Page, Scrantom, Sprouse, Tucker & Ford is an established, progressive law firm with a reputation for providing a full line of quality legal services to businesses, individuals and governmental entities principally located in Columbus, Georgia, and the

Page, Scrantom, Sprouse, Tucker & Ford, P.C.

surrounding area. One of the oldest and largest law firms in the area, with 30 attorneys and a support staff of 34, the firm is a leader in the fields of business, corporate, tax, estate planning and employment law, as well as commercial, general and insurance defense litigation. The offices of the firm are located at 1043 Third Avenue, near the heart of uptown Columbus.

The firm was founded as Slade & Swift in 1902 to practice corporate and business law, areas which continue to constitute a major segment of the firm's practice. The firm's interest in tax law dates back to the days of Herman Swift, who was one of the first income tax lawyers in the country and who held the distinction of being President

Franklin Delano Roosevelt's Georgia attorney. Today, the firm provides specialized tax counsel in connection with mergers and acquisitions, sales, partnerships, tax audits, employee benefits, public charities and private foundations.

The banking law services provided by the firm include commercial lending, project financing, asset-based and other structured lending, acquisitions, bond-related financing and regulatory matters.

The firm's labor and employment practice, one of the fastest growing areas of practice within the firm, includes employer representation in connection with employment contracts, terminations and defending age, sex and other discrimination charges. The firm represents companies before the EEOC, the NLRB and other federal and state agencies, as well as in court proceedings.

The firm's real estate practice includes providing counsel on commercial, industrial and residential real property matters, financing and restructuring, leasing, zoning and industrial development bond financing.

Page, Scrantom, Sprouse, Tucker & Ford has long engaged in a sophisticated estate planning practice involving the preparation of wills, charitable and noncharitable trusts, family limited partnerships and private foundations, along with providing

assistance in connection with the administration of estates and trusts. In addition, the firm represents a number of public charities and other nonprofit organizations.

Over the years, the firm has fostered and encourages participation by its attorneys and staff in local and state professional, civic and charitable organizations and activities with the goals of bettering professional skills and contributing to the growth, development and quality of life in Columbus and the surrounding area. The firm recently has undergone a major technological upgrade so as to enhance its ability to provide quality, timely and cost-effective legal services to its clients.

Page, Scrantom, Sprouse, Tucker & Ford faces the new millennium with plans for cutting-edge technological savvy and the ability to serve every aspect of someone's legal needs. Says the firm's president, William Scrantom: "We want to have enough expertise in this building, so that nobody has to go anywhere else." ➔

One of the oldest and largest law firms in the area, with 30 attorneys and a support staff of 34, Page, Scrantom, Sprouse, Tucker & Ford is a leader in the fields of business, corporate, tax, estate planning and employment law, as well as commercial, general and insurance defense litigation.

Photo by Jim Cawthorne.

Tom's Foods has been an institution on the Columbus landscape since 1925, when a young mechanical inventor named Tom Huston received peanuts from farmers in payment for some of his mechanical inventions. Huston then designed a mechanical

Tom's Foods Inc.

Tom Huston put roasted peanuts into a narrow cellophane package patented in 1926 and dubbed them in a triangular label as "Tom's Toasted Peanuts."

peanut sheller and a roasting process for the shelled peanuts. He put roasted peanuts into a narrow cellophane package patented in 1926, dubbed them in a triangular label as "Tom's Toasted Peanuts," and set out to sell them through independent distributors.

With that, the Tom Huston Peanut Company was launched, and four years later, the enterprising young man was featured in *Time* magazine as "The Farmer Boy Who Became Peanut King."

Tom's Foods, with peanut silos that reach 144 feet into the Columbus skyline off Tenth Avenue, is one of the largest purchasers of peanuts in the Southeast, and the toasted peanut remains one of the company's best-selling products. Today, the triangular label bearing the Tom's logo is a symbol of freshness and quality on one of the broadest product lines of quality snack foods in the industry. Built on the success of the lowly goober, Tom's Foods produces

Tom's snack foods can be found in vending machines, grocery stores, and convenience stores in all 50 states. Its modern, high-speed bakery in Columbus produces enough crackers each year to circle the earth at the equator more than three times when laid end to end.

and distributes more than 300 snack food products, including candy (Peanut Butter Log, Salted Nut Roll, Peanut Plank, Coconut Slice, My Buddy, and others), baked goods (fig bars, cookies, and snack cakes, etc.), cracker sandwiches (many varieties of peanut butter-filled, cheese-filled, and sweet-filled crackers), and chips (potato chips, corn chips, extruded items, popcorn, and pork skins in a variety of flavors). Its modern, high-speed bakery in Columbus produces enough crackers each year to circle the earth at the equator more than three times when laid end to end.

Tom's snack foods can be found in vending machines, grocery stores, and convenience stores in all 50 states. Unlike the major snack food companies who focus on multiple-serving packages, Tom's concentrates on smaller, single-serve packaging. Most of Tom's products are distributed through a large network of independent distributors who ensure that Tom's products arrive on store shelves and in their vending machines in a fresh and timely manner.

Located on 38 acres in the downtown area, Tom's three Columbus plants, which employ 800 of the company's 1,650 employees, produce its candy, peanut, and baked goods and cracker products. Tom's

chips and extruded items are produced in its plants in Perry, Florida; Knoxville, Tennessee; Corsicana, Texas; and Fresno, California. Including warehouse space, Tom's facilities exceed 1 million square feet.

Tom Huston didn't get to enjoy the fruits of his labor, however, as business reverses in another of his business ventures (frozen peaches) during the Depression in the 1930s caused him to lose his peanut company. The bank that held the note on the business hired Walter Richards as president of the company in 1932. Richards and several other investors bought the company from the bank and ran it independently until 1966, when it was acquired by corporate giant General Mills. In 1983, the company was purchased by a British company, Rowntree-Mackintosh, who operated it for five years. A group of local investors bought the company in 1988 and held it until it was acquired by a Chicago investment firm, Heico Acquisitions, in 1993.

Two mayors of Columbus have come from Tom's, as well as the current Phenix City Mayor Peggy Martin, who still works for Tom's. For many years, Tom's and its employees have provided support for just about every worthwhile cause or activity in the Columbus/Phenix City area, being a proud part of the area's past, as well as its future. ❧

Georgia Power Company is as intricately woven into the history of Columbus as the Chattahoochee River is woven into the landscape of the Valley. Since it entered the local market in 1930, the investor-owned utility has been committed to providing electricity to customers, playing a major role in the recruitment of new businesses and industries, and developing the best recreation facilities in the state.

For many people in the Chattahoochee Valley, the late 1800s and early 1900s were the years the lights came on. In 1922, the Gas Light Company of Columbus merged with the Columbus Power Company and the Columbus Railroad Company to form the Columbus Electric and Power Company. It wasn't until 1930, when Georgia Power Company, chartered in 1908, acquired the assets of the Columbus Electric and Power Co., that the use of hydroelectric power to illuminate households became widespread.

Today, Georgia Power's West Region serves 124,000 customers, including 74,000 in Columbus, and employs more than 200. With taxes exceeding $1.8 million, it is Columbus's largest taxpayer. Good stewardship of its land and resources has helped

Even back in 1930, Georgia Power was looking forward to the future and the progress of the Columbus area.

Georgia Power keep its rates nearly 15 percent below the national average.

Working closely with Chambers of Commerce, city government, and other utility companies, the economic development arm of Georgia Power makes it a key player in enticing companies to locate in the area. Through its Georgia Resource Center, Georgia Power provides the latest information on living and doing business in the state.

Locally, Georgia Power utilizes the power of the Chattahoochee River's falling water to generate electricity through hydropower production. From the 1820s to the early 1900s, the power of the Chattahoochee River was first used to run the giant sawmills, grain processors, and textile mills that dotted its banks. In the 1830s, the first dam was constructed to divert water to the business district.

Though today only a small percentage of Georgia Power's electricity is generated from the Chattahoochee, the river and its dams continue to be major assets both to the company and the community. Georgia Power dams create some of the most beautiful lakes found in the state.

Nine dams span the river from West Point to Columbus; six of them generate hydroelectric power for Georgia Power. The Chattahoochee Hydro Group can produce 290,000 kilowatts of electric power, enough to provide electricity for more than 36,000 homes in the region.

One of the smallest dams in the system, North Highlands Dam was built in 1899 and generates 29,600 kilowatts. Oliver Dam, the first remote controlled hydroelectric generating facility in the Georgia Power system, was constructed in 1959 and has the capacity to generate 60,000 kilowatts. The 70-foot-high

concrete dam creates the beautiful 2,150-acre Lake Oliver.

Goat Rock Dam was constructed in 1912 and has the capacity to generate 26,000 kilowatts of energy. Goat Rock Lake, covering 1,050 acres and boasting 25 miles of

Georgia Power Company

Oliver Dam, located on the Chattahoochee River downstream of Goat Rock, is one of the newest and most modern of Georgia Power's hydroelectric generating facilities.

coastline, is one of the smallest and least developed pristine lakes on the river.

Built in 1926 and capable of producing 173,000 kilowatts, Bartletts Ferry Dam creates Lake Harding, the largest and most popular lake in Georgia Power Company's Chattahoochee HydroGroup. Further up the river are the Riverview Dam, built in 1918, and the Langdale Dam, built in 1908.

Though the electric utility faces changes in technology and the challenge of pending deregulation, Georgia Power, a unit of the Southern Company, will continue its long tradition of service to the community it serves. Georgia Power continues to be "A citizen wherever we serve." ◆

The Progress of COLUMBUS and GEORGIA

The world contains few spots so definitely marked for progress as Columbus. In the heart of the swiftly-growing Southeast, it is a strategic location for plants to serve this rich market.

Decentralization of Industry, the need to produce at the center of each major market, is forcing American business to search for precisely the advantages Columbus can offer.

None can question the future of Georgia or of the Southeast. We pledge our best efforts towards building a greater Columbus.

Columbus Electric & Power Company

R. M. HARDING, Manager

S Since 1931, Robinson, Grimes & Company has provided outstanding financial advisory services to its clients. The largest Certified Public Accounting (CPA) firm in the region and one of the largest independent CPA firms in the Southeast,

Robinson, Grimes & Company, P.C.

RG & Co. is a full-service accounting firm with a reputation for providing a diversified mix of innovative services with special emphasis on personal attention to clients.

Based on its commitment to be large enough to offer clients a wide range of professional services, yet small enough to maintain and nurture personal attention, RG & Co. currently employs a team of 50. Business and individual clients look to the firm for services in the areas of tax, auditing and accounting, management advising, and computer systems design and consulting. Advice and assistance are provided in estate and financial planning, business succession planning, and related business services.

Located in its own 18,000-square-foot facility on Whitesville Road, RG & Co. is divided into three departments—tax, audit

Developing lasting relationships with its clients through personal attention and quality services is important to RG & Co. Firm owners are (seated, left to right) Lev Norman, Jay Pease, Clinton Gilmore, Jim Stokes (standing) Charlie Johnson, Alton Duncan, Scott Voynich, Ron Thomas, and Greg Voynich.

and accounting, and management advisory services. Though its CPAs have areas of specialization, each still maintains a high degree of competence in all three to help clients see the opportunities beyond the numbers.

The tax department works with both business clients and individuals to provide integrated tax planning and help in the development of appropriate tax strategies. The professional staff prepares and reviews all required tax filings, including income tax, franchise/property tax, pension/profit sharing reports, and amended returns/carryback claims. Tax professionals at RG & Co. work closely with clients to provide estate planning services and coordinate the team effort of related estate and trust services.

The audit and accounting department provides assurance services including audits, reviews, and compilations for commercial enterprises as well as governmental entities. Its professionals are skilled in preparing forecasts and projections and making recommendations about internal controls and best business practices. RG & Co. also helps clients develop their accounting systems and resolve problems within those systems.

The management advisory services department offers a broad range of services. Through its Systems Group, a team of consulting professionals help business clients evaluate and select computer hardware and software, expand into multiuser systems, install and use a number of accounting systems, and set up operational procedures

Members of the Robinson, Grimes & Company team are committed to being large enough to offer clients a wide range of professional services, yet small enough to maintain and nurture personal attention.

for security, unexpected loss of data, and correction of existing problems. The department offers systems review to examine and make recommendations regarding the effectiveness of existing accounting systems, procedures, budgeting, and overhead. Special projects are also performed to provide assistance with graphic analysis, financial projections, investment analysis, and other areas. Financial planning is offered to help clients plan for profitability, define financial objectives, and establish programs to meet business and personal financial goals.

The firm is a member of the Securities and Exchange Commission Practice Section of the American Institute of CPAs. Its members regularly hold leadership positions in the Georgia Society of CPAs and the American Institute of CPAs, participating at the local, state, and national levels.

Developing lasting relationships with its clients through personal attention and quality services is important to RG & Co. and will continue to be key into the millennium as the firm addresses new areas of service, and as it meets the evolving needs of this new age of opportunity. ❧

Litho-Krome exists because of one man's passion. The man was Columbus native J. Tom Morgan Jr., and his passion was print-making. In lithographic circles, his name is inked in under that of Currier and Ives and others who have made significant contributions to the profession. Morgan's key

The high quality of printing at the small Columbus storefront landed the company numerous national accounts, including Nehi soft drinks, Borden ice cream, Lenox china, Cartier jewelry, the Timken Co. calendars, and Hallmark cards.

contribution was four-color lithography, a technique he invented that revolutionized the printmaking industry and placed his famous *Wine and Cheese* print in a display on historic lithographic printing in the Smithsonian Institution in Washington, D.C. He also introduced to the printing world Litho-Krome Black, a system of printing black and white illustrations of photographic quality.

Ink started running in Morgan's veins when he joined Commercial Printers Inc. in Columbus in the 1930s. He later bought the company and changed its name to Litho-Krome, "litho" meaning "print" and "krome" meaning "color." The high quality of printing at the small Columbus store-front landed the company numerous national accounts, including Nehi soft drinks, Borden ice cream, Lenox china, Cartier jewelry, the Timken Co. calendars, and Hallmark cards.

Morgan set the standards of quality at Litho-Krome, ones that to this day remain. Indeed, he would not have sold the business on Thirteenth Street to Hallmark Cards of Kansas City, Missouri, in 1979 had they not shared his commitment to quality. Hallmark's advertising slogan,

In 1979, Morgan sold the business on Thirteenth Street to Hallmark Cards of Kansas City, Missouri, because they share his commitment to quality.

"When you care enough to send the very best," might well read, "When you care enough to be the very best." It's a philosophy that has spilled over to the workforce, said Litho-Krome President John Hasting.

Litho-Krome's relationship with Hallmark dates back to 1955 and has grown progressively through the years as technology made it possible for the plant to produce the quality product for which Hallmark is known. Hallmark grew from 10 percent of Litho-Krome's business in 1964 to 75 percent by 1972. Litho-Krome, a wholly owned subsidiary of Hallmark, employs 275. Hallmark and Ambassador greeting cards make up 50 percent of the plant's production and Hallmark Business Expressions cards, 25 percent.

While the Hallmark card business is expected to remain stable in the future, the company's growth will be in the brochures, annual reports, and catalogs Litho-Krome produces for companies. "The volumes [for Hallmark] won't decrease but the commercial business will, over time, become bigger than the Hallmark portion," Hasting said.

Another exciting venue for Litho-Krome in the new millennium is in the reproduction of original works of art using digital processes that give near-perfect color reproduction. The Columbus facility is already producing three-dimensional copies of oil paintings on canvas using computer technology that captures all the details, down to the brush strokes.

Using the process, the company printed 15 of the 29 best selling works of art in the

country in 1997. *U.S.Art,* a consumer art publication, presented Litho-Krome with a lifetime achievement award in 1997, the first time a printer has ever won the award.

The key ingredient to the company's success is simple—a workforce with a

Litho-Krome

passion for their work. Like Tom Morgan, they have ink in their veins, and that's the best compliment a printer can be paid. ❧

Tom Morgan set the standards of quality at Litho-Krome, ones that to this day remain.

M Mike Greenblatt says there's nothing sexy about selling toilet paper. But that's okay. You don't need sexy when sales have doubled to $20 million in the last seven years and the future looks as bright as a copper penny.

Columbus Paper Company

The Columbus company, located in a 60,000-square-foot building on Joy Road, is a distributor of paper products, janitorial supplies, and industrial packaging materials. Its line of paper goods for home or office includes such items as toilet paper, napkins, cups, paper plates, computer paper, copy paper, mailroom supplies, and adding machine paper. In the janitorial line, it carries bleach, brooms, degreasers, detergents, floor-care products, garbage can liners, and disposable aprons, caps, coveralls, and gloves. Industrial packaging offerings include meat trays, corrugated boxes, plastic bags, and packing materials used in industrial settings. It also leases and sells industrial-sized vacuum cleaners, floor waxers, and carpet cleaners. It operates distribution facilities in Macon, Georgia, and Montgomery, Alabama.

The upswing in sales in recent years is the result of industrial growth in Columbus and its other market areas and to a change in company strategy. Its workforce has expanded from 60 to 80 employees in the last four years, and its target area now reaches the fringes of Atlanta. It has also seen strong growth at Mid-State Paper, its Macon branch, in the last four years as the facility established itself as a player in the community.

The company's market strategy has been overhauled, too, and now leans heavily toward industrial packaging, which makes up 65 to 70 percent of sales.

Columbus Paper is more than a distributor, Greenblatt said. "We consider ourselves a solution-based distributor. We love to go into a company that has a problem and figure out a solution. There is a whole host of companies that can sell what we sell. We do not have a monopoly in our industry, but we do have a unique ability to problem solve for our customers."

Unlike many of its competitors,

Columbus Paper is proud to be a part of the community.

Columbus Paper, with its computer systems and data links, is "extremely technology advanced for our industry," Greenblatt said. "We want to make sure we're on the cutting edge as far as technology is concerned."

Greenblatt predicts that in the next five years, Columbus Paper will be searching for its fourth location, probably near the Florida panhandle or in north Georgia, where it can serve the Georgia/Tennessee area. Both are growth markets.

Columbus Paper Co. was founded in 1933 by Greenblatt's grandfather, Mike A. Greenblatt, who sold school supplies and paper products on a cash-and-carry basis. His father, Ben Greenblatt, took over the company's leadership in 1955, expanding the company to open Ben-Mar Paper Co. in Montgomery. Both men emphasized providing hometown service for hometown people. That's true of Columbus Paper today.

"We deal mainly with local companies who like to keep their dollars in town with local people," Greenblatt said. "Having a local presence and a local feeling is something you can't replace in our industry." ❧

For four generations, Reaves Wrecking Company, Inc. has played its part in changing the face of Columbus and surrounding communities. The building demolition company has removed everything from community blight to elegant estates, from mantels and molding for remodeling work to total demolition of factories, schools, courthouses, and hospitals.

Its wrecking ball leveled such landmarks as the old Waverly Hotel, the Columbus Municipal Airport, the Columbus Municipal Auditorium, the old Columbus Police Station, the Fieldcrest Mills, and the Meritas Mills in preparation for new construction. It cleaned up fire-gutted sites such as the old Archer Hosiery Mill and the Kress Building downtown. And it tore down some notable homes that had fallen into disrepair, including the Blanchard-Howard House at 1208 Fourth Avenue, the old Hardaway Home at 1508 Third Avenue, the James Shorter House, which became St. Joseph's Academy and was one of the oldest structures in Georgia devoted to education, and the D. A. Turner home on Wynnton Road, which later became Trinity School.

Not everything was lost, however. Since 1981, President Bill Reaves and his wife, Nancy, with an eye for the historic, have salvaged many one-of-a-kind architectural elements such as doors, mantels, windows, columns, and newel posts to sell at their retail business, the Yesteryear Shop at 1027 Seventh Avenue. The wrecking company also cleans and resells old bricks and heart pine lumber from some of its demolition projects.

Reaves Wrecking leveled its first building in Columbus in 1946 when William R. Reaves hired his first crew and bought his first truck. Delighted when his son, Dewey, moved from Albany, Georgia, nine years later to work with him in the growing company, Reaves renamed the company W. R. Reaves and Son Wrecking Company.

Following the death of the elder Reaves in 1964, Dewey Reaves bought his father's interest in the company from his estate and renamed it Reaves Wrecking Company.

Later that same year, Bill Reaves, who grew up with a Tonka truck in one hand and a hammer in the other, joined his father in the business and in 1979, on his father's retirement, bought it.

The fourth generation to wield the wrecking ball, Craig Reaves, Bill's son, joined the business in 1987, bringing ideas for diversification. In 1990, after certification by Georgia Institute of Technology, Craig founded Abatement by Reaves Inc., a company licensed in Georgia, Alabama, and Florida to remove asbestos and lead from buildings. As the Reaves companies grew and conditions changed regarding waste disposal in Columbus, father and son opened a 60-acre landfill in Russell County, Alabama, called Pine Hollow Inc. in 1994 for disposal of construction and demolition wastes. The inert landfill serves

at a reasonable price, Reaves said. "It is important to all the Reaves family that we operate our businesses in an exemplary manner, with integrity, honesty, and dependability." ❧

Reaves Wrecking Company, Inc.

For four generations, Reaves Wrecking Company Inc. has played its part in changing the face of Columbus and surrounding communities. The building demolition company has removed everything from community blight to elegant estates, from mantels and molding for remodeling work to total demolition of factories, schools, courthouses, and hospitals.

16 counties and is one of 125 permitted landfills in the state. A fourth business, Containers by Reaves, is a roll-off container service that provides trash containers for construction and demolition sites.

The Reaves family of companies employs 25 to 35, depending on the amount of work underway.

With the approach of the millennium, Reaves will continue to provide the Columbus area with high quality service

Chapter Four

The Modern Era

The Chattahoochee Riverwalk is a center-piece in uptown revitalization and the city's financial district, and is attracting attention from numerous other American cities. It is to be anchored at the north end by Oliver Dam and at the southern terminus by the National Infantry Museum at Fort Benning. Photo by Jim Cawthorne.

The 1950s

The 1950s was the decade that sparked urban sprawl and brought forth the emergence of shopping as a pastime. War was long-forgotten and material gain became more of a desire than a need. Farming had only a tiny presence in the overall economy scheme and "progress" had become the new buzzword. Census records listed 80.6 percent of the county's population as urban but only 67.5 percent resided in the city. Downtown was hopping though, with shoppers and businessmen swarming like ants and parking spaces becoming impossible to find. None of which was surprising as the city was the commercial center for over 150,000 people on both sides of the river.

Despite the popularity of downtown, a few outlying clusters of retail businesses sprang up. Small groups of stores appeared in Rose Hill on Hamilton Road, by the junction of Buena Vista and Wynnton Roads, and near Fort Benning at Baker Village Center and the Traffic Circle Shopping Center. The city's first true shopping center, however, was actually completed in 1939. Called St. Elmo it pushed wares in the former Wildwood Park area for decades. Up until the '50s, the outlying stores did nothing to compete with the downtown district.

The city's growth brought more retailers to the downtown area but sufficient parking was never added. It wasn't long before shoppers became so disgruntled by the lack of parking that they traveled further for goods. This in turn spurred the retailers on. The Cross Country Plaza, built in 1956, became the prized jewel in the shopping collection and culminated the trend to shop away from downtown.

Many doctors, dentists, and service companies followed the merchants in the move from the central city. No longer focused on the downtown hub, residents began buying homes further away and new retailers and churches clustered in the resulting neighborhoods. Bigger became equated with better and so Columbus Square, the region's first air-conditioned mall arrived on the scene in 1965. An even larger shopping complex, Peachtree Mall, appeared ten years later.

The move to the suburbs was neither as rapid nor as complete as similar moves in other cities in America. Nonetheless, it caused significant concern and efforts were quickly initiated to revitalize the downtown area. A large part of the revitalization movement was a renewed emphasis on

As Columbus began its urban sprawl, sightings like this weren't so uncommon. Photo by Herb Cawthorne.

It was the decade of the '50s that brought forth the emergence of shopping as a pastime. Now throughout Columbus' Entertainment and Arts District lies a wonderland of unique shops. Here visitors are shopping for antiques and one-of-a-kind artistic works in the popular Riverside Galleria. Photo by Steven Duffey.

Photo by Herb Cawthorne.

Though Columbus is growing in leaps and bounds, preserving tradition is still a favored and beloved duty. But there's plenty of pleasure in remembering the past as well. In the quaint Magnolia & Ivy Tea Room, tea is served at the proper English hour of four with the entire traditional spread. Time period costumes and accessories are often worn by patrons wanting a touch of an elegant past. Photo by Steven Duffey.

The Columbus Museum. Photo by Jim Cawthorne.

cultural and educational development. That emphasis brought about the area's first museum, which opened on March 29, 1953, and Columbus College, which was established as the 17th unit of the University of Georgia system on May 14, 1958. The college opened its doors for the first time in September that same year with 13 faculty members and 263 students.

Older cultural establishments were revitalized or reopened. The line-up included the Columbus Symphony Orchestra, the Columbus Little Theatre, and the Springer Opera House, which had been scheduled for demolition.

The Three Arts League found a permanent home for the performing arts in the old Royal Theatre. They renovated the old building and renamed it the Three Arts Theatre. Previously the League had moved performances from place to place, namely the auditorium of the Chase Conservatory in the 1930s, the auditorium of the Ninth Street USO during World War II, and the Jordan High School auditorium in later years. ❖

(Right) The Columbus Museum garden. Photo by Jim Cawthorne.

Heritage Park pays tribute to the agricultural and industrial history of Columbus with these statues of a foundryman and a farmer. Photos by Jim Cawthorne.

(Right) The AFLAC Tower dominates the Columbus skyline. Photo by Jim Cawthorne.

The 1960s

Preserving the past remained a popular activity. The Confederate ironclad *Jackson* was drug from the mud of the Chattahoochee and donated to the soon-to-be-built Confederate Naval museum. The *Chattahoochee* was also rescued from the depths of the river, complete with two almost-intact engines produced by the Columbus Iron Works during the Civil War. The vessel and its engines were given to the new museum as well. Both recoveries were exasperating endeavors that took several efforts to complete. However, they were extremely popular undertakings in the 1960s.

On the very last day of the year 1969, the city grew through annexation of all but a small area of Muscogee County thus adding 42.5 square miles and over 103,000 people. It was a move rapidly undertaken to meet the 1970 census deadline. The census would determine the amount of state aid the city would qualify for throughout the next decade. Mayor J.R. Allen led the move to capture some $12 million in state funding and thus move all residents into a new age.

With less than 5 percent of the county area still outside city limits, the popular mayor soon turned an eye towards consoli-

Mrs. Mary C. Bl
Teacher - First Grade

(Below) Education is a top priority in Columbus. Wynnton School, serving Columbus students for over 150 years, is the oldest continually occupied educational facility in the state. Photo by Jim Cawthorne.

BENNING HILLS ELEMENTARY SCHOOL
Columbus, Georgia
1963-64

L. B. Hickson
Principal

Reading, writing, and arithmetic... A 1963 Benning Hills Elementary School class photograph. Courtesy of Mary de Wit.

Kinfolk's Corner used to be a booming gathering place for area residents after a hard day's work or on a lazy Saturday morning. It was here that "kinfolks" met to catch a ride and shoot the breeze.

(Right) Columbus Government Center. Photo by Jim Cawthorne

talk shows pounded and pondered the issue from both viewpoints reaching a crescendo on election day, April 11, 1962.

The city vote was pretty close but the majority still said no to the merger. The county vote showed a much larger distaste up.

In 1967, consolidation was attempted again. The city commission proposed the establishment of a new consolidation-study committee. To everyone's surprise, the county commission agreed to cooperate. The Georgia Legislature passed the enabling act in January 1969 creating the commission and specifying its duties and limits.

The 15 member commission was to study the two governments and all matters pertaining to a unified government. It could not, however, make or recommend any changes to the state courts, sheriff's department, the Muscogee County School District, or Bibb City. The 15 members selected to serve on the commission were Dr. Thomas Whitley, Ellis Swint, Ray Dowling, Wilbur Glenn, W.E. Harrell, Bobby D. Hydrick, Harold Jambon, G. Gunby Jordan, Jr., Bruce Land, Martelle Layfield, Jr., Nolan Murrah, Robert Patterson, William B. Turner, John Wynn, and J. Gordon Young. It soon became obvious that there was a lack of nonwhite representation.

Rather than have to return to the legislators to correct this omission, four black community leaders were asked to serve as advisory members. They were Albert Thompson, M.F. Jackson, Dr. Robert T. Wright, and Gordon H. Kitchen.

The commission was funded equally by the county and the city. The study was conducted with every effort given to public awareness of the activities and findings of the commission and its various sub-committees. When the completed draft of the charter was submitted to the Judge of the Muscogee County Court on April 1, 1970, a full-scale campaign in support of the move was launched by the Chamber and various interested citizens. Public endorsements were gathered, town meetings were held, and the news media heralded the merits of consolidation. No serious opposition ever arose and 1970 voters approved adoption of the charter with a four-to-one margin. It would be just in time for the city's greatest challenge yet.... ❖

dation of the two governments. The merging of the health departments over 30 years ago and the school systems 20 years ago were convincing precedents to follow. Many thought consolidation of the governments was an obvious and logical solution to double taxation and wasteful duplication in services and official structure. It was not to be that simple, however. Both sides of the issue struggled to present their side and many a temper was invoked.

Proponents of consolidation had facts and benefits on their side. Opponents promoted a more emotional argument based primarily on the fear of loss of control by the people. Political advertisements, editorials, cartoons, posters, billboards, and radio

IN HONOR
OF
OUR VETERANS

The 1970s

An influential bi-racial citizens committee and widespread cooperation among the people had helped Columbus deal peacefully with racial issues through the 1960s. Integration of all restaurants, theaters, and most public facilities was complete by the end of the decade. Restrictive seating on city buses had been eliminated, but the schools had yet to be desegregated. In July 1971 the desegregation plan of the Muscogee County School District was approved by the federal courts and the school board was ordered to implement the plan in September. As news of the decision got around, unexpected racial violence rocked the city.

Many said the riots were instigated by outsiders, others disagreed. But either way, the fires burned just as hot. A series of fire bombings cost the city an estimated $2 million from property damage, ruined businesses, lost payrolls, and the costs for added security from police and fire departments. The new consolidated government's speedy action seemed to prove that it, rather than a dual government, was in a better position to deal with a major crisis. The city council quickly gave Mayor J.R. Allen emergency powers to deal expediently with the problem. Mayor Allen took a firm but fair stance in resolving the problem and the city settled down as quickly as it had exploded. Redoubled efforts to reach an equitable understanding between the races became the order of the day.

Roads came into focus again in the '70s. Transportation and road construction had lagged in the 1950s and the city was now omitted from established travel patterns. Even the federal government left Columbus and Fort Benning out of its plans for a massive system of interstate highways designed to move military equipment and personnel in times of emergency. It was obvious to Columbusites that something must be done to connect the city with other major areas. I-185 connecting Columbus to I-85 was finally completed in 1979 making Columbus into a kind of suburb of the state's capital. Other roads and bypasses were completed in this period and the city finally obtained the means to transport efficiently over ground.

The old Iron Works building was restored and transformed into the Iron Works Trade and Convention Center. The grand opening was four days prior to the opening of the new interstate. Columbus was now literally on the map due to the new road systems and now it had a convention center to attract conventioneers, party-goers, exhibits, and tourists. The old, abandoned Empire Mill across the street from the Iron Works remained vacant until developed by a group of local investors into a prestigious Hilton Hotel in June of 1982. As expected, the Iron Works became infinitely more popular with the addition of a hotel. The two restorations coupled with I-185 was a much needed shot in the arm for downtown revitalization efforts.

On the north end of town, Gunby Jordan came up with the idea to host a golf tournament when he learned of an opening on the Professional Golf Association (PGA) Tour's calendar. The first year, the event offered a $60,000 purse and was named the Green Island Invitational Tournament. In 1971, the Columbus event became the Southern Open Tournament but it was still held at the Green Island Country Club. Later the event became so popular on the PGA tour that it moved to

(Left) 1998 Buick Challenge winner, Steve Elkington. Photo by Jim Cawthorne.

nearby Callaway Gardens to better accommodate the crowds of fans. The Southern
Open, later called the Buick Challenge, laid
the groundwork for other national and
international sporting events to eventually
call Columbus home. ➷

*The Iron Works Trade and Convention Center
acts like is a tremendous magnet by attracting people, events, and business to Columbus.
Photo by Herb Cawthorne.*

The 1980s

Finally connected to the interstate, Columbus was no longer isolated. But the city wanted to be much more than a tiny little blip on the state road map. It wasn't long before plans were put into action to make Columbus a significant transportation hub. It worked. The city, once standing at the end of a two-lane road as the lonely destination of a most exhaustive trip, now stood dead center of I-185, South Georgia Parkway (Corridor Z), the Fall Line Freeway, and U.S. 27. Some of these roadways took years to complete but it didn't matter. The city was patient and time delivered the pay-off in due course.

Revitalization of downtown included a name change for the area: Uptown Columbus. The new name was announced among much fanfare and excitement. Historic restorations continued in an outbreak of modern day offices, restaurants, and gathering places in some old buildings and a collection of museums among others. It was a time of high expectations, fond memories, and fast rolling money in the profits of old and new industry alike. People began the journey back to the center city… a journey that would continue for the next two decades.

Gaiety accompanied the money made in those days like a swooning lover. Three competitive hot air balloon events featured 15 balloons competing in intricate maneuvers. Their graceful colors billowed above the city in the culminating ascension competition at sunrise on the morning of the very first Steeplechase. Pre-race parties were held all over the city and at Callaway Gardens where the race would be held. A concert by the Columbus Jazz Band was held at the Iron Works; an Ascot Ball at the Springer Opera House. There was a "people chase," a "bike chase," and a delicious food fair called "Taste of Columbus." There was considerable pulpit-pounding as churches objected to their congregations watching the horses rather than warming the pews. Nevertheless, the graceful thoroughbreds still pound their way up steep inclines and around sharp turns, stretching out, muscles straining, soaring up and over the jumps to this very day. ❧

Photo by Jim Cawthorne.

Nature enthusiasts can walk among a very large and exotic collection of butterflies from around the world in the natural setting of the Cecil B. Day Butterfly Center at Callaway Gardens. Courtesy of Callaway Gardens.

The Steeplechase at Callaway Gardens always attracts big, colorful, and festive crowds. Courtesy of Callaway Gardens.

Loft apartments in Uptown Columbus are in high demand. Located along the Riverwalk, throughout the entertainment district, and within the financial district, they are major draws to people who like to be in the center of city life and close enough to walk to work. Photo by Steven Duffey.

T Excellence in health care and community service has been a tradition at St. Francis Hospital since the Sisters of St. Francis of Millvale opened its doors to the public in 1950. Although the Sisters have gone, the commitment continues at the

St. Francis Hospital

private, acute-care community hospital on Manchester Expressway.

St. Francis offers inpatient, outpatient, and emergency room services and enjoys a regional reputation for excellence in cardiac care.

St. Francis Hospital was built on the outskirts of the city by the Sisters on pastureland donated by J. W. Woodruff Sr. Funding the building of a Catholic hospital in a predominantly non-Catholic city was no easy undertaking, but it was one Dr. Bert Tillery and banker Jack Key Sr. approached with passion. Fiercely determined, they and the Sisters raised in two years the $1.9 million needed to build the hospital.

On April 17, 1950, the original 154-bed hospital served its first patient. The Sisters continued to own and operate the hospital until 1969, when they deeded over its assets to the St. Francis Hospital Board of Trustees. From 1969 to 1993, the hospital

*St. Francis operates a health education and on-site health screening store in Peachtree Mall called **Health Matters**. More than 40,000 people annually use the service's blood pressure checks, participate in its mall walking program, or attend its on-site educational classes or health screenings.*

continued to be managed by the Sisters of St. Francis. Then in 1993, the board signed a management contract with the SSM Health Care System of St. Louis to take over management duties. Michael E. Garrigan arrived in July 1993 and became the first lay president in the history of the hospital. In December 1997, this agreement ended and the board contracted directly with Garrigan to continue to serve as president and chief executive officer.

To serve the needs of those in this region within a large radius of Columbus, St. Francis currently has 292 beds on its main campus and 84 beds at The Bradley Center of St. Francis, its mental health facility. It employs over 1,400 people and has more than 250 board certified physicians on its medical staff.

The hospital is accredited by the Joint Commission on Accreditation of Healthcare Organizations and received recognition for its "best practice" Infection Control Program, making it a model for hospitals across the nation.

Several renovation programs have improved the quality of care and the ambiance at St. Francis in recent years. Renovation of the second floor Intermediate Cardiac Care Unit and the third and fourth patient floors was completed in 1997 with added private rooms, open nurses' stations, and improved aesthetics. In 1998, a $9.3-million project added a new central energy facility and a new front entrance and lobby to make the hospital more efficient and customer friendly.

More construction is on the drawing board for the hospital, as is a host of new programs, as it moves into the millennium. Says Chief Executive Michael Garrigan about the future: "St. Francis is stronger clinically and financially than it ever has been . . . . This hospital will definitely be a major player in the health care arena, not only in the city of Columbus but in this area of Georgia and Alabama."

St. Francis Hospital was built on the outskirts of the city by the Sisters of St. Francis on pastureland donated by J. W. Woodruff Sr.

He continues: "At the same time we're developing new programs, we're going to continue to develop new relationships. Quality is being entered into every facet of the operation at St. Francis. Another thing that we're trying to do is to develop a higher quality workforce, and, as with any organization, the quality of its workforce is probably its most important component in terms of success of the organization."

"We're looking specifically at programs to further accommodate and provide services for the senior population, including independent and dependent living arrangements. We are also looking at developing a number of off-campus locations that would accommodate surgical procedures and outpatient activities. We're also looking at developing a number of programs that are not traditionally hospital-based but are more preventive in nature."

The Heart Institute of St. Francis

The Heart Institute of St. Francis is widely recognized as the region's premier source for the diagnosis, treatment, and rehabilitation of patients with heart problems. Highly experienced cardiologists and surgeons, supported by a skilled professional staff, provide total cardiac care from the most advanced diagnostic procedures to the area's only open-heart surgery program—from cardiac catheterizations and balloon angioplasty to an innovative rehabilitation program.

Since the first open-heart procedure in 1974, St. Francis has been dedicated to providing comprehensive cardiac care with the most advanced procedures and state-of-the-art equipment. St. Francis was the first hospital in the area to perform open-heart surgery, the first to perform balloon angioplasty and automatic defibrillator implant procedures, and the first to perform atherectomies and homografts (human tissue implants). Over the years, The Heart Institute of St. Francis has been established as the region's first choice for excellence in cardiac care.

In the case of a cardiac emergency, every second counts. In order to provide patients with fast and effective emergency treatment, The Heart Institute of St. Francis provides specially equipped cardiac rooms located in the emergency department. This area is staffed around-the-clock by highly skilled personnel experienced with and sensitive to the needs of cardiac patients.

The Heart Institute of St. Francis utilizes the latest diagnostic procedures to provide accurate analysis and determine treatment for patients with cardiovascular disease. These procedures range from non-invasive tests such as the electrocardiogram

Light the Spirit is St. Francis' gift to the community during the holiday season as the hospital is aglow with lights and a life-size manger scene.

(EKG), stress tests, nuclear cardiolite studies, echocardiograms, and Doppler flow studies to the more complex and sophisticated tests such as coronary angiograms. Many of these tests can be performed on an outpatient basis. They can help evaluate heart and blood vessel abnormalities or produce images of the heart muscle and valves. In addition, St. Francis cardiologists

have performed over 15,000 cardiac catheterizations in the most sophisticated and comprehensive cardiac diagnostic laboratory in the Columbus area.

The Heart Institute of St. Francis provides cardiovascular and thoracic surgical treatment for a variety of diseases. Surgical intervention is available for coronary artery disease, valvular heart disease, congenital heart disease, acute and chronic diseases of the thoracic aorta, pulmonary diseases of all kinds, esophageal diseases, diseases of mediastinum, pleura, chest wall, and diaphragm, pacemaker implantation, and implantable defibrillators. In case of coronary artery disease, when other treatments are not indicated to correct the problem, coronary artery bypass surgery (CABG) may be necessary. After the recovery period, most patients return to a normal, active life.

The Critical Care and Intermediate Cardiac Care units at The Heart Institute of St. Francis are equipped to care for cardiac patients in need of constant monitoring. These units are staffed by specially trained nurses and utilize state-of-the-art computer cardiac monitoring systems and other lifesaving equipments which enable the nurses and medical staff to continuously manage the progress of each patient.

The Cardiopulmonary Rehabilitation Program is designed for people recovering from heart or lung problems. The overall goal is to help complete the recovery process and assist the patient in returning to an active, productive lifestyle.

Although the cardiopulmonary rehabilitation staff directs the rehabilitation program, the patient continues to be under the care of his or her personal physician. The referring physician will receive reports on patients' progress and will be consulted as needed on matters of care and treatment. Counseling, lectures, and group discussions for patients and their family are an important part of the rehabilitation and recovery program.

The Heart Institute of St. Francis shares

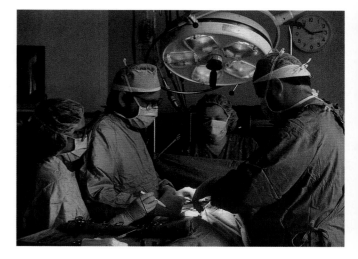

Highly experienced cardiologists and surgeons, supported by a skilled professional staff, provide total cardiac care from the most advanced diagnostic procedures to the area's only open-heart surgery program.

its expertise with physicians and hospitals through a partnership for care called the Heart Network. The Network is a system designed to deliver state-of-the-art emergency intervention quickly to patients throughout the west Georgia and east Alabama region. Through the Heart Network program, physicians and hospitals in surrounding communities can be afforded access to services which include heart emergency services, physician consultation, assistance with transfers, and educational programs.

The Bradley Center of St. Francis

The Bradley Center of St. Francis is a unique mental health resource committed to establishing wellness for the whole person—emotionally, socially, spiritually, and physically. St. Francis services, which include outpatient counseling, addiction treatment, inpatient and day treatment, support groups, and educational programs, work together to enhance the quality of life for individuals, families, and the community.

The Outpatient Program at The Bradley Center of St. Francis provides professional, qualified licensed staff to assist individuals and families in resolving problems, concerns, or changes that are impacting their lives. Services are designed to allow people to maintain their daily schedules while getting help with life problems. Clients can schedule appointments at times that are convenient to them. Outpatient Services include individual, group, marital, and

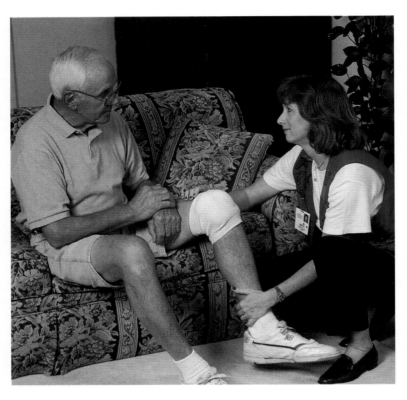

Home Care of St. Francis serves patients in 10 counties in west Georgia.

family counseling, diagnostic evaluations, and psychological testing.

The Pathway at The Bradley Center of St. Francis leads the way in providing substance abuse services in the community. As the oldest hospital-based treatment program in Columbus, the staff has years of experience in assessment, education, and counseling. In addition, St. Francis specializes in the treatment of dual diagnosis, the combination of mental or emotional ailments with substance abuse or addiction. Services at The Pathway are individualized according to each client's age, needs, and resources.

St. Francis' inpatient and day treatment programs provide a warm, caring, and structured approach to help adolescents overcome psychiatric disorders or substance abuse programs. The day program is less costly for patients not requiring the 24-hour structure of inpatient care. It provides patients with comprehensive, intensive treatment five days a week and the convenience of returning home in the evenings. Transportation is also available for many patients.

Home Care of St. Francis

To provide quality home health care to patients in their own homes, St. Francis entered the home health arena in 1995.

Home Care of St. Francis serves patients in 10 counties in west Georgia. The highly qualified staff of skilled nurses, certified home health aides, medical social workers, and physical, speech, and occupational therapists makes approximately 200,000 house calls each year.

Home Medical Equipment of St. Francis

Striving to meet the complete needs of its patients, Home Medical Equipment of St. Francis provides the largest selection of quality home medical equipment and services in the region. Clinically trained professionals help patients select the most cost-effective solutions to best meet their specific needs—from wheelchairs, beds, or diabetic supplies to many hard-to-find items. They work closely with physicians, visiting nurses, case managers, and other caregivers. In addition, the staff ensures thorough understanding of the equipment through follow-up at the hospital or home.

Health Dynamics of St. Francis

Health Dynamics of St. Francis offers interdisciplinary outpatient rehabilitation services including comprehensive neurological rehabilitation, orthopedic, physical and occupational therapy, industrial medicine, and exercise programs. A highly skilled and caring staff provides individualized treatment in a state-of-the-art medical/rehabilitation facility. Its goals are to challenge patients to reach their maximum level of community function and provide fitness/wellness clients supervised exercise and educational opportunities to enhance a healthy lifestyle. Continually striving for improvement, services are evaluated and patient outcomes are measured to ensure that care is efficient as well as effective.

Wound Care Center® of St. Francis

The Wound Care Center® of St. Francis

is a unique health service dedicated to caring for people with wounds that have resisted healing. A team of experienced doctors and nurses combine knowledge in all areas of wound management with the most advanced medical technology.

The Wound Care Center® of St. Francis is part of a nationwide network of Wound Care Centers that have established an impressive record in healing wounds that others thought hopeless, including many that might have required amputations.

Thousands of patients have come to the Wound Care Center for treatment of their wounds that have resisted healing despite months, or even years, of traditional treatment. For most patients, Wound Care programs have resulted in complete healing in just a few months.

Outreach and Wellness Programs

From its inception, St. Francis has responded to the community's need for medical information. That tradition continues through its outreach and wellness programs.

Ask-A-Nurse is a 24-hour, seven-day-a-week health information and referral service. The registered nurse on the other end of the line is often a godsend to a worried parent with a feverish baby or to someone who is concerned that their indigestion might be a heart attack. The dedicated service, started in 1988, answers more than 86,000 calls a year.

When St. Francis came up with the idea of setting up a health education and on-site

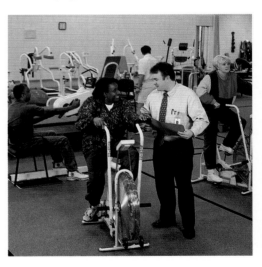

Health Dynamics of St. Francis offers interdisciplinary outpatient rehabilitation services including comprehensive neurological rehabilitation, orthopedic, physical and occupational therapy, industrial medicine, and exercise programs.

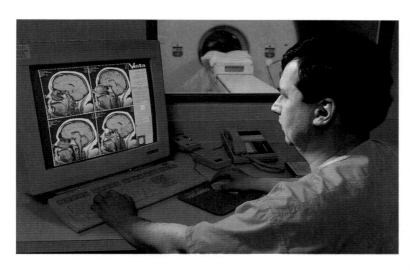

State-of-the-art equipment and technology keep St. Francis on the diagnostic cutting edge of health care.

health screening store in Peachtree Mall in 1995, some people wondered about the efficacy of this program. But the venture, **Health Matters,** has been wildly successful. More than 40,000 people annually use the service's blood pressure checks, participate in its mall walking program, or attend its on-site educational classes or health screenings.

Recognizing that physical and spiritual wellness go hand in hand, the hospital's **Parish Nurse Program** was started in the early 1990s and reaches out to those in the religious community. More than 30 congregations provide health ministries through the use of parish nurses.

St. Francis also extends its message of wellness to the business community through on-site health fairs, where employees can participate in health screenings and receive information on health-related topics.

St. Francis sponsors **SafetyCab** during the holiday season to reduce the number of DUI-related accidents and fatalities in the community. In its 16th year, SafetyCab offers a free ride home from holiday parties, bars, and restaurants from December 10 to January 1. Between 250 to 300 drinking drivers use the service annually.

The hospital is proud of its involvement with Pacelli High School, St. Anne School, and Eddy Middle School through the **Partners-in-Education Program,** an initiative of the Greater Columbus Chamber of Commerce that pairs businesses with schools to enrich them both.

The **St. Francis Hospital Auxiliary** has provided volunteer and monetary

assistance to the hospital since 1958. Assisting on patient floors and the information desk, working in the gift shop and pushing the cheer cart, more than 315 volunteers have given in excess of 650,000 hours. The Auxiliary has also donated more than $1.5 million to support projects within the hospital, including the Intensive Care Unit, equipment for cardiac rehabilitation, video endoscopy equipment, and the cardiac diagnostic unit. It offers annual scholarships to students in the health care profession. ✒

Excellence in health care and community service has been a tradition at St. Francis Hospital since the Sisters of St. Francis opened its doors to the community in 1950.

In the world of sports medicine, Columbus is a leader because of one man, Dr. Jack C. Hughston. As one of the founders of the sports medicine disciplines, he has helped lead the world to the realization that the physician must understand

The Hughston Clinic, P.C.

how an injury occurred to understand how to treat the injury. Through his observations of high school and collegiate athletes, Dr. Hughston saw that athletic injuries occurred differently from other types of injuries. These typically high-impact mechanisms of injury caused damage to specific structures in these athletes. In addition, unlike many nonathletes, athletes expected to resume their former level of activity as soon as possible. Therefore, treatment needed to be tailored to these injuries and to the expectations of the patient. Applying this knowledge, Dr. Hughston found that treatment techniques used for athletes also could benefit other patients, such as industry workers, recreational athletes, and nonathletes.

Today, The Hughston Clinic, P.C., at 6262 Veterans Parkway, is a leading center for the prevention and treatment of injuries and diseases of the musculoskeletal system. The Clinic boasts a highly skilled and experienced staff of 50 physicians who practice comprehensive orthopaedic sports medicine, family medicine, and occupational medicine. Its 22 locations include 16

The Hughston Clinic, P.C. is a leading center for the prevention and treatment of injuries and diseases of the musculoskeletal system.

clinics in Georgia, three in Colorado, two in Alabama, and one in South Carolina.

The Clinic's physicians, fellows, and athletic trainers are dedicated to continuing the community service program that Dr. Hughston started 50 years ago. They volunteer their time and experience to high school and collegiate athletic programs, providing comprehensive preparticipation physical examinations and working with coaches on injury prevention strategies.

The Hughston Clinic, P.C. is part of a family of services that include Hughston Management Services, an organization that offers health care management services to physicians and physician practices; Hughston Orthopaedic Network, a statewide network of orthopaedic providers; Hughston Sports Medicine Foundation, Inc., a nonprofit research and education organization; Hughston Health

As one of the founders of the sports medicine disciplines, Dr. Jack C. Hughston has helped lead the world to the realization that the physician must understand how an injury occurred to understand how to treat the injury.

and Wellness, a facility concerned with wellness; and Hughston Diagnostics, a provider of comprehensive imaging services including magnetic resonance imaging, computerized tomography scans, and electromyograms.

Not willing to rest on its laurels—and they are many—The Hughston Clinic, P.C. looks forward to a future in which its research and treatment programs will improve the quality of life for people of all ages and all levels of activity. ➜

Like Jack Hughston, George McCluskey Jr. was a trailblazer. Not only did he enter the new and rapidly emerging field of physical therapy when he opened his private practice in 1955, but he also became one of the first physical therapists in the nation to be associated with the new discipline of sports medicine. In 1970, his business, known as Rehabilitation Services of Columbus, Inc., became the second

Rehabilitation Services has more than 300 employees in 24 locations in Georgia, Alabama, South Carolina, and North Carolina, and its clients include world-famous athletes.

privately owned physical therapy company in the country to become incorporated.

As the fields of physical therapy and sports medicine grew, so did McCluskey's company. As time passed, the company realized that its knowledge of sports injuries was also applicable to other types of injuries. As a result, all of Rehabilitation Services' clients, regardless of the cause of their injuries, benefited. Today, Rehabilitation Services has more than 300 employees in 24 locations in Georgia, Alabama, South Carolina, and North Carolina, and its clients include world-famous athletes. The high caliber and skill of its therapists have created an international reputation for the company.

As its stable of services increased and its locations multiplied, Rehabilitation Services became the holding company for a number of organizations under its umbrella. Human Performance and Rehabilitation Centers, Inc. operate more than ten private practices located throughout the southeastern United States. Services include Physical and Occupational

Therapy, Spine Rehabilitation, Pediatric Rehabilitation, Electrophysiology, Industrial Rehabilitation, and Outreach and Fitness. Rehabilitation Contract Services, Inc. provides a broad array of both inpatient and outpatient rehabilitation services to hospitals, schools, and health care facilities. Services include Physical and Occupational Therapy, Pediatric Rehabilitation, Electrophysiology, Neurophysiological Monitoring Services, and Recreational Therapy. Committed Fitness Systems, Inc. provides specialty health and fitness programs. Medical and Health Resources, Inc. is a state-of-the-art facility specializing in the fabricating and fitting of orthotics and prosthetics. Medical and Health Resources also provides respiratory services and is a supplier for home medical equipment. Work Assessment and Readiness offers industrial rehabilitation programs, including functional capacity evaluations, impairment ratings, injury prevention programs, job site analysis, on-site physical therapy, occupational health services, and post-employment screenings. The Southern Rehab Alliance, LLC is a network of rehabilitation providers that handles managed care contracting and patient care. McCluskey Education and Research Foundation, Inc. is a nonprofit foundation that has played a major role in promoting the rehabilitation profession through education and research activities.

Rehabilitation Services' excellent reputation for quality care and its commitment to education and research have led to a long list of awards for the company and its founder, including the 1998 Georgia Family Business of the Year Award in the large business category presented by the Family Enterprise Center of Kennesaw State University and *Georgia Trend* magazine. Six family members continue the tradition of excellence that George McCluskey began. The company has also been the recipient of the American Physical Therapy Association's 1995 Best Private Practice Award Nationally, and the senior

McCluskey was named the 1997 Small Business Person of the Year Nationally by the Small Business Council of America.

Through the decades, community involvement has been the hallmark of Rehabilitation Services as exemplified

Rehabilitation Services of Columbus, Inc.

by the creation of the Institute of Athletic Health Care and Research, Inc., which is a sports medicine outreach program cofounded with the Hughston Clinic.

Rehabilitation Services, headquartered on Veterans Parkway, is banking on its people to secure its future. "It's our people who define who we are," said President Brian McCluskey. "Our focus always has been and always will be on interaction with our patients. Our people make that happen."

Rehabilitation Services is not looking "to see how big we can get" in the future, McCluskey said. "We want to see how good we can get. But if being better makes us bigger, that's okay too." ◆

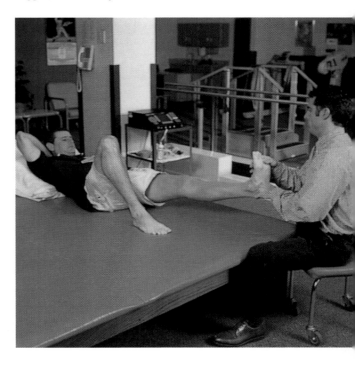

Rehabilitation Services' excellent reputation for quality care and its commitment to education and research has led to a long list of awards for the company and its founder.

Dr. Jack Hughston's dream of a comprehensive sports medicine facility was realized in 1984, when the Hospital Corporation of America built the Hughston Sports Medicine Hospital. A 100-acre tree-shaded campus located in north Columbus

Hughston Sports Medicine Hospital

was the setting for the nation's first hospital specifically designed for the treatment of musculoskeletal/sports injuries. The campus, which also includes the Hughston Clinic, the Hughston Sports Medicine Foundation, and Rehabilitation Services of Columbus, offers the entire spectrum of orthopaedic services.

Today, this specialty hospital provides services for sports injuries, joint replacement, back treatment, short-term rehabilitation, stroke rehabilitation, and general orthopaedics. In addition, it serves as a state-of-the-art teaching hospital for Fellows from the Hughston Sports Medicine Foundation.

Hughston physicians treat orthopaedic disorders, diseases, and injuries. When surgery is required, both inpatient and outpatient surgical procedures are performed in the hospital's eight operating

suites. Equipped with the latest in surgical equipment, the hospital offers maximum protection for the patient and the latest treatment options to the physician. The hospital contains all private rooms, suites, and oversized beds and doors.

An on-site radiology department performs traditional x-rays, as well as nuclear medicine, CT scans, and MRIs.

Following surgery, each patient receives follow-up treatment from the operating physician and a registered physical therapist who works with the physician to develop a personalized physical therapy program.

Hughston Sports Medicine Hospital is committed to patient satisfaction. The facility's Patient CARE Representative makes sure that the patient and the patient's family are as comfortable as possible. Hughston believes—and has incorporated into its mission statement—that each individual is unique and of intrinsic worth; that all who enter its doors will be treated with compassion and kindness; that business should be conducted with absolute honesty, integrity, and fairness; and that members of the health care team should be treated with loyalty, dignity, and respect.

On these values Hughston Sports Medicine Hospital has built a reputation that knows no boundaries, drawing patients from as far away as Spain, Brazil, and England. People from across the country and around the world come to Hughston for diagnoses they can count on and treatment they can trust.

Hughston Sports Medicine Hospital is owned by Columbia/HCA Healthcare Corporation, which operates more than 300 hospitals in the United States, England, and Switzerland. For the past three years Hughston was ranked in the top one percent of all Columbia/HCA hospitals in patient satisfaction.

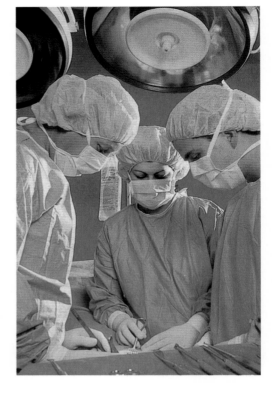

Both inpatient and outpatient surgical procedures are performed in the hospital's eight operating suites. Equipped with the latest in surgical equipment, the hospital offers maximum protection for the patient and the latest treatment options to the physician.

Hugh Tappan, the hospital's president and chief executive officer, says of the future: "In the next decade, we will continue to promote the Hughston campus as the premier orthopaedic site in America as well as to work collaboratively with local providers and insurance companies to provide Columbus and the surrounding communities with the highest level of orthopaedic care available."

As a new millennium dawns, the Hughston Sports Medicine Hospital stands as a tribute to Dr. Jack C. Hughston, a man who dreamed of excellence and envisioned the possibilities in a new field of study, whose vision chartered the course of sports medicine, whose experience and expertise taught hundreds of physicians, and whose dedication improved the quality of life for patients not only in Columbus but also throughout the world. ❖

A 100-acre tree-shaded campus located in north Columbus is the setting for the nation's first hospital specifically designed for the treatment of musculoskeletal/sports injuries, Hughston Sports Medicine Hospital.

Recognizing the importance of education and research in the field of sports medicine, Dr. Jack C. Hughston founded the Hughston Sports Medicine Foundation, Inc. in 1968 as a nonprofit research and education center for the study of musculoskeletal wellness. An outgrowth of The Hughston Clinic, P.C., the Foundation was created "to help people in all walks of life attain the highest possible levels of musculoskeletal health, fitness, and athletic prowess by providing national and international leadership in orthopaedic and sports medicine research, education, and communication."

Education is the cornerstone of the Foundation. Its educational mission includes a prestigious sports medicine fellowship program that draws orthopaedic and primary care physicians from all over the world to train at the renowned Hughston Sports Medicine Center. The Foundation receives more than 100 applications each year for the coveted year-long fellowship positions. Physicians who have completed their fellowships now practice throughout the world using the skills and knowledge they learned working with one of the founders of the sports medicine disciplines—Dr. Jack Hughston.

In addition to fellowship opportunities, the Foundation offers postgraduate continuing education programs. Physicians,

An outgrowth of The Hughston Clinic, P.C., the Hughston Sports Medicine Foundation was created "to help people in all walks of life attain the highest possible levels of musculoskeletal health, fitness, and athletic prowess by providing national and international leadership in orthopaedic and sports medicine research, education, and communication."

nurses, athletic trainers, educators, coaches, and paramedics who participate in these programs learn innovative injury prevention and treatment techniques that they can apply in the clinic, on the field, or in the classroom.

Located on the 100-acre Hughston Sports Medicine Center campus, the Foundation houses the Surgical Education Center, a 150-seat auditorium, television and illustration studios, a research laboratory, a medical writing department, and a comprehensive orthopaedic library. In keeping with its goal to educate, the Foundation's library serves as a resource in the study of sports medicine and orthopaedics. The library offers not only books and journals but also the latest in audiotapes, videotapes, sound slide programs, and computer programs. These services are available to medical professionals and to the lay public. The Foundation also offers medical writers, medical illustrators, and audiovisual personnel devoted to helping physicians communicate their knowledge and research through words, pictures, and audiovisual media.

Dr. Hughston has passed along his conviction that to treat an injury is not enough; a physician must continue to learn and to share that knowledge. That is why research plays such an important role in the mission of the Foundation. Physicians conduct state-of-the-art research in biomechanics, pharmaceutical trials, surgical techniques, and instrumentation. Researchers also conduct numerous studies related to orthopaedics and sports medicine to help maintain quality of care for The Hughston Clinic's patients.

Holding fast to its mission of research, education, and communication, the Hughston Sports Medicine Foundation, Inc. will continue to build on the traditions that Dr. Jack Hughston started 50 years ago. ➔

Hughston Sports Medicine Foundation, Inc.

Recognizing the importance of education and research in the field of sports medicine, Dr. Jack C. Hughston founded the Hughston Sports Medicine Foundation, Inc. in 1968 as a nonprofit research and education center for the study of musculoskeletal wellness.

At AFLAC Incorporated, success is more than black ink on a ledger. It's about being there when a policyholder's child is diagnosed with cancer, or when an injured breadwinner can't work to support the family, or when an elderly parent has to go

AFLAC Incorporated

into a long-term care facility.

It's about fostering in its employees an attitude of caring about the community and the world in which they live and about working to make that world better. AFLAC employees can be found wherever something special is going on in the community. An example of the company's caring is its multimillion-dollar renovation and expansion of the pediatric oncology unit at Egleston Children's Hospital in Atlanta, which was completed in 1998. The AFLAC Cancer Center at Egleston is now the largest children's cancer center in the Southeast.

That AFLAC is financially successful is

undisputed. The company's headquarters are on its 66-acre Wynnton Road campus, with state-of-the-art facilities and the 19-story AFLAC tower. AFLAC is the leading provider of supplemental insurance sold at workplaces across the United States and the largest foreign insurer in Japan. It insures 40 million people worldwide, boasts a workforce of over 4,000, sells its products through 30,000 agents, and reports to 130,000 shareholders.

With assets of $29 billion and revenues of more than $7.3 billion, AFLAC's rate of return to investors compounds at 22 percent annually. AFLAC is a Fortune 500 company, a position it holds from internal growth—not acquisitions—and is listed on the New York Stock Exchange, the Pacific Stock Exchange, and the Tokyo Stock Exchange.

The company consistently receives high ratings on financial condition and operating performance by independent rating services. Both Standard and Poor's and Duff & Phelps give it an "AA" rating for claims-paying ability, and A.M. Best gives the company an "A + ."

The company was founded in 1955 by John, Paul, and William Amos, three

plished," said AFLAC President Dan Amos. "They risked their own capital to start a business in a very competitive industry and then took AFLAC from a small Georgia insurance company to an international supplemental insurance giant. My goal is to build on their legacy and take AFLAC to new levels of success in the United States and Japan for the ultimate benefit of the company's shareholders, policyholders, and employees."

Several events have been critical to AFLAC's success. In 1958, it introduced one of the first cancer expense insurance policies in the United States, a product that was basically its mainstay for almost 30 years. Though the insurance was sold only in Georgia and Alabama initially, sales by the 1960s had expanded throughout the Southeast. Today, AFLAC supplemental insurance is sold in all 50 states as well as U.S. territories.

In 1974, AFLAC became the second foreign company in history licensed to sell insurance products in Japan. Today, AFLAC is the largest foreign insurer in Japan and ranks among the top four most profitable foreign companies doing business in any industry in Japan. Of the companies listed on the Tokyo Stock Exchange, 97 percent offer AFLAC products to their employees. AFLAC insures 30 million people in Japan, representing about 23 percent of the total population. AFLAC Japan accounts for two-thirds of AFLAC's after-tax earnings, a percentage expected to decrease as AFLAC U.S. continues its growth trend.

In the 1980s, under the leadership of Chairman Paul Amos and President and CEO Dan Amos, the company began strategically positioning itself to compete in a changing insurance market. Part of the repositioning included introducing an expanded product line of supplemental policies that would include its flagship, cancer expense protection, as well as accident, sickness, disability, hospital indemnity, intensive care, short- and long-term disability, long-term care, term life, and Medicare supplement policies. The new products now account for 75 percent of new sales in the United States. The best selling policy in the United States has been the accident/disability policy for four consecutive years.

In 1992, AFLAC expanded its portfolio of supplemental products in Japan. Since

Headquartered on a 66-acre campus on Wynnton Road, AFLAC is the leading provider of supplemental insurance sold at workplaces across the United States and the largest foreign insurer in Japan.

brothers who took a risk that paid off in dividends. "My father, Paul, and my uncles, John and Bill, founded AFLAC 40 years ago. I'm still in awe of what they accom-

Under the leadership of AFLAC President Daniel P. Amos, the company is striving for new levels of success in the United States and Japan.

1989, AFLAC has repatriated more than $1 billion of its profits in Japan to the United States.

"I've been very proud that the product-broadening initiative we started several years ago has been an unqualified success in both our primary markets," Dan Amos said. "We've also made significant strides expanding our distribution system to grow AFLAC's customer base to more than 40 million people worldwide. And through advertising, we've dramatically increased AFLAC's name awareness, propelling sales and increasing our efforts recruiting new sales associates. In financial terms, we've met or exceeded our earnings targets every year since I became CEO in 1990."

An independent study showed that between 1990 and 1998, AFLAC's name recognition soared from 2 percent to 62 percent, a coup the company attributes to its national advertising during major sporting events such as the Olympics, the Super Bowl, the World Series, National Hockey League games, the Major League Baseball All-Star Game, and college football games, in addition to network and cable broadcasts. It also advertises in national publications such as *Fortune* magazine.

AFLAC continues to be a company on the move. In 1998, it completed a $15-million, 133,000-square-foot customer call center in Columbus to handle its projected sales growth through the millennium.

"My goal is for AFLAC to continue its historical record of strong growth," Amos said. "I want our company to stay true to the core principals upon which it was founded—the greatest product value in the market, excellent customer service, conservative investment management. At the same time, I want us to embrace change—innovative technology, new and needed products, evolving insurance distribution channels. I think if we combine the foundations of the past with the best of the future, AFLAC will continue to provide its employees with a great place to work, its policyholders with the best supplemental insurance products, and its shareholders with a strong investment."

Through financial growth and dedication to service, value, and caring, AFLAC will continue to impact individuals and families across the world well beyond the year 2000. ◈

The company was founded in 1955 by (left to right) Paul, John, and William Amos, three brothers who took a risk that paid off in dividends.

Buy a six-pack of bottled Coca-Cola anywhere in the world and there's a 50-percent chance that the coated paperboard that holds it was manufactured in Cottonton, Alabama, at Mead Coated Board's Mahrt Mill.

Mead Coated Board

The Mahrt Mill, located on 1,400 acres just 25 minutes south of Phenix City, produces two grades of Mead Coated Natural Kraft™ paperboard. Carrier Kote® is a paperboard used for beverage packaging for soft drinks, beer, mineral water, and other products with high moisture levels. Custom Kote™ is a strong, glossy-surface paperboard used to hold dry foods, frozen foods, candy, pharmaceuticals, hardware, housewares, sporting goods, and baked goods. Both grades make their way to stores around the world.

Mead Coated Board is headquartered in Phenix City, Alabama, in a comfortably elegant building that overlooks the Chattahoochee River. Completed in 1996, the 35,000-square-foot facility houses the division's sales, marketing, financial services, information services, woodlands, solid

Mead Coated Board is a manufacturing division of the Mead Corporation, one of the world's largest manufacturers of quality paper for printing and business use.

wood products sales, and human resources departments. These operations, with the exception of the woodlands group, which was in Columbus, were located in Atlanta prior to the headquarters relocation to Phenix City.

The division's main manufacturing facility, the Mahrt Mill, employs 750. Two sawmills for cutting lumber, one in Cottonton, and the other in Greenville, Georgia, are operated by the Wood Products Group and employ 125 each. Mead Coated Board's European headquarters is in Vienna, Austria, with a sales office in London, England. It also owns a sheeting facility in Venlo, The Netherlands. Both the Mahrt Mill and the Venlo sheeting plant are ISO 9002 certified facilities.

The Mead Coated Board division employs 1,300 and dispenses an annual payroll of $75 million, much of it into the local economy.

The Mahrt Mill was built in 1966 by Alabama/Georgia Kraft at an initial cost of $45 million. Originally, it manufactured linerboard but gradually moved into the production of coated board. Mead

The Mahrt Mill, located on 1,400 acres just 25 minutes south of Phenix City, produces two grades of Mead Coated Natural Kraft™ paperboard.

Corporation acquired the Mahrt Mill in 1988, naming it for Al Mahrt, a top officer of the Mead Corporation and one who played a key role in developing the paperboard business.

In 1989, the mill underwent a $580-million, two-year expansion that doubled its size and made room for one of the largest and widest pieces of machinery in the world, one that would produce a high gloss paperboard to be used by the food industry.

Mead Coated Board is a manufacturing division of the Mead Corporation, one of the world's largest manufacturers of quality paper for printing and business use. The Mead Corporation was founded in 1846 in Ohio by Colonel Daniel Mead to produce book and other printing papers. Today, it is a $3.5-billion forest products company headquartered in Dayton, Ohio. It manages, through the Woodlands Group,

550,000 acres of timberlands in Georgia and Alabama that supply hardwoods and softwoods for Mead Coated Board.

The process of making the paperboard starts with the buzz of the power saw as loggers cut hardwoods like oak and soft woods such as Loblolly and Southern pines. About 30 percent of the wood is harvested from Mead-owned or leased woodlands within a 100-mile radius of the Mahrt Mill. The remainder is purchased from other logging operations.

Once at the wood yard, the logs go to the debarking drum, which strips them of the bark and then into a chipper run with a 3,000 horsepower motor. The leftover wood product is then prepared for chipping. The wood chips are conveyed to separate piles, one for hardwood and another for softwood. It's the blending of these different types of fibers that gives the coated board its strength and smoothness. The higher the ratio of hardwood fiber, the smoother, and more printable, the paper product.

The chips are then moved to the pulp mill, where they are cooked seven hours in a continuous digester, a tower 265 feet tall. The cooking time and temperature are carefully controlled. The pulp is washed and then sent to storage tanks. Different types of pulp are pulled in correct proportions from the storage tanks to the paperboard machines. The machines form, press, and dry the board. Then, it moves through a series of rollers that smooth the surface before it is coated and polished so that it can be printed on. Finally, the paperboard is wound into huge rolls for shipping on railcars and trucks to converting plants.

Very little is wasted at the Mahrt mill. It meets 80 percent of its own energy requirements by burning bark, leftover wood chips from the chipping process, and the "black liquor" produced in cooking the pulp.

Always aware of its effect on the environment, including the Chattahoochee River, Mead reuses many times the 23 million gallons of water it pumps out of the river each day. Before the water is returned to the river, it is cleaned and clarified according to governmental standards.

Mead Coated Board is more than just a major manufacturer in the Columbus/ Phenix City area; it's a caring corporate citizen. It understands that an investment in the community is an investment in the quality of life for its employees. In 1996, the company provided a major grant to

help develop the Space Science Center, complete with a Challenger Learning Center, for children in Columbus; supported the Muscogee Education Excellence Foundation to recognize public school educators; supported the Columbus Museum, the Columbus Symphony, and the Springer Theatre; and partnered with environmental groups in an urban forestry program.

As it positions itself for the new millennium, Mead Coated Board will continue its push to deliver high performing paperboard and outstanding customer service, said Jack Goldfrank, president and chief executive officer of Mead Coated Board. And it will continue to take seriously its commitment to renewable natural resources, sustainable forest management, and minimal environmental impact. "Our environment is a force we do not take for granted," he said. ❧

Through its Woodlands Group, Mead manages 550,000 acres of timberlands in Georgia and Alabama that supply hardwoods and softwoods for Mead Coated Board.

The process of making the paperboard starts with the buzz of the power saw as loggers cut hardwoods like oak and soft woods such as Loblolly and Southern pines.

WWhat does Columbus-based Johnston Industries, Inc., an "old textile company," have in common with National Football League touchdowns, California infrastructure rehabilitation, cheering fans at the NBA finals, and Brooks Brothers suits?

Johnston Industries, Inc.

The answers may be surprising. Since 1983, Johnston's Southern Phenix mill has woven the three-ply polyester fabric liner that goes into all Wilson™ brand footballs used by the National Football League as well as footballs used by half the college teams in the country.

In 1998, the company's Vectorply® composite reinforcement fabric, engineered with pride in Phenix City, Alabama, was used in a new high-tech jacketing system to reinforce the concrete bridge columns on the Yolo Causeway in northern California, providing additional stability in the event of an earthquake. This exciting application promises to be the first of many.

Johnston's Wellington Contract Fabrics launched every standing ovation during the 1997 and 1998 NBA finals. The seats in both the Delta Center in Salt Lake City and the United Center in Chicago are

Johnston's corporate office building is located at the corner of Thirteenth Street and Second Avenue in Columbus, Georgia.

The inner lining of the Wilson football is produced exclusively at the Southern Phenix Textile facility in Phenix City.

upholstered with fabrics designed and manufactured by Johnston Industries.

Johnston's Textest, a certified laboratory located in nearby Valley, Alabama, is used by Brooks Brothers and other manufacturers of fine apparel to ensure conformity with their stringent performance requirements.

Johnston Industries is a $300-million-plus diversified manufacturer of woven and nonwoven textile fabrics that employs 2,700 workers at plants in Georgia, Alabama, and Iowa. Of those, 1,170 are employed locally in Columbus and Phenix City. Johnston, a recognized leader in the textile industry as an innovator and customer-oriented company, produces fabrics that turn up in the most unexpected

places, including the light posts on the Riverwalk, in sandpaper, rubber belts, mops, and automobiles. Johnston's products are exported from Georgia and Alabama to approximately 30 countries on 6 continents, and many of Johnston's customers export goods containing Johnston products, indicating that Johnston is a true world-class manufacturer.

Johnston, well-known to those industrial users of textile products that require the highest performance characteristics, is little known to the average consumer. However, the furniture, automobiles, recreational equipment, and many, many other products that you encounter every day quite possibly have a Johnston fabric as a component—often innovative ways that you might not ever imagine a textile product might be used.

Johnston's Columbus mill, established in 1899 on the banks of the Chattahoochee River, produces high specification industrial fabrics used in abrasives, automotive belts, and filtrations, as well as fabrics used in the home furnishing markets. The Columbus mill, along with the Opp and Micolas mills in Opp, Alabama, form Johnston's highly successful and award-winning Greige Fabrics Division.

Johnston's Finished Fabrics Division includes two Phenix City plants, Southern Phenix Textiles and Stitchbond, as well as

the Shawmut Complex Finishing and Distribution operation in Valley, Alabama. Johnston's most diverse division, Finished Fabrics, spins, weaves, dyes, and finishes woven and nonwoven fabrics, as well as maintains a certified testing facility. The Shawmut Finishing facility includes environmentally friendly aqueous-based fabric finishing ranges, providing unique value-added finishes to many Johnston Fabrics.

The Fiber Products Division is a strong friend of the environment, converting textile waste into a wide range of quality fibers and by-products that are sold to a broad international market base. The fiber recycling process begins at the Division's Utilization Plant in Valley, Alabama, where textile waste is reprocessed into usable raw materials for sale. Much of Utilization's production is consumed at the division's pad production plants in Lanett, Alabama, and DeWitt, Iowa, where the fibers are processed into pads for use in bedding, automotive, and many other applications.

Johnston's newest operation, Johnston Industries Composite Reinforcements in Phenix City, Alabama, is in many ways its most exciting. This operation designs and produces highly engineered noncrimp multiaxial fabrics of carbon, kevlar, or fiberglass for applications ranging from skateboards to NASA rockets, including the launch vehicle used to boost the Lunar Prospector off to the moon. What are the potential applications for this new technology? Anywhere that superior weight and strength characteristics are desired, including Olympic sports equipment, sports cars, and transportation equipment, infrastructure rehabilitation, yachts, to thousands of applications that have not yet been envisioned.

In 1994, Johnston Industries, a New York Stock Exchange listed company, moved its headquarters from New York to Columbus, a city on the go in the heart of Johnston's operations. Johnston has invested heavily in the Columbus area and has steadily expanded its presence in the area, providing employment opportunities at all levels. Johnston's high-caliber workforce is committed to success through customer satisfaction.

Johnston has long been recognized as an innovator in its industry. It has been the recipient of *Textile World Magazine's* Textile Company of the Year and Model Mill Award; ATI's Award for Innovation as the most innovative textile company in America; and numerous awards from customers in recognition of superior performance. ➔

The concrete bridge columns of the Yolo Causeway in northern California are reinforced with Vectorply, made at Johnston's Composite Reinforcements location.

Automotive belts contain fabric woven by the Greige Fabrics Division Columbus Mill, located on First Avenue in Columbus, Georgia.

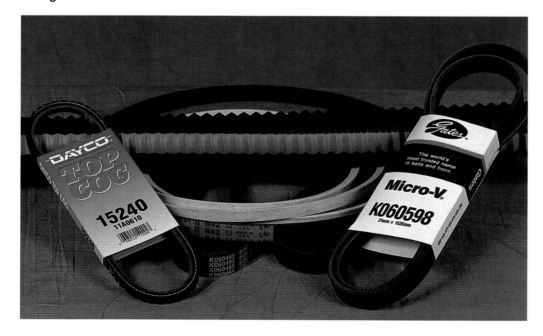

Sammy Howard grew up on Dillingham Street, just blocks from some of Phenix City's most notorious gambling houses. In the late 1990s, as he looks across the area where he used to romp with his buddies, he sees a much different picture. Mead

West Chattahoochee Development Council

Coated Board's corporate headquarters, Fred Peak's renovated real estate development office, a handsome amphitheater, and a Riverwalk have replaced dilapidated buildings and neglected landscaping. As a long-time proponent of the city and as mayor of Phenix City from 1995 through 1998, Howard had a hand in facilitating the change.

Howard, president of CB&T Bank of Russell County and a former high school coach, and his team solicited input from local residents to find out what they wanted for their city and then came up with a game plan to help them get it. Phenix 2000, an economic development organization headed by Executive Director Paul Alexander, was part of that team. Howard and other local business leaders founded Phenix 2000 in 1987 to promote economic development in the Phenix City/Russell County area. As it developed, it changed its focus from industrial recruitment to that of consulting and supporting the leadership of the city in commercial, residential, and other aspects of productive development. This proactive approach led to a new name for the organization, the West Chattahoochee Development Council.

The Chattahoochee River, once considered a barrier between Phenix City and

Columbus, is now a link. The synergy that occurred in the late 1990s in Columbus with the revitalization of downtown with a $100-million Total System Services campus, a $60-million RiverCenter for the Performing Arts, a new Thirteenth Street Bridge, and other developments spread across the river like wildfire. All it took was a spark ignited by Howard and others to set Phenix City aflame with its own brand of synergy.

In 1995, an assessment team of community residents took a long, hard look at the city and came back with recommendations that became the backbone of Phenix Forward, an $18.4-million city-wide improvement plan.

After voters approved funding of these projects with a one-cent sales tax and a hike in garbage and utility fees in 1997, the city rolled up its collective sleeves and went to work. More than 100 miles of streets were resurfaced. The public library was moved into a new building that doubled its space and provided state-of-the-art facilities. Two new fire stations were built; the police department was renovated and new equipment purchased; a $1-million RiverWalk was begun; and a new animal shelter was built. All recreational facilities in the city were updated. The city's computer system was upgraded. Water and sewer extensions were constructed to

The Mead Corporation spent $6 million to move its Coated Board Division headquarters to Phenix City.

handle new capacity and take advantage of growth opportunities. New buses were bought for the city's transportation system. Projects not part of Phenix Forward were completed as well, including the addition of a new softball and baseball complex, eight new tennis courts, and a clubhouse at Idle Hour Park.

The city's proactive approach and enthusiasm for improving the quality of life for its citizens and beautifying its environment led to an unexpected increase in economic development activity for this city of 28,000 nestled on the west bank of the Chattahoochee. Commercial developments, industrial locations, and new residential/commercial developments sprang up. The fact that the Mead Corporation had spent $6 million to move its Coated Board Division headquarters to Phenix City didn't hurt the cause. Neither did the 1995 creation of the $1.2-million, 1,500-seat Phenix City Amphitheater on the banks of the river to provide an entertainment site for visitors at the 1996 Summer Olympics' Women's Fast Pitch Softball venue in Columbus.

The synergy created by these projects led to a $38-million investment by Continental Carbon Company and a $2.4-million investment by Cosmyl Inc. that created 125 new jobs at the two companies. Kudzu, a

The Dillingham Street view of Mayor Howard's childhood looks much different today.

The Phenix City Amphitheater, on the banks of the river, provided an entertainment site for visitors at the 1996 Summer Olympics' Women's Fast Pitch Softball venue in Columbus.

Development Company of Phenix City and The Jordan Company of Columbus, began construction of a 200-acre upscale residential and commercial development. The development, McIntosh Creek, was named after Chief William McIntosh of the Creek Nation, who lived in the Chattahoochee Valley.

Local groups also stepped up their efforts to improve the quality of life in the city. The Phenix City Arts Council opened an 1,800-square-foot arts education center and gallery near Moon Lake, and the Friends of Idle Hour Park raised funds to open the Idle Hour Nature Trail.

Down Highway 431, the extended water lines helped bring in a new hotel and other retail establishments and a 300-lot residential subdivision, boosting the economy on the south end of town.

Added to the mix is the fact that the Phenix City area is one of the fastest growing regions in Alabama with double-digit population growth, according to figures released by the U.S. Census Bureau.

But the city isn't finished yet. The momentum is expected to extend well into the new millennium as forward-looking supporters pick up the torch. The local community newspaper, *The Phenix Citizen,* and the Phenix Cable Company have heavily promoted the "can-do" attitude. Phenix City has moved forward and is ready to turn "Vision into Action," the name of the city's development package. To ensure the best possible future growth direction, "Project West Chattahoochee," a comprehensive master plan, is underway. On the drawing board as it approaches the millennium are plans to continue the city's rebirth by concentrating on riverfront

development. The plans include the redevelopment of the area near the river that is occupied by Riverview Court Apartments, a Housing and Urban Development project, and the completion of the Fifth Avenue Extension and Interchange project, which will provide a north/south access corridor through the city and open additional riverfront property for commercial and upscale residential development.

"We're very proud of what has been accomplished," Howard said. "I love this city. I want to be sure our grandchildren love this city." ❖

"homegrown," innovative custom headwear manufacturer built a $3.1-million facility that increased its employment to 150, and Olvedi Equipment Company invested $500,000, creating 30 new skilled jobs. Phenix Regional Hospital, to the tune of $10 million, expanded and upgraded its facilities and added two new stand-alone clinics.

Good things kept happening. In 1998, Wal-Mart Corporation built a $12-million, 200,000-square-foot SuperCenter on the U.S. Highway 280 Bypass in Phenix City, creating 200 new jobs and pumping $500,000 into city coffers through sales and property taxes. The project was the largest retail investment in the city's history and generated additional developments in the area.

Also in 1998, Warr Jordan Development, a joint venture project between Warr

It was a proud day in May of 1988 when Matsushita Electric Industrial Co., Ltd. (MEI), Matsushita Battery Industrial Co., Ltd. (MBI), and Eastman Kodak broke ground for a battery manufacturing facility in Columbus. In an atmosphere charged

Matsushita Battery Industrial Corp. of America

with excitement as U.S. and Japanese flags unfurled in the breeze, city government officials beamed, and Matsushita and Kodak company officials smiled. Little did any of them realize that the growth this company would experience would lead to the building of four plants in Columbus, nor did they imagine the role it would play as an outstanding corporate citizen.

Matsushita's first plant in Columbus, Matsushita-Ultra Tech. Battery Corporation (MUTEC), is a joint venture between Rochester, New York-based Eastman Kodak Company and Osaka, Japan-based Matsushita. The 265,000-square-foot plant began production of alkaline batteries for the consumer market in 1989, making it

In 1996, MBIA opened its fourth plant in Corporate Ridge—the MBIA-Materials Division (MBIA-MD). The $15-million, 30,000-square-foot facility, located on the MUTEC property, employs approximately 50 people.

one of only a few companies in the world to manufacture this kind of battery.

Located on a beautifully manicured 80-acre site at One Mutec Drive in Corporate Ridge Industrial Park, MUTEC manufactures alkaline batteries in sizes C, D, AA, AAA, 9-volt, and J cell, a specialty battery used in special devices. The batteries are sold under the well-known Kodak and Panasonic labels. Producing over 2.5 million batteries per day on machinery developed and manufactured by its parent company, the Columbus facility succeeded so well in its first six years of operation that for five of those six years it was the leader of Matsushita's 20-plus manufacturing operations in North America. Sales of the long-life, high-output alkaline batteries, used in cell phones, calculators, and other high-tech consumer devices, were so great they drove employment up to 450. High-volume sales also led to an expansion in 1992, and another in 1998 that increased the plant's manufacturing space to approximately 350,000 square feet.

Smiles at the

Matsushita's first plant in Columbus, Matsushita-Ultra Tech. Battery Corporation (MUTEC), is a joint venture between Rochester, New York-based Eastman Kodak Company and Osaka, Japan-based Matsushita. The 265,000-square-foot plant began production of alkaline batteries for the consumer market in 1989.

groundbreaking would have been even broader had the participants known that the plant was only the first of four the company would build in the city.

In 1991, Matsushita broke ground for a second plant—Matsushita Storage Battery Corporation of America, later to be MBIA's Storage Battery Division (MBIA-SBD). The new $39-million, 118,000-square-foot plant manufactures sealed lead acid storage batteries and is located on 30 acres adjacent to MUTEC at One Battery Boulevard. The Storage Battery Division, which employs approximately 425, and has undergone several expansions to its present size of 135,000 square feet, manufactures sealed-lead acid batteries under the Panasonic brand for alarm devices, medical equipment, exit signs, emergency lights, and uninterrupted power supply systems. Keeping up with the latest technology, the company also manufactures batteries for desktop UPS system units that sense a power failure and perform a controlled shutdown of computer systems to prevent crashes.

To bring its Columbus holdings under one umbrella and to provide a structure for future expansion, MEI and MBI in a corporate reorganization in 1993 created a new

The Storage Battery Division, which employs approximately 425, and has undergone several expansions to its present size of 135,000 square feet, manufactures sealed-lead acid batteries under the Panasonic brand for alarm devices, medical equipment, exit signs, emergency lights, and uninterrupted power supply systems.

wholly-owned subsidiary called Matsushita Battery Industrial Corporation of America (MBIA). Under its auspices fall the Storage Battery Division, the Lithium Battery Division, and the Materials Division. MUTEC is a separate corporation from MBIA. MBIA and MUTEC report to Matsushita Battery Industrial Co. (MBI), which is a subsidiary of MEI. The president of both corporations is Masuo "Mark" Shintani. Batteries manufactured in Columbus find their way to domestic and international markets.

The Columbus economy received another boost in 1994, when the company broke ground for its third plant in Corporate Ridge. The $25-million, 80,000-square-foot MBIA-Lithium Battery Division (MBIA-LD) manufactures three sizes of lithium camera batteries. Located on 20 acres, at One Panasonic Drive in Corporate Ridge Industrial Park, MBIA-LD employs approximately 100, and manufactures batteries for Panasonic and Panasonic's private label customers.

In 1996, MBIA opened its fourth plant in Corporate Ridge—the MBIA-Materials Division (MBIA-MD). The $15-million, 30,000-square-foot facility, located on the MUTEC property, employs approximately 50 people and produces cylindrical steel battery casings, called DI cans (Draw and Ironing), for use in the alkaline batteries produced by MUTEC, lithium batteries produced by MBIA in Columbus, as well as for the nickel-cadmium batteries produced by the MBIA-California Division (MBIA-CD) at its factory in Tijuana, Mexico.

Matsushita cares about producing quality products while protecting the environment, a long-held corporate philosophy. MUTEC is ISO 9000 certified for quality, and all the Columbus plants are ISO 14000 (environmentally friendly) certified.

The Columbus plants have been trendsetters for other organizations in Matsushita's United States operations. Pilot programs on employee relations, the four-day work week, and general employment policies that have worked here have been adopted at other plants.

Matsushita is committed to the health and welfare of its employees, a standard set by Konosuke Matsushita, who in 1918 founded the company and led it to become the 11th largest industrial organization in the world. His philosophy of "People Before Products" is standard operating procedure in all Matsushita plants. As a result of the company's commitment to caring, the plants enjoy a stable workforce willing to learn the skills necessary to operate the sensitive machinery used in battery production.

Matsushita's Columbus plants take seriously their commitment to the community. Since 1991, the company has enjoyed an active partnership with Fort Middle School through the Partners-in-Education program. The company conducts an annual Japanese Culture Week for students, offers incentive programs to recognize students' achievements, attends school functions, provides tours of the plant, and includes teachers in its training programs. In turn, students create the company's holiday card each December, participate in the company's March of Dimes Walkathon, and include the company in special events.

MBIA's parent company has a long and impressive history of growth. Since its founding in 1918 in Osaka, the $62-billion Matsushita Electric Industrial Co. Ltd. has grown from a small electrical manufacturer into one of the world's largest manufacturers of quality electric and electronic products for the consumer, business, and industrial markets. The company's 14,000 products are sold internationally in more than 160 countries around the world under the well-known Panasonic, National, Technics, and Quasar brand names.

With its finger on the pulse of technology, Matsushita anticipates further growth as it designs products, perfects manufacturing processes, and creates new products to meet the needs of a technologically changing world. ◈

The $25-million, 80,000-square-foot MBIA-Lithium Battery Division (MBIA-LD) manufactures three sizes of lithium camera batteries.

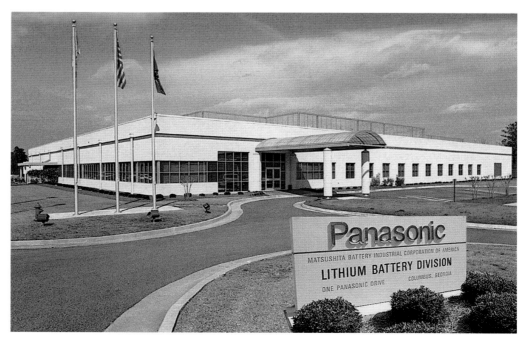

Sun Chemical's Polychrome Division began operations in Columbus during 1990. On January 1, 1998, Sun Chemical and Eastman Kodak Company formed Kodak Polychrome Graphics as an equally owned joint venture.

Kodak Polychrome Graphics

Since it began production in 1990, Kodak Polychrome Graphics has engraved its image on the Columbus community. Oddly though, this almost didn't happen. Another community had received the company's stamp of approval for its relocation.

Kodak Polychrome Graphics' site in Corporate Ridge Industrial Park is the result of a commitment by its parent company—then Dainippon Ink and Chemicals—to expand operations, invest in customer service and product quality, and operate efficiently. In the late 1980s, an intensive search began for a new location. From an original list of 31 site options, the list was narrowed to two Southern cities, Columbus being one. Both cities met the stringent criteria set, but Columbus was not initially selected.

Ordinarily, that would be the end of the story. But a combination of two things precipitated a reconsideration. First, unanticipated difficulties arose at the South Carolina site that had been selected. Second, Columbus officials, the Greater Columbus Chamber of Commerce, and the Georgia Department of Industry, Trade, and Tourism were tenacious in maintaining their contacts with the company, even after the South Carolina site had been selected. Although the Columbus officials were unaware of the problems arising at the other site, company officials were impressed with the persistence of the Columbus delegation.

When construction deadlines approached and issues at the South Carolina site were yet unresolved, the company reopened discussions with Columbus. Within two months, land was cleared and construction began on an $80-million, state-of-the-art facility on a 57-acre site in Corporate Ridge Industrial Park. In July 1990, less than a year later, the finishing and distribution section of the plant began full operations. The administrative offices were opened in August 1990, and the manufacturing facility opened in December.

Columbus was not only hospitable to the company itself, but also played an important role in welcoming the workers' families relocating to the city. Relocation can often be difficult for families, but the Southern hospitality and spirit of cooperation in Columbus made for a happier transition.

The company's presence in Columbus continued to grow through the 1990s. In 1994, the plant underwent a $20-million expansion, adding two additional process lines to the site, and 1996 saw an expansion of the finishing operation.

Kodak Polychrome Graphics produces a full range of quality products and services for the graphic arts industry, including advanced digital imaging technologies through conventional lithographic plates and thermal plates for computer-to-plate solutions, and Kodak-brand graphic arts films and digital proofing products and color management solutions for the prepress and printing industry.

In Columbus, Kodak Polychrome Graphics produces more than 4,000 formats of press plates for all types of printing operations, from small commercial printers to large publication printers.

In Columbus, Kodak Polychrome Graphics produces more than 4,000 formats of press plates for all types of printing operations, from small commercial printers to large publication printers.

Kodak Polychrome Graphics, an equally owned joint venture between two of the most respected companies in the prepress and printing industries—Eastman Kodak Company and Sun Chemical Corporation—was founded on January 1, 1998. The company, a combination of Kodak's Graphics Market Division and Sun Chemical's Polychrome Division, produces a full range of quality products and services for the graphic arts industry, including advanced digital imaging technologies through conventional lithographic plates and thermal plates for computer-to-plate solutions, and

Kodak-branded graphic arts films, digital proofing products, and color management solutions for the prepress and printing industry. Its markets include commercial printers, trade shops, service bureaus, publishers, newspapers, book printers, packaging printers, and design studios.

Mark Stewart, chief executive officer at Kodak Polychrome Graphics, described the company as "an excellent marriage of two industry leaders that strikes a perfect balance of technology, manufacturing, and distribution expertise." The company, headquartered in Norwalk, Connecticut, and employing 4,000 people worldwide, reported sales in excess of $1.4 billion at the end of its first year. Operating out of three research and development centers and 10 manufacturing facilities, the company serves more than 120,000 customers in more than 85 countries throughout the world, from Australia to Venezuela, Belgium to the United Arab Emirates,

Singapore to Toronto, and all points in between.

The company's proprietary technology is moving Kodak Polychrome Graphics forward as a worldwide leader in the graphic arts industry. With manufacturing operations in the United States and Europe, a sister organization in Japan, a sales and marketing presence throughout the world, and strategic alliances with other important leaders in the industry, Kodak Polychrome Graphics is well placed for the new millennium.

As Jeffrey Jacobson, president of Kodak Polychrome Graphics in the United States and Canada, put it: "The powerful partnership embodied by our new company creates new opportunities and advantages for our customers and employees."

The partnership gives the company the vast research and development resources of Eastman Kodak Company and Sun Chemical Corporation. That partnership expanded again in April 1998, when Kodak Polychrome Graphics acquired Horsell Anitec from International Paper Company, a move that further strengthened the company's business prospects in the world marketplace.

Columbus's involvement with this worldwide leader began with determination and dedication in 1990. Today, the city is a key manufacturing component of Kodak Polychrome Graphics' global enterprises, helping to bring great ideas to print. ✦

The company's proprietary technology is moving Kodak Polychrome Graphics forward as a leader in the world graphic arts market.

Company President Bob Gilson loves to see sparks fly and hear the pounding of hammers on metal. Those are the sights and sounds of success at Industrial Metal Fabricators, a company that grows and changes as Columbus grows and changes.

Industrial Metal Fabricators

Industrial Metal Fabricators has evolved from a sheet metal shop begun in 1956 by Frank McManious, to an experienced and nationally known state-of-the-art metal working shop. Its once modest customer base of local companies has grown to include leaders in the aircraft, construction, paper, and tobacco industries, and federal, state, and local government agencies. Sixty percent of the company's business is for out-of-town customers.

In a 60,000-square-foot facility on Flat Rock Road, its trained and experienced engineers help customers design their product to meet their specific needs, while its production crews work to provide high quality metal fabrication.

Using computer-assisted plasma arc

Industrial Metal Fabricators' trained and experienced engineers help customers design their product to meet specific needs, while its production crews work to provide high quality metal fabrication.

burners and a plasma cutting system, the company cuts stainless steel, carbon steel, and aluminum in minutes, work that used to take days. Its crews are accomplished in the skills of the trade: welding, shearing, forming, punching, and rolling. Its paint shop is equipped to apply a wide variety of finishes.

Custom fabrications in heavy sheet metal and plate make up the bulk of the company's business. To meet demand and to keep up with the industry, the company has installed a new 350-ton capacity press brake.

To supplement its production work, Industrial Metal Fabricators took on a new project in 1996—making above-ground fuel storage tanks for Trusco Tank Inc. The storage tank, called the SuperVault MH and insulated with lightweight cement, is the first above-ground tank to be multi-hazard rated, meaning that it can be in a fire, punctured, or hit and still be recertified after repair. The tanks are used to store gasoline, diesel fuel, jet fuel, and hydraulic fluids.

In its early days, the company worked mostly with light sheet metal to meet the needs of the local textile industry. As textiles became a less dominant industry in the community and other companies came in, it found itself getting into light structural work, machine shop work, and heavy plate work. "One thing led to another. . . each time a new company came, we started doing something different. We've tried to grow and to be receptive to what's going on industry-wide," Gilson said. The company employs 45.

As the company grew in skill, it discovered a need to expand its reach. "Several years ago there wasn't enough business in Columbus to keep us busy and we started looking outside. Now, we ship work all over the country."

As the millennium approaches, the company will continue to change in response to industry needs. It is considering buying its first piece of state-of-the-art

Industrial Metal Fabricators has evolved from a sheet metal shop begun in 1956 to an experienced and nationally known state-of-the-art metal working shop.

laser equipment for cutting metal to position itself as a participant in other markets. "We've got to change with the times. We're looking at doing the things that will make us more productive and more competitive," Gilson said. "I don't see us getting a whole lot bigger, just getting better and more efficient with what we have." ❖

Never underestimate the power of a jingle. TIC Federal Credit Union put on an ad campaign several years ago with the catchy jingle "T-I-C for you and me" that had Columbus singing its song.

For members' convenience, TIC offers ATM cards, safe deposit boxes, 24-hour Touch-Tone teller, direct deposit and payroll deduction, traveler's checks, money orders, Saturday hours, drive-through windows, and warranty insurance.

But more than the jingle, it's the products and the service that bring more than 46,000 people in as members of the home-grown credit union which in 1998 boasted assets of $122 million and growing strong. Because it's a not-for-profit cooperative, TIC uses its revenues to improve existing services and to create new ones. The revenues have been responsible for TIC's growth into five offices throughout the city and the addition of eight automated teller machines. It has allowed TIC to expand its loan products to include home equity, recreation vehicle and boat loans, VISA credit cards, and mortgages. The earnings also result in higher dividend rates and lower loan rates for members.

TIC is a membership organization, and only members may use its services. The

National Credit Union Administration sets guidelines about who can join a federal credit union, but typically, it's for people who belong to a common group, such as the same employer, the same church, or the same military post.

TIC is a full-service credit union. Its share account—or savings account—yields great dividends along with the share draft account—a checking account with no minimum balance, no per-check charge, no monthly service charge, and overdraft protection.

Other products include unsecured and secured loans, home equity loans, VISA credit cards, new and used car loans, new and used recreational vehicle and boat loans, educational loans, Member Mortgage Services, and their Plan America financial planning center.

For members' convenience, TIC offers ATM cards, safe deposit boxes, 24-hour Touch-Tone teller, direct deposit and payroll deduction, traveler's checks, money orders, Saturday hours, drive-through windows, and warranty insurance, just to name a few.

TIC's roots go back to Fort Benning in February 1956, when a group of civilian personnel met to discuss the possibility of forming a credit union on post. The civilian group unanimously agreed to organize a credit union for Fort Benning's civilian personnel, later adding the Fort Benning military personnel.

In March 1956, the Bureau of Federal Credit Unions of the Department of Health, Education, and Welfare approved a charter for TIC Federal Credit Union to be located at the Infantry Center at Fort Benning, Georgia. Fifty civilian employees formed its membership. In 1965, Fort Benning military personnel joined the field of membership, and today the military makes up a significant portion of TIC's member base.

TIC Federal Credit Union first opened as The Infantry Center Federal Credit Union, later changing its name to TIC. In 1964, the credit union reached its first financial milestone—$1 million in assets. Since then, asset growth has been exponential. In

---

TIC Federal Credit Union

1970, it was at the $5 million mark; in 1979, at $15 million; in 1986, $55 million; 1992, $75 million; and 1996, the landmark $100 million.

Over the years, TIC has been involved in a number of mergers that kept credit union membership alive for the members of several smaller, struggling credit unions. In addition to the Dolly Madison and Kirven Department Store credit union mergers in the '80s, the City of Columbus Employees Credit Union merged with TIC in 1990. In 1995 the Columbus Health & Hospital Credit Union, the Kaydee Federal Credit Union, and the Gas Light Employees Credit Union merged with TIC.

Recognizing that members occasionally need assistance in organizing their financial affairs and planning for their futures, TIC began offering a service called Plan America, a personal financial management program, in 1992.

"T-I-C for you and me" has proven to be more than just a jingle. It's the song many in the area sing. ◈

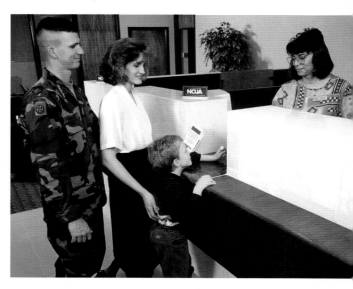

TIC is a full-service credit union.

Columbus State University stands as dramatic evidence of what can emerge from the dreams of visionary people and from the power of partnership.

Through its reputation for academic excellence, a dedicated faculty and staff,

Columbus State University

and numerous partnerships with private sector businesses, foundations, and individuals, the institution has grown from a state-supported college to a regional university that exercises significant influence on the region's educational, economic, and cultural life.

The university was founded by a group of individuals who dreamed of having a college in their community to open doors of opportunity to its citizens. Their efforts resulted in the creation in 1958 of Columbus College, a two-year college operated under the auspices of the University System of Georgia.

College leadership, with support from the academic and business communities, continued to push for growth and excellence. In 1966, the college received four-year status, and in 1973, it began offering graduate programs. The college also moved to a new campus on 132 acres in north Columbus in 1963. The institution's name was changed to Columbus State University in 1996.

With a student enrollment of 5,500 and a faculty and staff of 500, the university offers more than 70 majors, from one-year certificate programs to a six-year educational specialist degree. Undergraduate degrees are available in art, fine arts, music, science, education, nursing, and business administration; graduate degrees in science, education, music, and public administration; and one-year certificate programs in science and applied science. More than 17,000 students have graduated from CSU, with 9,000 of them staying in the Columbus area.

With a bold strategic plan to provide direction, CSU has answered the door when opportunities for collaboration knocked. Examples of its proactive leadership abound.

In the 1980s, when Total System Services was expanding but couldn't find enough computer programmers to meet its needs, CSU trained students for the company. By 1996, this model program had evolved into a statewide initiative called the Intellectual Capital Partnership Program, state-funded as an economic development tool to keep businesses in Georgia.

Another excellent example of public/private partnership is the university's Coca-Cola Space Science Center, which combines a Challenger Learning Center, an observatory, and an Omnisphere Theater.

Oxbow Meadows Environmental Learning Center opened in 1996 to provide opportunities for the study of natural habitats and other environmental phenomena.

Columbus State University stands as dramatic evidence of what can emerge from the dreams of visionary people and from the power of partnership.

To develop this community resource, the university, which operates the center, partnered with the City of Columbus, the school district, and the Columbus Water Works.

In response to a community need for cultural enrichment, CSU was at the forefront in putting together plans for the new $60-million RiverCenter for the Performing Arts. In addition to state-of-the-art performance halls for community and visiting productions, the facility houses the university's Schwob Department of Music.

CSU understands and embraces the power of partnership. "Columbus State is poised, because of long-standing community support, to be a major player in the further development of our community in the years ahead," says CSU President Frank Brown.

CSU is committed to the community it serves. "The progress it makes and the successes it realizes are a testament to strong community support through the years. We have no reason for being other than serving our region, our community." ➔

With a student enrollment of 5,500 and a faculty and staff of 500, Columbus State University offers more than 70 majors, from one-year certificate programs to a six-year educational specialist degree.

Take 300 pounds of sugar, blend in 30 pounds of eggs, and add 265 pounds of flour, and you have a good start on a batch of Zingers. It's not grandma's recipe, but the smell of cake cooking in the oven is just as enticing at the Dolly Madison Bakery in Blanchard Industrial Park on Victory Drive.

When the Columbus bakery opened in 1970, it was one of the most modern cake making facilities in the nation.

Success smells sweet at Dolly Madison, which reports annual sales of $25 million. Inside the 264,000-square-foot facility, workers whip up 2.7 million pounds of doughnuts, snack cakes, and cupcakes a week for distribution as far west as Kansas and as far north as Maine. In Twinkies alone, that's 816 a minute.

The Columbus bakery, which employs 750, is one of four Dolly Madison Bakeries owned by Interstate Brands Corporation. Others are in Columbus, Indiana; Emporia, Kansas; and Los Angeles. Interstate Brands is a subsidiary of Interstate Bakeries Corporation of Kansas City, Missouri.

When the Columbus bakery opened in 1970, it was one of the most modern cake making facilities in the nation. Following Interstate's purchase of Continental Baking Co. in 1995 from Ralston Purina Co., the bakery underwent a $2.7-million expansion to accommodate the production and distribution of Hostess products. The acquisition of Continental created the synergy to move Interstate from a regional baking company to a national, branded food company.

The Dolly Madison story began in 1937 when Roy Nafzinger created a new snack cake division of Interstate Bakeries. He named the venture Dolly Madison Bakeries after the wife of President James Madison.

Today, the mark of a Dolly Madison snack cake is still freshness and taste. The emphasis on quality products and excellent service carries over to all the 70 bakeries of Interstate Bakeries Corp., which together generate more than $3 billion in sales.

Interstate Bakeries Corp. is the largest wholesale baker and distributor of fresh bread and snack cake in the country. Its product lines include breads, snack cakes, croutons, and stuffing, and its bakeries deliver to grocery and convenience stores and company-operated thrift stores throughout the United States.

Its product labels include Wonder, Hostess, Home Pride, Beefsteak, Bread du Jour, Dolly Madison, Butternut, Merita, Weber's, Mickey, Millbrook, Eddy's, Holsum, Sweetheart, Cotton's Holsum, Mrs. Cubbison's, Marie Callender's, Colombo, Parisian, and Toscana. It also makes and distributes Roman Meal bread and Sun Maid raisin bread.

To compete in an increasingly tough and competitive baking industry, the company will follow an established game plan into the millennium, said Dan Futato, the bakery's general manager. "Continued emphasis on product quality, service to our customers, and building strong brand image are our primary objectives."

The plan also calls for building margin through strong brands; fueling growth

Dolly Madison— Interstate Baking Co.

through strategic acquisitions and product line diversity; staying competitive through capital investment; and maintaining a competitive edge through strong, positive performance and a streamlined operation.

Working three shifts, 24 hours a day, seven days a week, Dolly Madison employees take pride in their jobs. Their paychecks, which total $5.4 million a year, are, well, just frosting on the cake. ➔

Following Interstate's purchase of Continental Baking Co. in 1995 from Ralston Purina Co., the bakery underwent a $2.7-million expansion to accommodate the production and distribution of Hostess products.

Founded 1970

It's a bold new world out there. For banks to thrive in this age of bank mergers, advanced computer technology, and online banking, they have to be willing to grasp the future while holding on to the lessons of the past. And always, they have to

Regions Bank

remember the customer.

Change is nothing new to Regions Bank in Phenix City and Columbus. The federally chartered bank began operation in 1962 as Phenix National Bank in Phenix City. In 1974, it became affiliated with First Alabama Bancshares, Alabama's first multibank holding company.

First Alabama Bancshares was created in 1970 when three banks—First National Bank of Montgomery, First National Bank of Huntsville, and Exchange Security Bank of Birmingham—proposed an alliance that would, by the end of 1974, encompass 13 affiliate banks and 6 subsidiaries and double its assets from $543 million in 1971 to $1.2 billion. In 1975, the holding company changed the names of its affiliate banks, including the one in Phenix City, to First Alabama Bank to create a statewide identity. By 1981, First Alabama

Bancshares was a $2.6-billion multibank holding company with an impressive earnings record.

The 1970s and 1980s changed the banking industry significantly, as new laws allowed banks to offer new types of accounts, such as money market certificates of deposit (1978), interest bearing checking accounts (1981), and individual retirement accounts (1982).

Advances in computer and telephone technology also made possible Automated Teller Machines (ATMs). In 1986, the ALERT Network went on-line, giving First Alabama customers access to 24-hour banking services through hundreds of ATMs across the state.

In 1981, state regulators passed a law that allowed multibank holding companies to merge their affiliates into one statewide bank. First Alabama divided into five regions throughout Alabama with each retaining local management.

As interstate banking laws relaxed, First Alabama expanded into other states, moving first into the panhandle of Florida in 1987. The savings and loan association debacle provided the impetus for regulators to allow banks to buy failed savings and loans across state lines and, thus, opened the Georgia market. First Alabama moved across the Chattahoochee River into Columbus in 1991 with the acquisition of three offices of Fulton Federal Savings and

Loan. Regions continued its push into the state with further acquisitions. To reflect its growth in a regional market, First Alabama Bancshares changed its name to Regions Financial Corporation in 1994. In 1996, all First Alabama Banks became Regions Banks to correspond to the name of the parent company. The corporation is headquartered in Birmingham, Alabama.

Other acquisitions took it into Louisiana and Arkansas. In 1998, First Commercial Corporation, Arkansas' largest bank holding company, merged with Regions, making Regions the nation's 26th largest banking organization. At the time of the merger, Regions reported assets of $33 billion with 667 banking locations in nine southern states.

Into the millennium, Regions will remain customer-driven. In 1998, Regions Bank had four offices in Columbus and two in Phenix City, and plans were in the works for two additional locations on sites that reflect changing shopping patterns in the bi-city area. "Phenix City is growing just like Columbus is, so there are growth opportunities on both sides of the river," said Larry Cardin, president and chief executive officer of the local Regions Banks. ➔

Regions Bank is the nation's 26th largest banking organization, reporting assets of $35 billion with 700 banking locations in eight southern states. Locally, Regions Bank has four offices in Columbus and two in Phenix City, with plans for two additional locations.

A modern-day renaissance has occurred in this historic river town on the banks of the Chattahoochee River. Throughout the community, a new spirit of optimism has emerged with bricks and mortar as its symbol. Much of what is happening here has its roots in past years when the city's key

This statue of father and daughter, caught in a moment of sharing and inspiration where young and old are fellow sojourners in life, depicts the Pastoral Institute's mission of caring.

business and religious leaders embraced a concept of caring, of making a difference in the quality of life in the community in which they lived.

The Pastoral Institute was created as part of that community of caring. Founded in 1974 and supported by area businesses, congregations, and organizations, the Pastoral Institute has evolved into a not-for-profit organization that touches the lives of more than 40,000 people a year through counseling services, education programs, and corporate consultations that reach into all segments of the community.

Headquartered at 2022 15th Avenue in Columbus with satellite offices in Valley, Alabama, and Albany, Georgia, the Pastoral Institute consists of four centers under the leadership of Executive Director Ronald E. King, Ph.D. It employs 60 people.

The Counseling Center provides counseling for individuals, couples, and families on issues such as marital and family problems; personal struggles with depression, stress, and anxiety; coping with grief or loss; emotional problems associated with physical illness or accident; dilemmas with children, teenagers, and aging parents; issues related to separation, divorce, remarriage, and life in blended families; drug, alcohol, and other addictions; and spiritual issues.

The counselors of the Pastoral Institute are experienced licensed mental health professionals who specialize in the fields of psychiatry, psychology, marriage and family therapy, social work, professional counseling, and pastoral counseling.

The Center for Education and Training offers skills for living workshops on topics related to personal growth and family issues to the community; provides continuing education and professional development workshops for mental health professionals and clergy; and administers the Pastoral Institute's Pastoral Training Program. Master's- and doctoral-level students from throughout the country receive training through this certified program of the American Association of Pastoral Counselors. This division also offers support groups for individuals with specific needs, a speakers' bureau, and hosts a number of annual conferences featuring nationally known speakers.

The Business Resource Center addresses the needs of area businesses. Today, it coordinates individual and family counseling services through its Employee Assistance Program for the employees of more than 107 area companies. An Affiliate Provider Network offers counseling benefits to employees located in other parts of the country. Using a cadre of experienced trainers, The Business Resource Center provides customized management and employee training and organizational development for companies. When businesses and organizations experience workplace traumas, the Trauma and Crisis Response team goes on-site to provide group debriefings to help employees through those difficult times.

The Clergy Resource Center provides ministers of all denominations opportunities for personal, professional, and spiritual growth through individual counseling, workshops, and support groups. Clergy assessment and psychological testing, a national Clergy HelpLine, and a Pulpit Supply Program are also available. The Clergy-in-Crisis Program provides week-long intensive counseling in a tranquil retreat setting for ministers who need emotional, relational, and spiritual renewal. This division also coordinates counseling services to members of area congregations through the Congregational Assistance Program.

The Pastoral Institute

As the Pastoral Institute goes into the new millennium, it will continue to build on its history of providing hope, help, and healing. ❧

Since 1974, the Pastoral Institute has provided hope, help, and healing for those in need.

*P*eachtree Mall's roots in the fertile soil of Columbus run deep, resulting in lush growth and ample fruit. Developed on Manchester Expressway in 1975, it has evolved from a center of 451,000 square feet to an 820,000-square-foot upscale

Peachtree Mall

shopping experience whose 120 shops attract customers from 26 counties in Georgia and Alabama.

The real story is not just about the mall's growth, but about the effect of the community's growth on the mall and the partnership that has developed. Family-oriented events complement the mall's quality retail mix to provide an enjoyable atmosphere for shoppers of all ages. Arts and crafts shows, local school exhibits, symphony performances, flower shows, and costumed character visits are among the favorites. Peachtree Mall maintains its commitment to the city through involvement with a multitude of local organizations that work to support education, recreation, health services, performing arts, and numerous charitable efforts.

Developed and managed by Jim Wilson and Associates of Montgomery, Alabama, Peachtree Mall opened in 1975 with two anchor department stores—Gayfers and Montgomery Ward—and 59 specialty stores. Ten years later, the center added a new $10-million wing with 22 new specialty stores, including a 13-store, 400-seat

Innovative architectural style offers inviting entrances for shoppers.

food court, and a third anchor store—Parisian. The mall completed a $26.5-million renovation and expansion project in 1993-94, transforming it into the beautiful regional shopping mall that it is today. This renovation helped Peachtree Mall attract major retailers, including Eddie Bauer, The Disney Store, and Bath and Body Works, just to name a few. Long-term tenant Gayfers expanded by 54,000 square feet so it could move its home store from an outlying location into the mall. Innovative design made Gayfers a link between the existing mall and the expansion by adding a new wing, with JCPenney as the mall's fourth anchor store and 21 additional speciality shops, including the Mole Hole and The Gap. New skylights on vaulted ceilings opened up the interior of the mall, as did new paint, carpet, interior and exterior landscape design, mall entrances, and parking lot refurbishment, making it a true shopper's delight.

Changes to the exterior added a new eight-screen Carmike Cinema, a branch of Columbus Bank and Trust Co., and 30 percent more parking. The Peach-tree Mini Strip Shopping Center was remodeled and renamed The Plaza at Peachtree.

After a successful retail acquisition in 1998, Gayfers was renamed Dillard's.

The combination of shops and restaurants, in addition to the Jim Wilson and Associates team, employs in excess of 2,500 people. The energy and commitment of each dedicated employee is truly reflective in the beauty and atmosphere of the center.

"Thankfully, we are experiencing success with all the exciting development in the city, the need for better goods, and the desire for a better quality of life," said mall Manager Debbie Bailey. "Because of the continued growth in this community, the future is bright for our mall. Columbus is a land of opportunity and we strive to keep Peachtree Mall on the cutting edge of retail

Beautifully designed columns, skylights, and marble tile grace the fountain at Center Court.

development." Jim Wilson and Associates is committed to offer a quality shopping experience for the people of Columbus and the region. The developers are working to meet the challenge of the city's changing needs. ❧

Those familiar with hand tools know the J.H. Williams Hand Tool brand because of its long history of providing high-quality products for the professional tool user. J.H. Williams was founded by James Harvey Williams in 1882 on Long Island, New York. Although primarily a wrench manufacturer, Mr. Williams quickly became known as a pioneer in the standardization of industrial hand tools. In 1914, the company was relocated to Buffalo, New York, where it remained until 1982.

In 1946, J.H. Williams merged with United Greenfield. TRW, Inc. then acquired it in 1968, and relocated to Columbus, Georgia, where the current 125,000-square-foot facility was built on 26 acres on Jamesson Road. The plant's main function at this time was to provide socket products for the corporation.

During the late 1970s, markets were tightening, and by 1982 serious labor problems in the Buffalo, New York, facility resulted in all J.H. Williams operations being moved to Columbus. Shortly after being sold by TRW, Inc., Williams filed for bankruptcy. The 300-plus workforce dwindled, and with the reduced sales effort, Williams lost much of its marketshare to competitors.

Reminiscent of a phoenix rising from the ashes, J.H. Williams was resurrected in 1993, when it was acquired by the Snap-on Corporation. Snap-on is a $1.7-billion hand tool manufacturer that markets its

J.H. Williams chrome plates over 7 million parts annually.

high-quality products and services in 150 countries worldwide. J.H. Williams is a wholly-owned subsidiary under Snap-on's industrial products division. Being part of the Snap-on family has afforded Williams financial security, as well as access to cutting edge research and development opportunities necessary for continued growth and improvement.

Snap-on Corporation has ignited a spark at J.H. Williams that has fueled the growth at the Columbus facility. Currently, 182 people are employed at the Williams plant and perform manufacturing, marketing, sales, and customer service functions. Since the acquisition, revenues have doubled and Wiliams has been successful in capturing more than 10 percent of the United States industrial hand tool market. Williams is also expanding its influence in foreign markets. It currently has sales initiatives in Mexico, Canada, and South America, as well as the petrochemical industry in the Middle East.

Williams tools can be found on offshore oil rigs, in the shops of major manufacturers, shipbuilders, and in the toolboxes of

professional tool users nationwide. Using blanks and forgings provided by other Snap-on plants, the facility manufactures chrome plated and black oxide ratchets, sockets, wrenches, and drive tools for use in industry and construction. Williams

J.H.Williams–A Division of Snap-on

J.H. Williams has been in Columbus since 1976.

augments its manufactured line with such products as tool chests, torque tools, hammers, pliers, and screwdrivers to provide the professional hand tool user with a tool product for every need.

J.H. Williams has placed considerable emphasis on quality and service. The entire organization is committed to providing its customers with the highest quality products in a timely fashion. "The thing that delineates winners from losers is service," says Larry Burton, general manager. "By improving our service, we automatically grow our sales."

Going into the millennium, J.H. Williams is poised to become a major supplier in the growing U.S. consumer market. Burton expects this opportunity to enable J.H. Williams to continue to expand its Columbus facility. ◆

To shift a paradigm, sometimes you've got to change the angle in which people see themselves, and Weyerhaeuser did just that when it bought Westvaco's Container Division in Columbus in 1995.

"When we became part of this company,

Weyerhaeuser Containerboard Packaging

one of the first things we heard was the company vision—to be the best forest products company in the world," said General Manager Tom Pulley.

"That's a big statement. We thought, 'These guys really believe in their vision.' We didn't have a whole lot of ownership in that statement. That was their vision. It wasn't long before we realized they were serious. A little later, we had customers in for a presentation and we were talking about our vision and our values . . . and we were standing there saying, 'Our mission is to be the best forest products company in the world.' We realized that we were saying it too, and we believed it."

Already the Containerboard Packaging Business is on its way. With 45 box plants, 5 paper mills, 2 technical facilities, and a 12 percent market share, Weyerhaeuser is the largest producer of corrugated boxes in

the country. In fact, the box business accounts for 17 to 20 percent of sales for the diversified forest products company, establishing it as a core product.

The 145,000-square-foot Columbus facility—one of Weyerhaeuser's 45 box plants—designs, constructs, cuts, stamps, and labels more than 8 million boxes a month and reports annual sales of $38 million. Located in Columbus East Industrial Park, the plant, with 93 hourly employees, manufactures boxes to meet customers' packaging requirements, starting with computer-generated design and ending with a corrugated box ready for packing.

Though the technology has changed with the advent of the computer and improvements in equipment, corrugated boxes are still constructed using the processes in place 75 to 80 years ago, when boxes replaced wooden crates. Basically, a corrugated box is two sheets of paperboard with a center of corrugated medium held together by a cornstarch adhesive.

That's not expected to change, but the Containerboard Business will. Company strategy calls for continued growth through market share and acquisitions. The Columbus plant, with its own production, shipping,

Weyerhaeuser is the largest producer of corrugated boxes in the country.

customer service, and sales force, is expected to undergo a $2.5-million to $5-million expansion sometime after the beginning of the millennium.

Another goal is to achieve total customer satisfaction for its employees, the end users, and its shareholders. In addition to producing a high quality product, Weyerhaeuser is also aware of its environmental responsibilities. The Columbus plant, for instance, collects its waste materials for recycling at recycling facilities in the Containerboard Business.

Weyerhaeuser is a $12-billion Fortune 500 company. It owns and manages six million acres of timberland, making it the largest single landowner outside the federal government. Its pulp, paper, and packaging division manufactures wood pulp, coated and uncoated fine papers, newsprint, bleached paperboard, containerboard, and chemicals used in pulp and paper manufacturing processes. The timberlands and wood products division produces soft and hard wood lumber, plywood, composite products, and architectural doors.

Although the company is continually exploring new packaging solutions for its customers, one thing's for sure. You won't find the Columbus containerboard plant thinking too far outside the box. ❧

Located in Columbus East Industrial Park, Weyerhaeuser, with 93 hourly employees, manufactures boxes to meet customers' packaging requirements.

When Phillips Construction Company nails down a contract to build an office building or a manufacturing facility, the owner can be part of the team that makes it happen.

Phillips Construction is a general, full-service contractor, which offers commercial, industrial, and institutional building construction.

President R. Larry Phillips believes in "team-oriented construction," a concept where the owner, architect, engineers, and contractor work together for the successful completion of the project. In this partnering relationship, the participants develop mutual goals and strategies for meeting those goals. They also develop mechanisms for solving problems that save time and money and prevent problems from becoming disputes.

Phillips and two partners founded Phillips Construction in 1978 to specialize in pre-engineered steel building type projects. In 1983, he bought his partners' interest in the company and expanded it to include commercial, industrial, and institutional building construction. To complement those services, the company began offering project planning and analysis, site survey and soil analysis, guaranteed maximum cost estimates, and building and construction services. Architectural, engineering, and design services through association with professionals in each field have also been added to the mix.

Today, Phillips Construction is a general, full-service contractor located on Old Hamilton Road in north Columbus. It still offers its pre-engineered steel projects, but now constructs masonry, structural steel, and wood frame buildings as well. Employing 40 permanent, full-time construction professionals and using the skills of as many as 60 local subcontractors, Phillips Construction has built aircraft hangars and terminals, automobile dealerships, chemical plants, restaurants, office buildings, institutional buildings, condominiums, shopping centers, and retail stores.

Like most businesses, Phillips Construction has been impacted by the computer and improvements in communication technology. Buildings are designed on computers, and the information needed by subcontractors and suppliers is sent to them via the Internet or by fax. Although the technology has made it easier to design and build buildings and to communicate details, it's still the individual worker picking up lumber, mortaring bricks, and pouring concrete that turns a plan into a building. Even the "magic moment" when the next 100 years begins won't change the way construction is done. "In construction to actually get the project done, it's still just human beings out there working. There's no magic to it," Phillips said. "But this type of work is very fulfilling. Everything you see on a building has had a pair of hands on it. When a project is completed, there's a lot of pride in each of us who had a part in making it happen."

The construction of commercial and industrial buildings is inextricably linked to homebuilding, and a shift to a new millennium won't change that, Phillips said. "Our business follows residential construction by half a year to a year. If it goes down, we go down; if it goes up, we go up. When homebuilding is up, it's because people feel good about the economy and about their work and their ability to pay for the largest thing most of us ever purchase [our homes]."

Phillips Construction Company, Inc.

That same spirit works in corporations as well. When companies are wary of the economy, they are less likely to build. What contractors need is perspective, Phillips said. "When there's a lull in the economy, it's not the end of the world. Things are still happening. The momentum is still building. The need is growing." ❧

Phillips Construction Company believes in "team-oriented construction," a concept where the owner, architect, engineers, and contractor work together for the successful completion of the project.

There's something vastly exciting about soaring on the wings of eagles. Orville and Wilbur Wright felt it as their plane left the ground in Kitty Hawk, North Carolina, in 1903. So did Clyde V. Cessna in 1911, when he built and flew the first plane west of the

Cessna Columbus

Mississippi River. It's a fascination that continues today, and Cessna Columbus is glad of it.

Cessna Columbus is a manufacturer of detail parts and assemblies for large business jets such as the Excel, Cessna's small single-engine aircraft, and the Caravan utility turboprop, the workhorse of the air. Its main customer is the company Clyde Cessna founded in 1927 in Wichita, Kansas—Cessna Aircraft Company. It also manufactures parts for Gulfstream G4 and G5 luxury jets and Airbus planes that are manufactured in France, England, and Germany.

The 140,000-square-foot, $30-million plant located on 30 acres in Columbus East Industrial Park cuts, bends, forms, and assembles sheet metal into tail sections and control surfaces (parts that make planes manuever and take off). It began operations in 1984 as Precision Fabrication Center, a division of Fairchild Industries. In 1987,

Textron bought the plant and assigned it to operate under its Nashville, Tennessee, subsidiary, Textron Aerostructures, and in 1991 changed the name to Textron Aerospace Products. In 1996, Textron sold Aerostructures and reassigned the Columbus plant to Cessna Aircraft Company, another Textron subsidiary, to manufacture detail parts and subassemblies for single-engine light aircraft and business jets.

Cessna is a $2-billion wholly owned subsidiary of Textron, a Providence, Rhode Island-based diversified manufacturing and financial services company with annual revenues of $8 billion. Textron's product lines include E-Z-Go golf carts, Bell helicopters, and Speidel watches.

For a number of years, Cessna and other plane manufacturers ceased to produce single-engine piston aircraft because of high fuel prices and product liability issues in the 1980s. As a result, the Columbus plant's production dropped significantly, and its workforce of several hundred dwindled to 65.

From 1996 to 1998, the Columbus plant experienced a turnaround, growing at warp speed. The number of employees soared to 290 and sales from $3 million to $19 million. Capital investment surged from $50,000 to $1.1 million, and Cessna Columbus's customer base grew from one customer to four—Cessna, Wichita; Cessna, Independence; Aerostructures, Nashville; and Gulfstream, Oklahoma City.

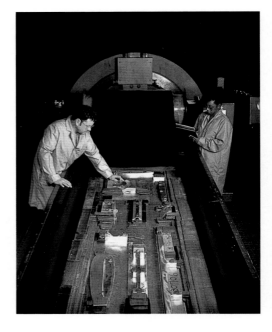

The 140,000-square-foot, $30-million plant located on 30 acres in Columbus East Industrial Park cuts, bends, forms, and assembles sheet metal into tail sections and control surfaces.

The tailwind behind the company's growth was in part due to a drop in gas prices and to the passage of the General Aviation Revitalization Act of 1994, which reformed product liability and brought the cost of liability insurance down.

Cessna Columbus's phenomenal growth is expected to continue into the millennium as its employee base climbs to 300 plus and revenues edge over the $20-million mark, said General Manager Rod Holter. Sales of Cessna airplanes, which account for 60 percent of the Columbus plant's production, are expected to rise to $2 billion as new products come off the drawing board and more people take to the sky. ◈

Cessna Columbus is a manufacturer of detail parts and assemblies for large business jets such as the Excel, Cessna's small single-engine aircraft, and the Caravan utility turboprop, the workhorse of the air.

Since 1981, the Columbus Convention and Visitors Bureau has been telling a story of heritage, people, and places, and the renaissance that is underway in Columbus. The story has been told to a burgeoning market called tourism. Many have discovered fascinating things to see and do here.

Columbus is an authentic river town. The bureau's marketing strategies—to promote the city for tourism, conventions, and trade shows—incorporate the romance and nostalgia of Columbus' history and the river.

"Columbus is the ideal convention site," says Brenda Price, executive director of the bureau. "We have outstanding convention facilities and a wide array of tourism locations in our area."

Tourism continues to boom with visitors exceeding the 1996 Olympic crowds. Nearly a million people overnight in Columbus annually and brought with them an economic benefit of $232 million in 1997.

The bureau's task is to fill the city's 2,700 hotel rooms and convention space by targeting motor coach and tour operators, conventions, religious groups, military reunions, minority-based tour groups, and sporting events.

Success is made on the city's unique-

Connecting the states of Georgia and Alabama is the Dillingham Street Bridge, originally designed and built by a master and his slave, Horace King. King had been set free, but the two men were such good friends that they continued to work together. In the foreground is the statue of Christopher Columbus on the Chattahoochee RiverWalk.

ness. The city retains its old-world charm, with 100-year-old houses, brick streets, Victorian gardens, and gazebos, as well as reminders of the city's role in the Civil War as found in a number of historic markers.

The Chattahoochee Riverwalk hugs the banks of the river. This is a place for families to bike, jog, or take a leisurely stroll. The river is home to the *Chattahoochee Princess* riverboat, an 1880s era paddlewheel riverboat, and the Coca-Cola Space Science Center nestles on its eastern bank.

Columbus offers a variety of museums. The Columbus Museum features traveling exhibits, a collection of works of nineteenth- and twentieth-century masters, a regional history gallery, and a gallery for young people. Fort Benning's National Infantry Museum presents the history of the infantry. The Woodruff Museum of Civil War Naval History focuses on naval contributions made by the Southern states. The Springer Opera House is the State Theater of Georgia and a national historic landmark.

Columbus Historic District, circa 1850 to 1870, epitomizes preservation efforts and the best uses of resources without compromising architectural integrity.

The Columbus Iron Works, now the Convention and Trade Center, was a munitions factory during the Civil War and still displays its early wares.

The South Commons Complex is the finest collection of sports facilities at one location. The centerpiece is the Columbus Civic Center. Opened in 1996, this 10,000-seat venue is home to the Columbus Cottonmouths hockey team. A new 2,500-

seat softball stadium features the Women's Professional Fast Pitch Softball team, Georgia Pride. The stadium, surrounded by a seven-field softball complex, provides Columbus with the opportunity to host any size softball event. Memorial Stadium is

Columbus Convention and Visitors Bureau

Filled with beautiful antebellum and Victorian homes and restored to their original splendor, the 26-block Columbus Historic District is a sight to behold. Special treats to tour in the district include: the home of Dr. John Pemberton, the originator of the formula for Coca-Cola, an original log cabin used by traders, and the oldest known home in Columbus.

a 17,000-seat football stadium that hosts college football powers Albany State and Fort Valley State, and the Tuskegee-Morehouse game, known as the Fountain City Classic. Historic Golden Park is a 4,500-seat baseball stadium that is home to the Columbus RedStixx. The stadium was the Olympic venue for the Women's Fast Pitch Softball competition in 1996.

"Every dollar that the bureau spends on promotions brings a hefty return," Price said. "Southern hospitality makes us real. The key is the personal touch in service. It's a community that takes pride in preserving the past while maintaining a vision for the future." ❧

The Historic Columbus Hilton has something a lot of hotels don't—character and ambiance. Guests are welcomed by the unique blend of the old and the new from the moment they walk into the atrium lobby with its 100-year-old brick and

Historic Columbus Hilton

exposed hewn wooden beams until they snuggle under the covers in their temperature-controlled rooms and flip on their television sets.

The historic 177-room, full-service hotel is built around the old Empire Mill, a grist mill operated by George W. Woodruff for milling corn meal and flour. The building had been a cotton warehouse from 1847 until Woodruff opened the mill in 1861. In 1982, the Columbus Hilton, in tune with preservation efforts of historic downtown properties, restored the original red brick walls and converted part of the mill into guest rooms, meeting rooms, and a tavern. The presidential and governor's suites on the mill side, with their polished heart of pine floors, period oak furnishings, beamed ceilings, and loft bedrooms have hosted such famous guests as Colin Powell, television news show host Barbara Walters, actress Jane Fonda, country music singers Reba McIntyre and Lee Ann Rimes, and Presidents Ronald Reagan and George Bush.

The modern section of the hotel is a six-story tower that offers comfort and convenience to business and meeting travelers. In these rooms, guests find easy chairs, a working desk with a phone for data ports, an honor bar, in-room movies, coffeemakers, hair dryers, and irons.

Located across the street from the Columbus Convention and Trade Center, the Hilton is the hotel of choice for convention and meeting planners. With seven meeting rooms that can seat an intimate group of 10 to a convention-sized group of 350, the Hilton is a choice meeting spot for businesses and organizations.

For light dining or a quiet cocktail, Hunter's Bar and Grill is located off the lobby. Guests may choose to dine on American fare in Pemberton's Cafe, named for John S. Pemberton, the Columbus

native who invented the formula for Coca-Cola.

Among the amenities at the Hilton are ATM machines, shoeshine services, an outdoor swimming pool, a health club, banquet facilities, room service, complimentary parking, shuttle service, and reservation service through a national reservation system.

In the heart of the Columbus historic district, the Hilton, which holds a Triple Star rating from the AAA Auto Club, provides ready access to a number of local attractions, including the Columbus Riverwalk, the Columbus Civic Center, Golden Park, the Olympic softball complex, the Coca-Cola Space Science Center, the Springer Opera House, and the Woodruff Museum of Civil War Naval History.

As the city grows, so does the Hilton, said General Manager Rick Greenwald. He's excited about the recent developments in the downtown area, especially the Total System Services campus, already under construction, which will bring thousands of employees downtown every day, and the RiverCenter for the Performing Arts, which is expected to open in 2000-2001

and attract local residents as well as tourist trade. A proposed entertainment/shopping district near the river will also impact the hotel as it approaches the millennium, perhaps to the extent that the hotel will add additional rooms, he said. ✒

Guests of the Historic Columbus Hilton are welcomed by the unique blend of the old and the new. The historic 177-room, full-service hotel is built around the old Empire Mill, a grist mill operated by George W. Woodruff for milling corn meal and flour.

Listening to Ted Freeman talk, it's obvious he loves his job. It's a quiet enthusiasm, one that engenders trust and assures his customers that from this man's company they'll get quality construction, fair prices, and good service.

Freeman is president of Freeman & Associates, a general contractor headquartered at 1454 54th Street in Columbus. The company builds commercial, industrial, health care, office, and retail facilities, and multifamily housing. With 60 to 70 employees and a host of subcontractors, the company generates from $12 million to $20 million in annual revenues.

The name Freeman & Associates is associated with some of the most impressive buildings in Columbus. On that list are the Columbus Regional Pediatric Center, Char-Broil, Kysor//Warren, Ruco Polymer Corporation, Morningside Baptist Church, the Columbus Cancer Center, One Arsenal Place, the Clubhouse at Maple Ridge Golf Community, Jay Auto Mall, the Downtown Elementary Magnet School, and numerous physicians' offices and shopping centers.

Its most visible presence, however, is in the construction of the $100-million Total System Services campus in downtown Columbus, a project which began in 1997. A joint venture with Beers Construction Co. of Atlanta, the five-year project which will result in 1 million square feet of building space, is the largest in Columbus's history.

Theodore "Ted" Freeman moved from LaGrange, Georgia, to Columbus in 1959 to join contractor Bob Carter's residential construction company. After a year, he became a partner in the company and encouraged its diversification into his specialties—multifamily housing, commercial, and industrial construction.

Following Carter's death in 1978, limited bonding capacity and financing slowed the company's growth but never stopped it. Though untested at the helm, Freeman, with his son Andy and Carter's son David beside him, put the company on the road to prosperity. In 1982, the Freemans purchased the Carters' interest in the company and renamed it Freeman & Associates Inc. Later that year, Freeman's son Mark sold his trucking business and purchased interest in the corporation. They have gradually surrounded themselves with quality people as corporate officers, including Randy Williams as vice president and director of management operations, Carol Freeman as office administrator and corporate secretary, and Vanessa Knight as assistant corporate secretary.

In the 1970s, while still part of Carter's company, Freeman helped build the city's first speculative building, a building shell used to attract companies to a community. Since then, Freeman & Associates has built more than a dozen of the buildings, which have a tremendous impact on the city's economic development.

The company has been heavily involved in building condominiums, retirement communities, and apartment complexes. On its list of accomplishments are Covenant Woods Retirement Community, Bull Creek, Quail Ridge, Hunter's Run, and Renaissance Villas Apartments.

Freeman & Associates works with its customers in a design-build process, which means that the company is involved from the idea stage to a completed facility. This type arrangement encourages a team approach and often results in cost savings to the customer. Or it can build from plans and specifications provided by clients, architects, and engineers, through negotiated and conventional bid processes.

Freeman & Associates is committed to its employees and its customers. The company emphasizes the importance of each person's job and rewards its employees with benefits, bonus plans, and profit sharing. As a result, employee turnover is low.

Most of the company's business comes from repeat business and referrals from

Freeman & Associates Inc.

satisfied customers. "We try to build something at a reasonable cost, finish it on time, and be there when something goes wrong," Freeman said. "That's what people want and that's what we try to give them so they'll keep coming back." ◆

Freeman & Associates works with its customers in a design-build process which means that the company is involved from the idea stage to a completed facility.

Freeman & Associates' most visible presence is with Freeman-Beers in the construction of the $100-million Total System Services campus in downtown Columbus.

Chances are when you walk into the grocery store and grab a steak or a gallon of milk, you don't give much thought to the refrigerated display case that keeps the products cool. That's just the way they want it at Kysor//Warren. Their product is

Kysor//Warren

At its Columbus East Industrial Park location, Kysor//Warren manufactures refrigerated display cases that are used to keep foods cold in grocery stores and other food outlets.

meant to be low profile. It's one of those products that doesn't get much attention but would be sorely missed if it weren't available.

At its Columbus East Industrial Park location, Kysor//Warren manufactures refrigerated display cases that are used to keep foods cold in grocery stores and other food outlets. At its Corporate Ridge location, it makes the refrigeration and electrical distribution systems that are located away from a store's customer area and provides power, air filtration and circulation, and temperature controls to the refrigerated display cases within the store. The two plants employ 600 and have annual sales that top $100 million.

Kysor//Warren came to Columbus in 1984 as Warren/Sherer, a division of Kysor Industrial Corp. of Cadillac, Michigan. It moved into a 135,000-square-foot speculative building on 20 acres in Columbus

East Industrial Park. The building was expanded in 1989 to 300,000 square feet.

In 1996, Kysor//Warren built a new $6.6-million, 154,000-square-foot facility in Corporate Ridge Industrial Park, adding 300 employees to its Columbus workforce.

In 1997, Chicago-based Scotsman Industries Inc. bought Kysor's commercial products division, which included the Columbus operations. Scotsman is a leading manufacturer of such refrigeration products as ice machines, drink and ice dispensers, refrigerators and freezers, display and deli cases, walk-in cold rooms, insulated panels, and food preparation workstations. It sells to the food service industry, the hospitality industry, supermarkets, convenience stores, mass merchandisers, and the health care industry. In addition to the domestic market, Scotsman distributes its products in over 100 countries.

Kysor//Warren's history reaches back to 1882, when J. H. Shannen began experimenting with walk-in coolers refrigerated with blocks of ice. By 1900, he had created a more efficient two-cycle refrigeration system that he sold to one of his customers, Virgil P. Warren of Atlanta. Warren and his father, George T. Warren, bought Shannen's interest in the company in 1909 and operated the company under the name Shannen Refrigeration and Butcher Supply Co. In 1922, the name was changed to The Warren Co. It wasn't until after World War

II that the company really took off and became one of the country's top suppliers of commercial refrigerators and condensing units. Today, Kysor//Warren is the second largest producer of commercial refrigeration equipment in the country.

Trends in the industry and mandated governmental regulations have impacted the company in recent years. Although the operation of display cases has remained constant, the style has changed from a boxy unit to a rounded European look with more plastic components, said Plant Manager Lee McDaniel. The systems side of the business has seen major changes, especially in the move toward greater energy efficiency and in the use of environmentally friendly refrigerants.

In the year 2000 and beyond, Kysor//Warren will focus on producing a quality product, continue its commitment to customer service, and maintain its place as an industry leader, McDaniel said. ❧

At its Corporate Ridge location, it makes the refrigeration and electrical distribution systems that are located away from a store's customer area and provides power, air filtration and circulation, and temperature controls to the refrigerated display cases within the store.

Meacham, Earley & Jones, P.C. began in 1986 when Chris Meacham opened his practice with an emphasis in real estate, corporate, business, and labor and employment law. The practice grew very quickly, and Karen Earley joined the firm in 1990, specializing in real estate. Since that time, the firm has added several additional lawyers, a sizable support staff, and expanded its professional practice areas.

The firm's facility is located at 5704 Veterans Parkway.

A regional firm, the clients of Meacham, Earley & Jones, P.C. come primarily from Columbus and Harris County, Georgia, Russell and Lee Counties, Alabama, and surrounding areas. Good lawyers and good business practitioners, the attorneys of this firm, some of whom are licensed in both Georgia and Alabama, concentrate their practices in different specialties, including real estate, corporate, business, domestic and family, wills and trusts, creditors' rights, general litigation, and labor and employment law.

In the area of residential and commercial real estate law, the firm assists individuals and corporations buying and selling real estate together with related licensing and zoning issues. The firm works closely with real estate developers and builders in planning new residential and commercial projects.

Though it represents large corporate enterprises, the corporate and business practice of the firm focuses on small and medium business entities, assisting those clients in maximizing the benefits and advantages of their business organization. The firm regularly provides advice to its various clients regarding the buying and selling of businesses, business expansions, mergers and acquisitions, service mark registrations, and trade name registrations.

The wills, estate, and trust department of the firm assists its clients with estate and financial planning issues, including the drafting of wills, the creation of trusts, and the probate of estates.

Employment law is one of the fastest growing areas of litigation in the Columbus area. The complexity of constantly changing employment law and the fact that few law firms specialize in this practice area have created a niche market for Meacham, Earley & Jones, P.C. The firm regularly assists its current and prospective clients in complying with wage-hour, discrimination, and sexual harassment laws, including major legislation involving the Americans With Disabilities Act and the Family and Medical Leave Act. "With the proliferation of federal and state legislation affecting just about everyone, compliance is a major concern for all employers," Meacham said. To further assist its clients, the firm routinely conducts in-house seminars tailored to meet the needs of specific employers.

The domestic and family law practice involves divorces, separations, adoptions, and issues concerning child custody and support. Compassion, understanding, and professionalism are fundamental concerns in this area of practice, and the firm strives to set the standard regarding such issues.

Dedication to their profession, commitment to their clients, and eager participation in continuing legal education programs are distinguishing characteristics of the

law firm of Meacham, Earley & Jones, P.C. Such activities, along with participation in community affairs, create an excitement for the attorneys of this firm over their professional growth and that of the Columbus community at large. ⬧➔

Meacham, Earley & Jones, P.C.

The attorneys at Meacham, Earley & Jones, P.C. are (left to right): T. Michael Jones, Donald Oulsnam, Karen Earley, M. Scott Phillips, and Christopher Meacham.

Since SouthTrust Bank forded the Chattahoochee River in 1989, it has maintained banks on both sides of the river serving the Columbus and Phenix City markets with its presence in both communities compounding daily. Its aggressive

SouthTrust Bank

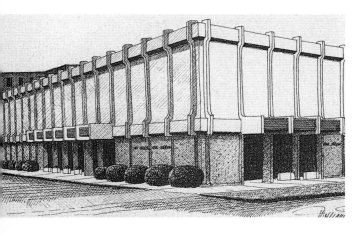

SouthTrust Bank, formerly the Trust Company of Columbus, offers its customers a full line of competitively priced banking products and services.

growth has netted 12 branches and 18 automated teller machines located in Columbus and Manchester, Georgia, and Phenix City and Smiths, Alabama. Its market bank holds over $400 million in deposits and employs more than 150. In Columbus alone, it holds 14 percent of the market share.

SouthTrust opened its first market bank in Phenix City in 1975. After the charter was moved to Columbus, the Phenix City bank was rechartered under an Alabama state charter.

"From a growth standpoint, we're real aggressive, not only in the Columbus and Phenix City markets, but the entire seven-state region," said bank President and CEO Mitch Hunt. In addition to our exceptional internal growth in the last nine years, in 1992, SouthTrust acquired BankSouth's Columbus operation, adding three banking locations. In 1994, it acquired First Columbus Community Bank and Trust, a five-year-old community bank. And in 1997, it purchased the Barnett Bank of

Southwest Georgia's locations, netting seven offices in the Columbus area and adding assets of over $250 million. "Through our acquisitions and new branch and ATM locations we've added, SouthTrust has become a convenient market bank in Columbus and Phenix City," added Hunt.

SouthTrust offers its customers a full line of competitively priced banking products and services, including a variety of checking accounts designed to meet the changing needs of a maturing customer. It offers specialty products such as the Just Checking account for young adults; Bankers Dozen Checking that combines a number of banking products and services with additional benefits such as insurance and travel discounts; and Silver Service interest-bearing checking for customers age 50 and over. SouthTrust customers have access to check cards, credit cards, safe deposit boxes, and certificates of deposit among many other products and services. SouthTrust Online allows busy customers to bank from their homes or offices using their computers. Through its bank-related subsidiaries, SouthTrust customers have local access to personal and home mortgage loans, life insurance, asset and trust management, full-service securities, and discount brokerage.

Customer service comes first at SouthTrust. The corporation believes so strongly in accuracy, responsiveness, promptness, reliability, and courtesy that it backs up those qualities with a guarantee. If, for instance, the bank makes a mistake on a transaction, it credits the customer's account with $10, or if a customer waits longer than five minutes in a teller line,

$1 is given to the customer on the spot.

As the millennium approaches, SouthTrust is focused on continuing to provide convenient, competitive products and services by taking advantage of the rapidly changing and improving technological arena. "We will continue to grow in this market, particularly focusing on the existing customer base," Hunt said. "Our objective in this market is to have our customers utilize us for more of their services."

SouthTrust, headquartered in Birmingham, Alabama, operates more than 600 offices and bank-related affiliates in Alabama, Florida, Georgia, Mississippi, North Carolina, South Carolina, Tennessee, and Texas. With assets of $39 billion, it is the 21st largest bank holding company in the nation and the fifth largest in the Southeast. The corporation was formed in 1972 in a merger between Birmingham Trust National Bank and First National Bank of Dothan. ✒

Since SouthTrust Bank forded the Chattahoochee River in 1989, it has maintained banks on both sides of the river serving the Columbus and Phenix City markets with its presence in both communities compounding daily.

Photo by Jim Cawthorne.

Chapter Five

The Millennium Milieu

Like an island in a sea of trees, Columbus beckons the traveler to stop for a respite. A multitude of city advantages light up the future for Columbus. Photo by Steven Duffey.

(Right) The Hale Bopp Comet as sighted over Columbus skies in 1997. Columbus State University's Coca Cola Space and Science Center attracts Columbus residents and visitors alike—to view the stars and to journey into the skies. Photo by Andy Waddell and Steve Armstrong.

Paving the road to a new millennium, Columbus made way for the new Total System Services Campus. Photo by Jim Cawthorne.

In the midst of the millennium countdown, many in the U.S. are struck with 'les terreurs de l'an mil," the terrors of the new millennium. This is nothing new nor uniquely American. The year 1000 A.D. was met with the same expectations from European cultures.

Abbo of Fleury wrote circa 994-996 A.D., "De fine quoque mundi coram populo sermonem in Ecclesia Parisiorum adolescentulus audivi, quod statim finito mille annorum numero Antichristus adveniret, et non longo post tempore universale iudicium succederet: cui praedicationi ex Evangeliis ac Apocalypsi et libro Danielis, qua potui virtute, resistiti." *Concerning the end of the world, as a youth I heard a sermon in a church in Paris that as soon as the number of a thousand years should come, the Antichrist would come, and not long thereafter, the Last Judgement would follow; which preaching I resisted with all my strength from the Evangels and the Apocalypse and the book of Daniel.*

The times were thought to be consumed with terrors that seemed confirmed in the appearance of Halley's Comet in 989 and the seemingly endless portrayal of signs like fire from the heavens, widespread famine and plagues, the birth of a monstrously deformed child, and peace councils where peace had not existed before. In the 990s, the fevered preachings of Aelfric and Wulfistan were filled with images of the Last Judgement that were specifically linked to the year 1000 and the unleashing of the Antichrist. They pointed often to the Bible and drew conclusions from the disasters all around. The last Carolingian dynasty toppled under malicious circumstances and was seen as the removal of the final hindrance to the arrival of the Antichrist. Riots formed sporadically and spontaneously in the streets and hostile mobs destroyed churches. Many leaders of the time made pilgrimages to Jerusalem to either await Christ's return or to seek sanctuary from the Antichrist.

Even so, not everyone predicted disaster. The optimistic saw good omens everywhere. For the first time in world history, Russia, Hungary, and Poland embraced Christianity just two decades before the fateful birth of the millennium. Otto III was crowned Holy Roman emperor in 996 and was considered the last great hope for church unification. Shortly after his coronation, Otto was joined by Pope Sylvester II, a like-minded reformer who also dreamed of church unity. The pious expected the two to eradicate corruption and the dividing lines between the Eastern and Western churches. The believers thought that this would occur for the sake of the Lord as predicted by the new millennium, the new age of peace.

Neither group was right. The final dawning of the feared millennium was not attended by the Antichrist. And, Otto never united the church. Instead, the Italian peninsula rebelled against the

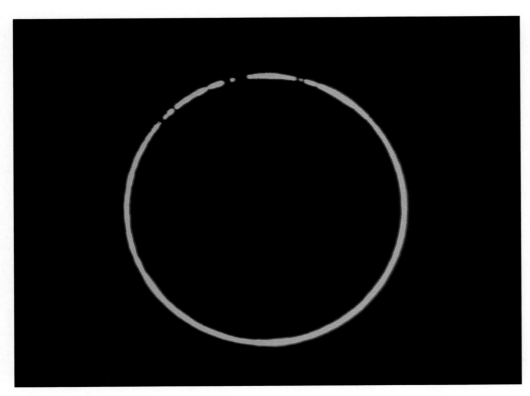

This rare complete solar eclipse in August of 1984 held Columbus residents spellbound for hours in their yards and in parking lots all over the city. Photo by Herb Cawthorne.

German Otto, his Byzantine kinfolk, and the French pope. However, it was his mistress, the widow of a Roman rebel Otto had killed, who poisoned him in 1002. She poisoned Pope Sylvester a year later. Unity as a millennial event was a total flop.

The crises to society eventually passed and "la mutation de l'an mil," changes in society during and after the millennium, transformed the world as it was known then.

One thousand years later the millennium is surrounded by many of the same hopes and fears. But, there are two significant differences: Israel and the 2000 year cycle. The New Testament compares the Kingdom of God to the growth of a fig tree. Some say the figurative speech refers to Israel and that the Second Coming is near when Israel becomes a nation. It did...in 1948. Many prophets who predict the end of time place the apocalyptic Armageddon in Israel so developments there are certainly of interest and tend to gather some interesting speculations. In 1967, Israel reclaimed much of Jerusalem from Jordan. The war between the U.S. and Iraq in 1991 was also thought to signal the beginning of the end.

As to the infamous 2000 year cycle: Abraham and Issac, significant biblical figures who are considered the patriarchs who established a covenant between God and mankind, were born around 2000 B.C (first Abraham and sometime later Issac,

but both within a timeframe set around the 2000 B.C. period). Christians believe that Christ was born 2000 years later. This new millennium places man exactly 2000 years after that. To many believers this means that human history is 6000 years old. The year 2000 A.D. begins the 7000th year of human history which would then also be the beginning of the 1000 years of peace on earth under the rule of Jesus. This belief is based largely on the mathematics presented in Peter's Second Letter "One day with the Lord is as a thousand years." The new millennium, to them, is similar to the seventh day of creation... the period of holiness and rest.

However, Christianity is not the only religious belief among humans. The millennium is therefore momentous to some and inconsequential to others. By the Chinese lunar calendar the year is 4696, 304 years away from the next millennium. Roughly 1.2 billion people, therefore, see the year 2000 A.D. as a nonevent. Hindus are now in a calendrical cycle predicted to end in the world's total annihilation... but their cycle has over 350,000 years to go. Jews start their calendar from the biblical Creation; the year 2000 A.D. will be the year 5760 to them and thus no big deal. However, some rabbis believe the Messiah will arrive about 240 years from now. The Muslims begin their calendar from the prophet Muhammad's move from Mecca to Medina. 2000 A.D. translates to the Islamic year of 1420. The Muslims totally ignored the one millennium they have had so far because the Islamic day of doom was predicted by Muhammad at 50,000 years... no where close to the current year of 1418 (1998).

Roughly one-third of the world cares a great deal about the new millennium, one-third will notice it but assigns it no particular importance, and one-third will ignore it completely.

Columbus, Georgia, sits deep in the South and is firmly entrenched in the Bible belt. Religion is, and always has been, a significant factor in daily life. However, the make-up of the city's people is universally diverse with most of the world's nationalities and cultures represented in the mix. Within this paradox of old and new world, of Southern tradition and worldly sophistication, is a precognition of many possible futures. As to the matter of "les terreurs de l'an mil," look deep within the collective

heart and soul of the city, and there you will find the answer....

Uptown Columbus is circled by churches. They are among the oldest buildings in the city and have since stood watch over all that has happened here. At the feet of these magnificent structures lie rubble and chaos. The turmoil began innocently enough.

In 1993, Columbus was faced with a state mandate to upgrade the city's combined sewage overflow system. The mandate also applied to several cities in Georgia in a serious attempt to clean up the environment. The clean-up, however, cost big money. The city did not have sufficient funding to comply. So, taxpayers were asked to vote for a one-cent sales tax to rectify the problem. If the sales tax referendum was not passed, the citizens were told, then an increase would be added to the water bills of all residents. One way or the other, the city was determined to fix the problem... not so much because of the mandate, after all many other cities have virtually ignored the demand, but because it was the right thing to do.

The projects proposed to be covered by the sales tax included the combined sewage solution, a new public safety administration building, additional funding for Parks and Recreation, new sidewalks, and a new 10,000 seat civic center to replace the dilapidated Municipal Auditorium. On March 16, 1993, Columbusites voted overwhelmingly in favor of the sales tax.

Shortly thereafter, former Mayor Frank Martin and several civic leaders traveled to Atlanta to attend a "Georgians For Better Transportation" meeting at the Nikko hotel in Buckhead (Atlanta). Wyck Knox, who at that time was on the Atlanta Olympic Committee, mentioned to Martin in casual conversation that Marietta had voted down a one-cent sales tax that had been earmarked to build a softball complex for the newly awarded venue. No money meant that there was now no venue for women's fast-pitch softball and bidding would begin again.

Martin rounded up the Columbus group and, standing in a corner of the hotel lobby just outside the ballroom, they discussed the chance remark and what it could mean to Columbus. A discussion that, while set aside for the banquet, resumed on the CB&T private plane on the way home and again at a 7:30 a.m. breakfast meeting in the boardroom at Synovus the next day. A formal 23 page proposal was quickly drawn up and sent to the Atlanta Committee for Olympic Games (ACOG).

Competition for the Olympic Venue was intense between Columbus, Albany, Atlanta, Augusta, Clayton County, Cobb County, Macon, and Savannah. On August 6, 1993, ACOG President Billy Payne announced that Columbus would be the site for the 1996 Olympic Softball Competition.

Serendipity was a major factor. Here stood the Columbus group with $22 million a year cash-flow from the sales tax in hand

First Baptist Church. Photo by Jim Cawthorne.

The city of Columbus was laid out with the churches as their foundation stones...

Temple Israel. Photo by Jim Cawthorne.

(Left) First Presbyterian Church. Photo by Jim Cawthorne.

(Above) Holy Family Catholic Church. Photo by Jim Cawthorne.

(Left) St. Luke Methodist Church. Photo by Jim Cawthorne.

and 90 acres of city-owned land that required no demolition and had, in fact, been slated for construction of ten softball fields for public recreation. The Columbus Consolidated Government's Parks and Recreation Department was quick to change the plans to eight fields at Olympic specifications.

ACOG President Billy Payne tells this story about dealing with Columbus and other communities on the Olympic Games: "As we dealt with a multitude of satellite venues and locations, there always seemed to be unlimited desire on the part of the respective communities outside Atlanta to be a part of the Olympics. And, yet, in most cases, as those decisions were made and everybody got down to the real business of getting the job done, their enthusiasm proportionally decreased. We used to kind of laugh, because when the reality of having to invest funds and the reality of having to contribute to the preparation of the venue and its operation hit all these communities, we would then get into some very difficult negotiations about getting the job done on time, and who was going to do what, and enforcing the commitments that had been made when they proposed to do it in the first instance.

Having said that, I remember specifically

(Above) St. James A.M.E. Church. Photo by Jim Cawthorne.

(Left) Trinity Episcopal Church. Photo by Jim Cawthorne.

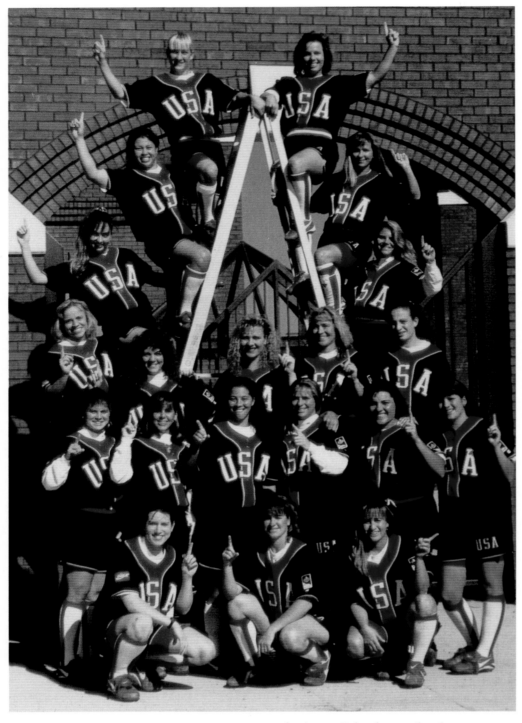

Visitors from all over the world came to Columbus to cheer on the USA Women's softball team to win the first Olympic gold medal for softball. Photo by Herb Cawthorne.

referring to Columbus as the clear exception to that and perhaps the city, that from day one, took the ball and ran with it, and never once tried to renege or modify the commitment they had made. Columbus did precisely what they said they would do. It was refreshing, it was wonderful, and I think it was very much indicative of the support that existed in the community for the Olympics.

Columbus was a great experience for us through all the years of preparation and, most importantly, in the enthusiasm in which they embraced the games and conducted themselves during the games. It was a home run in every respect."

The Olympic softball games drew visitors from all over the world to Columbus,

but tourists eventually go home. Columbus, however, was determined to hold on to the glory and the tourist dollars earned by high-visibility sports events. Before the Olympic games ended, perhaps even before they began, Columbus announced its intent to become the softball capital of the world.

Columbus raked in big bucks in their sports infancy: $21 million in 1995, $42 million in 1996, $25 million in 1997, and an estimated total of $27 million on 1998 bookings. Most events are too competitive for cities to do much more than break even; the big bucks listed here weren't collected at the gate but in the coffers of retail stores, hotels, restaurants, malls, gas stations, and the city's sales tax office. Columbus expects to draw even bigger dollars in the future having now earned a great reputation and the experience to compete more efficiently.

The city's efforts in overall economic development and in establishing an edge in competing for big name sports are substantially aided by the notoriety and name recognition that comes with hosting the big games. Roughly 20 percent of all events held in Columbus are televised into millions of households by the likes of ESPN and Fox Sports South.

Since the Olympics, the city has hosted NCAA national championship games, SEC conference championships, and a myriad of other national and regional championships and play-offs. In May 1998, the city hosted the NAIA (National Association of Intercollegiate Athletics) regional championship. The day after the NAIA event, the SEC softball championships began. In June 1998, the city hosted an international competition, Junior Superball. The competitors were girls 18 and under from the USA, Australia, Puerto Rico, and the Czech Republic.

Columbus averages hosting 35 events a year, mostly on week-ends. That's an extremely aggressive schedule; most communities only try to do about 15 or 20 in a year. On weekdays, Columbus youth leagues, charity players, and business teams play on the same fields as the major competitors.

But softball isn't the only game in town. Regional youth soccer championship games are played at Woodruff Farm Soccer Complex. The recent $2.5 million dollar expansion added five more international size fields. Regional and national tennis championships are also held in Cooper

Creek Park. Plus, the Cottonmouth hockey team, the RedStixx professional baseball team, and the Georgia Pride women's fast-pitch softball team are doing well. A long list of successes in basketball, baseball, softball, hockey, tennis, wrestling, and soccer is more than the average Olympic legacy.

The tax referendum ended up building the Olympic venue and a sports legacy, none of which had even been imagined before the sales tax vote. Yet another welcome surprise sprang from the public coffers: the riverwalk.

When the riverfront effort first began, it was only a subcommittee of the Chamber of Commerce because, according to Peggy Theus, chairman of the Riverfront Development Committee, no one actually thought anything would ever come of the idea. In fact, Theus said local folks often laughed at her and a handful of others who promoted the idea of making the river the front door to the city rather than a back-door embarrassment. But she and the others were driven by a passion deep-seated in a personal belief that the Riverwalk was both a good idea and a realistic endeavor. "God's not making any more rivers," said Theus. "It was like I could see it, you know, I just felt it, other people did, too. It was a passion combined with competitive spirit." The group of believers hit the Columbus circuit, determined to share their vision and gather supporters.

"I would just about beg to get on any program I could, Rotary or whatever," said Theus. At the beginning of the presentation, Theus would show slides she had taken in successful cities. Ed Burdeshaw of Hecht, Burdeshaw, Johnson, Kidd, & Clark Architects, who also ended up designing the Riverwalk, would then show what Theus and Burdeshaw liked to call opportunity shots. They were pictures of ugly sites along the Chattahoochee that had development potential. The presentation was made for over a year to any group that would listen.

One day the duo was presenting their plea before the Downtown Rotary Club. In the audience was Billy Turner, president of Columbus Water Works, who was already struggling with the mandate to clean up the combined sewage overflow (CSO). As he listened to the presentation, it occurred to him that the Riverwalk could be built directly over the CSO as it was already planned to run parallel to the river. And

Living legend and Medal of Honor winner, Colonel R. Nett, carrying the Olympic Torch. Photo by Jim Cawthorne.

Gold medal fans in historic Golden Park! Photo by Jim Cawthorne.

Columbus is well on its way to being the soft-ball capital of the world with the new state-of-the-art South Commons Softball Complex. Photo by Herb Cawthorne.

that was how the Riverwalk project was jump-started from dream to reality.

Clearing the way for construction of the new Riverwalk required moving some existing structures, one of which was the gas company. The main gas line serving Columbus crossed the Chattahoochee and had ruptured. United Cities informed state and federal authorities immediately and installed a temporary patch. Bobby Gaylor, then with United Cities Gas Company and now City Manager of Phenix City, says that while he was deciding on a more perma-nent solution, Matt Swift and Peggy Theus, both of W.C. Bradley Company, approached

him with the suggestion of moving the company's Bay Avenue site to make way for a riverwalk. The city came forward at this point and offered United Cities Gas a land swap deal if the gas company would agree to move to Victory Drive. Gaylor agreed.

The move created a logistical and envi-ronmental nightmare. Twenty-five feet below the surface, unbeknownst to anyone, coal tar was leaching into the river. The stuff dated back to 1854 when coal was used to produce methane gas to light the streetlights in downtown Columbus. It was unclear who was technically responsible

Ushering in the new millennium... the 1999-2000 Columbus City Council. Photo Jim Cawthorne.

for clean-up since the city had a part in past operations, Georgia Power Company had once owned the gas company, and then United Cities owned the place. In similar scenarios in other cities, the parties have tangled in courtrooms for years to settle the issue. But, that didn't happen in Columbus; the actual clean-up was finished within 18 months. The Columbus Consolidated Government, Georgia Power, and United Cities Gas shared the costs and moved ahead.

So it was that with each new addition, something had to move or be torn down. The result was that Columbus moved

through the millennium countdown, the 1990s, as a rubble-strewn and incredibly industrious city. The new Civic Center was built as were the Olympic softball fields, the CSO project, and the Riverwalk. Amongst the new structures were several renovations including Golden Park and Memorial Stadium. Private money was donated to assist the city in funding all these efforts simultaneously.

But even these grand efforts were only the beginning of the renaissance movement in Columbus during the 1990s.

Total System Services Inc. (TSYS) new uptown campus continued more or less on schedule. The north extension of the Riverwalk, from 12th to 14th streets and part of the TSYS campus, was funded by a public/private partnership at a cost of $2-$3 million. Historic preservations amongst the new TSYS construction includes the Mott House, which will be used for client training and administrative uses, and a number of elements from other historic properties. The old Carnegie Library's entrance way and one of the big window framings will be incorporated into the Riverwalk as will several plaques and cornerstones off of the old mills. The foundation of Mill 4 has been saved and is being converted into a green space, also as part of the Riverwalk.

The TSYS campus anchors one end of the uptown area while the Civic Center and South Commons anchors the other and

revitalized uptown business and entertainment districts fill in the middle.

The TSYS campus and expanded workforce is the central focus of the day; the campus being a gigantic manifestation of the city's hopes and dreams. But, many a company either relocated or expanded in Columbus throughout the 1980s and 1990s. The last ten years alone—that being from 1988 to 1998—saw 122 companies expand or move to town for a cumulative total of $1,451,946,600 in capital investments and 14,680 new jobs. The list reads like a corporate America's who's who: AFLAC, Oneda, MUTEC, Bradley Center, Wal-Mart, Sam's, HomeQuarters, Johnston Industries, GNB Battery Corp., Callaway Chemical, Cott Beverages, Textron, Swift Spinning, Citizen's Mortgage, Swift Textiles, Kodak Polychrome Graphics, MBIA Lithium Plant, Pratt & Whitney, Healthtrust, Inc., Fieldcrest Cannon, Hollis Eye Institute, Charbroil, Inc., OptiRay, and many others. The Riverclub sprang into being on the north end of the downtown Riverwalk section and the Harmony Club changed ownership and became The Estates. The Greater Columbus Chamber of Commerce became the new name for the Columbus Chamber of Commerce and it continued to lead aggressive initiatives to sustain growth in the city.

Construction wise, the Muscogee County School District is one of the biggest deals of its time... at least in terms of costs. The six

(Top) The new Columbus Public Safety building. Photo by Jim Cawthorne.

(Above) Columbus Police Department Honor Guard in front of the memorial statue which pays tribute to the city's public safety defenders who gave their lives to protect others. This beautiful statue has been moved from in front of the Government Center into the second floor atrium of the new Public Safety Building pictured above. Photo by Jim Cawthorne.

year construction program is funded by state funds and local sales tax revenues for a total estimated cost of $156 million. The program includes 52 projects, 10 of which are new schools and the rest are renovations and modifications of existing schools.

Culture and the arts underwent several major renovation and construction projects in the 1990s, too. Talbotton Road was slated for widening but that meant the demise of the old Three Arts Theater... home of

the Columbus Symphony. The choices were to allow the symphony to die a quiet death as other cities had done, or to raise the funds to find a new home for the program and cover its operation costs. The consensus was to preserve the symphony. Location became a subject of intense debate as two camps developed; one wanted the symphony moved to the Columbus State University campus, the other wanted a downtown site. Eventually the downtown camp prevailed.

However, no existing downtown facility was suitable to house the symphony. A new one would have to be built. Fundraising was a problem as several arts organizations were launching capital campaigns at the same time. Columbus State University agreed to move its music department downtown and share a facility with the Columbus Symphony, which opened more funding routes and led to help from the Board of Regents. It also facilitated a pledge of support from Governor Zell Miller that resulted in $17 million in state funding for the new Performing Arts Center since named RiverCenter.

The Georgia legislature appropriated $2 million of the approved $17 million for the purposes of planning the particulars of the new center and the Georgia Department of Community Development kicked in another

Columbus' youth are healthy and energetic. Photo by Steven Duffey.

If patients could choose where to get sick, they would do well to choose Columbus. The Pediatric Center is one of the many medical facilities in Columbus. Photo by Jim Cawthorne.

$250,000. A project development team consisting of State Representative Calvin Symre as chairman, Dr. Frank Brown as secretary/treasurer, Rozier Dedwylder as project manager, and Mayor Bobby Peters and Rick McKnight as general members was formed by the Columbus legislative delegation to plan, oversee design, and implement the construction of the new facility.

Regular meetings were held to confer with the state team, which included the Office of Planning and Budget, Georgia State Financing and Investment Commission, Board of Regents, Department of Natural Resources, and the Attorney General's Office. The job could have been completed from there and Columbus would have been within its rights to call the whole affair a win. Instead, they were just warming up.

While all of the above was in the works, local foundations were flooded with requests from most of the arts and cultural organizations including the new Performing Arts Center. Rather than simply process the requests and divvy up the money as best as could be done, the trustees of the Bradley-Turner Foundation took a proactive approach and proposed a cooperative effort among the competing organizations and agencies to form a single fundraising effort. If such could be done, the Bradley-Turner Foundation promised a $20 million challenge to be matched dollar for dollar by the community. It came to be known as the Columbus Challenge.

Two thousand eighty-three ordinary citizens answered the challenge as did numerous foundations and businesses. Anonymous donations were frequent and large... $2 million came from a foundation outside of Columbus and four gifts of $500,000 were delivered with no name attached. The Columbus Consolidated Government donated the property where the RiverCenter is being built for an in-kind gift valued at $1 million. Mayor Peters' administration became the first to put funding for the arts in the city budget with an initial commitment of $35,000 that was subsequently raised to $50,000.

The $20 million challenge was met so enthusiastically by so many people that the Bradley-Turner Foundation raised the stakes to $25 million. The citizens of Columbus responded with $28.4 million, exceeding the latest challenge by $3.4 million. The total of all monies collected at last count, including state and city donations, funding from foundations and businesses, the matching funds from the Bradley-Turner Foundation, and public donations was over $86.4 million.

The Columbus Challenge is by most accounts the largest fundraising campaign of its kind in the South and among the largest nationally. Eight of the top cultural organizations operating in the city agreed to set aside individual concerns, competition for the entertainment dollar, and rivalry for donor attention in favor of an effort aimed at a common good for the entire city... not just for the arts. In return for their active support in spite of their initial fears, the Columbus Museum will receive $8 million, the Springer Opera House $6

(Above) The new $100 million Total System Services, Inc. TSYS is one of the largest credit card processors in the world. Photo by Jim Cawthorne.

(Right) Artistic rendering of the Port Columbus National Museum of Civil War Naval History being constructed at the south end of South Commons. Scheduled to open in late 2000, the museum—in addition to its comprehensive collection—will also feature the latest in interactive exhibits. Courtesy of Hecht, Burdeshaw, Johnson Kidd and Clark, Inc. Architects.

The new $67 million RiverCenter For The Performing Arts, a 245,000-square-foot facility, will feature the state's largest symphony hall with over 2,000 seats, a 450-seat recital hall with a $1 million handmade pipe organ, and a 150-seat "black-box" theater. It will also be home to Columbus State University's Schwob Department of Music. Photo by Jim Cawthorne.

(Above) The Columbus Civic Center—a world class facility. Photo by Jim Cawthorne.

(Right) The Cottonmouths, Columbus' very own hockey team. Photo by Jim Cawthorne.

million, the yet to be built Port Columbus National Museum of Civil War Naval History (formerly the Woodruff Museum of Civil War Naval History) gets $5 million, the Columbus Symphony netted $2.5 million plus a new home, the Coca-Cola Space Science Center was awarded $1 million, the Liberty Theater $1 million, the Historic Columbus Foundation got $1 million, and the RiverCenter for the Performing Arts

gained $27 million.

Campaign costs to the community was only .07 percent, including consultant fees and postage costs, according to Tom Black, Organizations Chairman for Community Projects Foundation, the organization that coordinated response to the Columbus Challenge.

The Columbus Museum is planning to use its endowment to strengthen educational programs, reach underserved audiences, and improve its exhibitions. The Springer Opera House, on the other hand, is undergoing a much needed face-lift including the restoration of original artwork. Restoration efforts on the official state theater (and one of only a handful of theaters designated as national historic landmarks) began in 1964 and have floundered for 35 years for lack of funding. With funding finally available, the restoration will be complete in every detail, even the wallpaper and decor will be based on authentic period design from the turn of the century.

The Springer is also adding a multi-purpose hall that can be used for dinner theater, meetings, receptions, and events for children. The third floor of the theater is being revamped into lodging for faculty and performing artists. In the past, the Springer has been renting apartments and lodging interns, faculty, and teachers in private homes. Beyond the savings in rental costs, the Springer gained a new advantage... top performing artists tend to favor theaters with private quarters for security and privacy reasons.

The Columbus Symphony's endowment is ear-marked for operating costs and to increase its music and educational programming. The Liberty Theater will use its funds to complete renovations and establish an operating endowment. The Coca-Cola Space Science Center is protected by an endowment for future operating costs and now has sufficient monies to add to its community education efforts. In 1998, students watched the eclipse from the Coca-Cola Space Science Center in real-time from Aruba.

The Port Columbus National Museum of Civil War Naval History is building a new 38,000 square foot facility on the Riverwalk that features two recreated confederate ships and a living museum with a covered bridge, two batteries on the banks of the river, barracks built to show how sailors lived back then, and a sawmill to show how they built the boats during the war. Meanwhile fellow preservationist, the Historic Columbus Foundation is planning on using its money to continue restoration of the 7th Street Historic District, increase facade loans, and construct Heritage Park that will connect the Historic District to the Coca-Cola Space Science Center.

The centerpiece of the new park will be

a water course replicating the Chattahoochee River complete with a miniature waterfall. The falling water turns a turbine, and below the falls floats a mini-replica of the W.C. Bradley steamboat. A time-line will mark the water's borders and chronicle the history of the river from 1850 until 1900, the city's industrial period. Along the banks of the water stands a series of statues, replicas, and plaques to tell the story of the city's economic heritage. A small brick kiln demonstrates how clay deposited by the river was transformed into bricks. Statues representing workers from the time period will be posed and dressed according

Tomoko Okuzawa cools a watermelon in her native Kiryu, Japan, Columbus' sister city. Photo by Jim Cawthorne.

The Pemberton House, a tribute to Columbus' most famous pharmacist, John Pemberton, the creator of the Coca-Cola beverage. Photo by Jim Cawthorne.

(Above) The Columbus Museum has a strong and far-reaching presence in Columbus. Photo by Jim Cawthorne.

(Right) Not all learning takes place in the classroom as shown by this youngster who is experiencing the wonder and color of Transformations, a discovery area for children at The Columbus Museum. Photo by Steven Duffey.

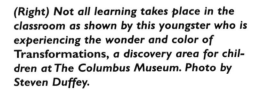

The Springer Opera House, a national historic landmark and the state's official theater, was renovated in 1999 at a cost of $11.3 million. Photo by Jim Cawthorne.

Columbus on the threshold of a new millennium. Photo by Jim Cawthorne.

Grill, as in the country western artists of the decade in the '80s, Spaghetti Warehouse, Owen-Brennan out of New Orleans, and Chesterfield's out of Mississippi and others are scoping out the uptown Columbus for prime locations now. Retailers, hotels, and housing developers are converging on the area to support the massive influx of workers by day, and of players and patrons by night.

Construction workers are literally everywhere and the market for skilled laborers has never been better, especially as there appears to be no end of building and renovating in sight. As said earlier, it all began innocently enough but it just keeps on going.

In short, the evidence seems to indicate that the millennium is seen by Columbus as a future of hope and blinding promise. The church bells ring every Sunday in uptown Columbus and throughout the suburbs. The Christians, Jews, Muslims, Hindus, and other faiths meet regularly in Columbus and peacefully coexist. Though these faiths may not use the same calendars, they do look forward with the same enthusiasm.

From crystal balls to hallowed halls, there isn't so much as a tremor of "les terreurs de l'an mil" in sight. ❧

to their labors. The city's most famous pharmacist, John Pemberton, the creator of the Coca-Cola beverage, will be embodied in stone and permanently seated on a bench in the park's Pemberton Plaza. Other Columbusites associated with Coke will also be represented, including Columbus-born Robert Winship Woodruff who made the drink available around the globe.

Combined, all of these developments provide a fertile field for other players. The first of the interested restaurants should be in place early in 1999. Alabama Bar &

(Right) The past, present and future in Columbus are virtually seamless. Surrounded by the lessons of long ago held in the here and now by a strong historic district, brick streets, educational parks, and works of artistic masters... and surrounded by the promise of yet-to-be tied to the land of now through the wonderment of technology. Photo by Steven Duffey.

Since it was established in 1991, Diaz-Verson Capital Investments has managed investments for large public and private pensions funds and high net-worth individuals. Its clients include the State of Georgia Employees Retirement System, the State of

Diaz-Verson Capital Investments L.L.C.

Georgia Teachers Retirement System, the Fulton-Dekalb Hospital Authority Foundation, and the Ohio Bureau of Workers' Compensation.

The firm, registered with the Securities and Exchange Commission and the State of Georgia as an investment advisor, invests for clients whose portfolios average $250,000 or more. Its average client invests $5.5 million.

The firm focuses on value equities, meaning that it invests in undervalued stocks with potential. For its clients, it

wants high return investments with low risk.

Diaz-Verson Capital Investments was founded by Salvador Diaz-Verson Jr., the Cuban-born son of a journalist. It is the only Hispanic-owned firm of its kind in Georgia. Prior to registering as an independent financial advisor, Diaz-Verson served for 8 years as president of AFLAC Inc. and for 14 years as chief investment officer responsible for managing the supplemental insurance company's global fixed income and equity portfolio. Under his supervision, AFLAC's portfolio grew from $45 million to $8 billion.

Diaz-Verson set out on his own in 1991 after the death of his brother-in-law, John B. Amos, founder of AFLAC. Like most new businesses, the first years were the hardest as he struggled to get his foot on the playing field. Once out there, the firm's lineup of managed funds started growing. Opportunities were so abundant, the firm opened offices in Atlanta and Miami to complement its office in Columbus. "We proved we could get the same returns and outperform the market, not every year, but over a five- to six-year period. We have been able to do that, and it has brought us credibility. I think that's what's driving us now," Diaz-Verson said.

Since it was established in 1991, Diaz-Verson Capital Investments has managed investments for large public and private pensions funds and high net-worth individuals.

At Diaz-Verson Capital Investments, the investment strategy always begins with the client. Investment managers help clients identify their financial goals and objectives and the levels of risk at which they are comfortable. Then, Diaz-Verson Capital Investments, using the latest in computer technology, finds investment opportunities that meet those goals and comfort levels. Applying a value-oriented approach to investing, the firm uses a proven investment discipline and process. Instead of reacting to Wall Street's trends and stampedes, Diaz-Verson responds to market changes based on action. "Our skills are in identifying the substance beneath market appearance, assessing movement, and anticipating change," Diaz-Verson said. After investing, managers keep clients informed of changing market conditions and other investment opportunities.

Increased communication through the Internet, more privatization of investments, and a lack of confidence in Social Security will bring more investors into the market looking for investment advisors as the millennium changes, Diaz-Verson said. ❧

Diaz-Verson Capital Investments was founded by Salvador Diaz-Verson Jr., the Cuban-born son of a journalist. It is the only Hispanic-owned firm of its kind in Georgia.

In 1993, Miramar Securities opened in Columbus as a sister company to Diaz-Verson Capital Investments. A full-service broker dealer, Miramar deals in stocks, corporate bonds, mutual funds, annuities, unit investment trusts, tax-free municipal bonds, U.S. treasuries, U.S. government and federal obligations, and mortgage-backed securities.

Miramar differs from Diaz-Verson Capital Investments in that it works with clients of all economic backgrounds, including those who have minimal funds for investing and the first-time investor. Its clients range from the person who walks in with $250 to invest to the $50-a-month investor to the $2.5-million investor.

Miramar Securities has $50 million under management, serves more than 250 accounts from its Columbus office, and has a branch office in Miami. It employs a diverse workforce of 15. Both offices have their own unique characteristics.

Recognizing that each person's financial situation and investment goals are different, Miramar personalizes each client's investment portfolio. "Our investment strategy is to take the individual person, whoever he or she is economically, and try to maximize where they need to be when they retire," said Lois N. Cohen, who has served as president of Miramar since 1994. "The average person who comes to us is somebody we work with in every aspect of his or her financial planning. We do the portfolio based on what the client wants."

Miramar brokers are licensed and registered members of the National Association of Securities Dealers, the Municipal Securities Rulemaking Board, and the firm is insured with the Securities Investor Protection Corporation.

Using little paid advertising, the firm takes advantage of educational opportunities, investment clubs, and seminars to promote itself. Much of its business is acquired through referrals, a feat not difficult because of its backing from Diaz-Verson, Cohen said.

For many years, Salvador Diaz-Verson has been a civic leader in Columbus, serving on such boards as United Way, St. Francis Hospital, the Metro Columbus Urban League, Uptown Columbus Inc., the Columbus Steeplechase, and the Greater Columbus Chamber of Commerce. But his reach extends far beyond the confines of home. He is also involved with the Latin American Association of Atlanta, the Fund for American Studies, the National Board of the Boys and Girls Clubs of America, the National Black College Hall of Fame, the Atlanta Hispanic Chamber of Commerce, State Industry Trade and Tourism Board, the International Board of the U.S.-Philippine Foundation, and a president's appointment to the Christopher Columbus Foundation Board. ❧

Miramar Securities, Inc.

Counter clockwise: Top right; Mike Majure, Vice President Diaz-Verson Capital Investments, L.L.C.; Scott Koser, Portfolio Manager, Diaz-Verson Capital Investments, L.L.C.; Lois Cohen, President, Miramar Securities, Inc.; Lourdes Diaz-Jones, Vice President, Miramar Securities, Inc.

Throughout its history, Columbus has had international connections. Even before its settlement, travelers roamed its soil, searching for items of value for rulers in faraway lands. From its official founding in 1828 by the descendants of immigrants to

Commission on International Relations and Cultural Liaison Encounters (CIRCLE)

its increasing global interactions today, the city has continued to touch, and be touched, by people and cultures from around the world.

Commerce has long paved the road between Columbus and other nations. In the 1800s, snow-white cotton from Southern fields and other consumable goods left the city's port on the

Chattahoochee River bound for foreign markets. In the early 1900s, Lummus Industries marketed and sold cotton gins in Russia and other countries. Expansion of twentieth-century technology, changes in trade laws, and ease of international travel made the world smaller in many ways and opened even greater opportunities for worldwide trade. As a result, products and services from Columbus are available globally. For example, denim made by Swift Denim is sewn into wearing apparel for people around the globe; credit cards are swiped through machines all over the world and the transactions routed to Total System Services; and insurance sold by AFLAC Inc. covers millions of people in Japan.

Likewise, foreign companies—among them Oneda, Matsushita Battery Industrial Corporation of America, and Marubeni Denim—have located plants in Columbus and have found it a great place to do business.

Fort Benning, too, has played a part in building bridges between nations. From its founding in 1920, Benning has sent soldiers to fight on foreign soils, exposing them to cultures unlike their own. Some

brought home spouses from across the ocean.

Against this historical background, new relationships were created when Columbus hosted the 1995 Super Ball Classic and the Women's Fast Pitch Softball competition in the 1996 Olympics. It became increasingly clear as athletes and fans from around the world converged on the city that Columbus's importance on the international scene was growing. The Commission on International Relations and Cultural Liaison Encounters, or CIRCLE as it's more commonly known, was created by city ordinance in 1996 to guide and nurture Columbus's international relations. CIRCLE, with its own bylaws, is a 12-member advisory board that reports to the Columbus Consolidated Government. Its mission is to promote and coordinate communication, contacts, and encounters

CIRCLE was created by city ordinance to guide and nurture Columbus's international relations. Its mission is to promote and coordinate communication, contacts, and encounters between Columbus and the people of other nations, and to facilitate cross-cultural communication and association among the various national groups in Columbus.

between Columbus and the people of other nations, and to facilitate cross-cultural communication and association among the various national groups in Columbus.

So CIRCLE, a self-sufficient entity appointed by the mayor and city council, advises the Columbus Consolidated Government on international concerns and interests; promotes international goodwill and understanding through programs and activities affecting social, cultural, educational, artistic, business and governmental contacts, and exchanges; serves as a link connecting the various groups in Columbus which represent other cultures; and arranges accommodations for official visitors from other countries to Columbus and for visits by Columbus citizens who act as emissaries to other countries.

Among CIRCLE's goals is that of nurturing the relationships with Columbus's sister cities, Kiryu, Japan, and Zugdidi, Georgia, (formerly the Republic of Georgia in the Soviet Union). The relationship with Zugdidi is relatively new, but that with Kiryu is long-standing. For more than 20 years, Columbus and Kiryu have been sister cities. Two large display cabinets on the Plaza level of the Government Center contain permanent displays of Japanese garments from Kiryu, a center of silk production.

The relationship is growing as visits between citizens of the two cities have multiplied and acquaintances have matured into friendships. There was, however, a need for an organization to work for its continued health and nurture. To answer that need, CIRCLE formed the Columbus Kiryu Club, an organization of local citizens who meet periodically to discuss various aspects of Japanese culture, such as politics, food, art, education, and the economy. Membership is open to anyone interested. In response, Kiryu in 1998 created a Kiryu Columbus Club.

At the urging of CIRCLE, the Kiryu Pavilion in the South Commons Softball Complex was named in celebration of the relationship. Earlier, a drinking fountain— the Kiryu Fountain—was built by Kiryu on the Chattahoochee Riverwalk in Columbus. CIRCLE was also responsible for a kiosk at the Columbus Metropolitan Airport that welcomes people to Columbus in six different languages.

On the Columbus State University campus, the Kiryu Garden is a beautiful reminder of the Kiryu-Columbus sisterhood. The garden also reflects CSU's active involvement in the relationship through the English Language Institute, which provides classes for exchange students from Kiryu.

Kiryu honored the relationship as well by naming one if its important downtown streets Columbus Street, and by creating on that street the Columbus Fountain, which replicates the Kiryu Fountain in Columbus. Representatives from CIRCLE were members of the Columbus delegation that attended the ceremony in Kiryu.

While working for world peace is a lofty ideal and seemingly out of reach, that is indeed what CIRCLE is doing. In the words of one CIRCLE member: "CIRCLE is, in essence and in its own small way, working for world peace, one friendship at a time." ➔

For more than 20 years, Columbus and Kiryu, Japan, have been sister cities. Visits between citizens of the two cities have multiplied and acquaintances have matured into friendships. Those present at the celebration marking the relationship's anniversary include Shirley Jaeger, Kiryu Mayor Hino, Columbus Mayor Peters, and Sal Diaz-Verson.

Founded in 1992, Beacon College is a not-for-profit, undergraduate interdenominational Christian liberal arts college offering associate of arts and bachelor of arts degrees. Founder and Chancellor Dr. Ronald E. Cottle sees Beacon College as the

Beacon College

fourth leg of the postsecondary educational table in the Columbus area, joining the region's university, its community college, and its technical/vocational school. Beacon is the only authorized Christian College that uniquely serves the greater Columbus area.

Beacon College achieved a major milestone by gaining its candidate status accreditation from the Transnational Association of Christian Colleges and Schools (TRACS) in less than five years. Through the TRACS recognition, Beacon participates in the Federal Student Financial Aid Program, which allows qualified students to be eligible for Pell Grants and other forms of student financial aid. It is also an approved provider of Veterans Administration benefits and is approved for international students by the Department of Immigration. The college is also authorized by the Georgia Nonpublic Postsecondary Education Commission (NPEC) and is a member of the Association of Christian Schools International (ACSI), which allows Beacon to grant Continuing Education Units (CEU) for teachers.

The purpose of Beacon College is to provide higher education within the context of

Founded in 1992, Beacon College is a not-for-profit, undergraduate interdenominational Christian liberal arts college offering associate of arts and bachelor of arts degrees.

Christian values with emphasis on high academic standards, practical application, and spiritual development, enabling individuals to lead a life of personal fulfillment and Christian citizenship and service. In addition to its associate of arts and bachelor of arts degrees, courses for personal or professional enrichment are also available. Beacon College offers day and evening classes in Biblical studies, general education, and professional studies.

Located in the Five Points neighborhood on Thirteenth Avenue in Columbus, the college is conveniently situated in the heart of the valley. The campus is currently comprised of five one-story buildings, the largest of which houses the administrative offices, classrooms, student lounge, and college library. Students have access to a well-stocked, quality library equipped on-line with GALILEO (Georgia Library Lending Online), an electronic system through which schools and colleges in the University System of Georgia share information. The service provides students access to hundreds of academic books and journals in addition to those physically located in the library. Beacon also has a television studio available for videotaping student presentations and Columbus Christian Bookstore, a full-service campus bookstore, from which students can purchase textbooks and supplies. A 200-seat chapel is also on campus and is used regularly for worship.

"Beacon is now poised for significant growth," Cottle said. He anticipates a tremendous increase in the student population, with 25 percent being international students. This expected growth will result in an expansion of facilities, faculty, and the number and scope of Beacon's degree programs. Development plans are

Beacon College provides higher education within the context of Christian values with emphasis on high academic standards, practical application, and spiritual development, enabling individuals to lead a life of personal fulfillment and Christian citizenship and service.

underway to build a 200-apartment student housing complex adjacent to the college, with a projected completion date in 1999. Robert George became the president in 1998 to spearhead the college's growth and development plans and to meet the challenge of bringing Beacon into the twenty-first century. ➔

The welcome mat is out at the Holiday Inn Center City. And the tourists are beating a path to the door. Already events at the new softball complex and soccer fields have come close to filling the 156 rooms at the Veterans Parkway hotel with parents, friends, and supporters of the teams.

And Jim Davis, owner of the hotel, expects occupancy to only get better as the revitalization of downtown Columbus continues with the completion of the Total System Services complex, the RiverCenter for the Performing Arts, and the Riverwalk. Located in the heart of the inner city, the hotel is where the action is.

"When we were looking for a location, it was clear that everybody was focused on the development of downtown Columbus—and there was no doubt that downtown Columbus needed quality hotel rooms."

He and his partners bought the hotel, which was previously a Ramada Inn, and began negotiations with Holiday Inn to become franchisees. The Holiday Inn hotel chain provides exceptional support to its member hotels through training, an exceptional reservation system, and high standards for maintenance and service. Currently, the Center City hotel receives 25 percent of its reservations through the corporate reservation system, a percentage that will increase as the hotel becomes more firmly established. "Holiday Inn is the number one hotel chain as far as recognition of the customer anywhere. Everybody knows what Holiday Inn is," Davis said.

After the agreement was completed, the hotel underwent a $1-million renovation, including completely redecorated guest rooms, lobby, and dining room. Of the 156 mid-priced rooms at the hotel, two are two-room suites.

Amenities include The Cotton Exchange Restaurant and Lounge, room service, an outdoor pool, exercise rooms, a barber/styling shop, and van service. The hotel also has a grab-and-go breakfast bar for the traveler who's in a hurry.

The hotel's conference and catering facilities can host meetings, conferences, reunions, and wedding receptions for groups as intimate as 10 persons or as large as 275 for a seated dinner or 350 with theater-style seating. Menu items can be as simple as a chef's salad or as elegant as Chicken Cordon Bleu and may be seated or buffet.

"This is a nice Holiday Inn with its own character, its own feel," Davis said. "Our exterior corridors turn into porches and our guests love them. You have the feeling of security because of the stuccoed walls. It's got a clean, Southern look. It doesn't fit the profile of a roadside inn. We aren't a cookie cutter property."

Holiday Inn is a family of hotels located in countries around the world. Its chain includes the no-frills Holiday Inn Express; Holiday Inn Select for the business tra-

Holiday Inn Center City

veler; the Holiday Inn hotel for business and leisure travelers; Holiday Inn SunSpree Resort in leisure destinations; and the Holiday Inn Garden Court in Europe and South Africa. ❧

The welcome mat is out at the Holiday Inn Center City. And the tourists are beating a path to the door.

Dougherty McKinnon & Luby is moving forward with Columbus into the next millennium. Constant change seems to be the order of the day, but the one thing that has not changed is the focus on results. Dougherty McKinnon & Luby combines

Dougherty McKinnon & Luby

the latest technology with the traditional value of personalized service to help clients achieve results. Even though the firm is located in Columbus, its proactive approach to helping clients achieve their goals has resulted in a client base that extends across the nation.

Under the guidance and leadership of (left to right) Dennis Luby and Len McKinnon, Dougherty McKinnon & Luby combines the latest technology with the traditional value of personalized service to help clients achieve results.

Dougherty McKinnon & Luby, LLC, Certified Public Accountants

The firm's clients include businesses of various sizes in a wide range of industries, including retail sales, wholesale distribution, construction, real estate development, hospitality, manufacturing, and the service industry. Individuals, nonprofit organizations, trusts, estates, investment partnerships, and other entities also avail themselves of the firm's services. Regardless of the type or size of the client, the services provided always revolve around helping clients achieve the results necessary to accomplish their goals.

Businesses look to the firm for traditional services such as bookkeeping, tax return preparation, and audits. They also rely on the firm's expertise in obtaining financing, acquiring other businesses, analyzing profitability, tax planning, compensation planning, succession planning, and other areas critical to achieving the goals of the business. Each business has unique needs, and Dougherty McKinnon & Luby provides the specific services required to meet those needs. Whether it is a trip to New York to arrange financing for a large business, or implementing a computerized accounting system for a small business, the firm is always ready to provide solutions to the business world.

Individual clients have very different goals, depending upon factors such as age, health, family requirements, and financial position. The firm assists clients in developing and implementing strategies to accomplish their goals, such as buying a home, financing college educations, diversifying investment portfolios, tax planning, retirement planning, estate planning, and transferring wealth to future generations. The firm's practice of coordinating closely with other professional advisors assures the client of obtaining the best advice with respect to each goal.

Dougherty McKinnon & Luby Benefit Services, LLC

Dougherty McKinnon & Luby Benefit Services was formed at the request of clients seeking responsive and accurate retirement plan administration services with flexibility in investments and plan options. The firm offers IRS-approved prototype retirement plan documents which allow the plan assets to be invested through insurance companies, brokerage firms, and

Dougherty McKinnon & Luby has built lasting relationships for four decades, providing customized services to businesses and individuals.

fee-based financial planners and advisors. The firm provides retirement plan design and consulting services, administration services, and government compliance services. Trained accounting and pension professionals work with employers to establish efficient procedures that coordinate the retirement plan administration process with the employer's payroll, human resources, and financial reporting departments. Services are customized for each client to assist them in attaining their objectives. The firm's rapid growth is directly attributable to its ability to work closely with various investment custodians and employers, ensuring efficient and effective results for all parties. State-of-the-art technology provides access to employer and investment information, resulting in timely allocation of income and contributions to participants' retirement accounts. The firm has the ability to work with daily, weekly, or monthly valuations which provide employers the flexibility to select a plan tailored to their specific needs.

As the world moves into the next millennium, business will continue to be based on relationships that are built on trust. Dougherty McKinnon & Luby has built these relationships for four decades and will continue to help clients achieve their goals. ❧

Patients always come first at River City Orthopaedics and Spine Center. From the time they call to make an appointment to the time they are dismissed from treatment, they can expect to be treated with respect and courtesy and to receive high quality treatment for their orthopaedic problems.

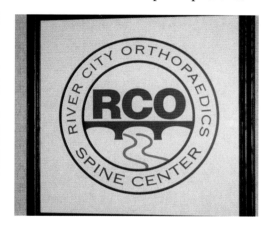

River City Orthopaedics and Spine Center keeps the "moral mission" of healing at the forefront of patient care by not only providing treatment for the affliction, but also by involving the patient in the healing process.

The center, located in the 1900 building at the Tenth Avenue Medical Plaza, was founded in January 1998 by a physician, Dr. Emory J. Alexander. An orthopaedic surgeon, Dr. Alexander treats a comprehensive range of spinal and muscular/skeletal disorders, including back strain, herniated disks, and spinal injuries. His primary specialty is in disorders of the spine and in spinal surgery. Dr. Alexander is also a fellowship trained hand and sports medicine specialist, in addition to his spine surgery expertise.

A former nurse and nurse anesthetist, Dr. Alexander received an M.D. degree from the University of Iowa in 1985. He completed an orthopaedic internship and residency program at Louisiana State University Medical Center in 1993, and served as chief resident of orthopaedic surgery at the university in 1992-93. In 1994, he completed a sports medicine fellowship at the Alabama Sports Medicine Institute and a hand fellowship at the University of Virginia. He completed a spine fellowship at the Baylor University College of Medicine in 1995.

In addition to residency and fellowship experience, Dr. Alexander served as an orthopaedic surgeon at the Hughston Orthopaedic Clinic in Columbus from 1995

to 1998. He has a number of research experiences and publications to his credit, as well as affiliations with such professional groups as the American Medical Association, the American Association of Orthopaedic Surgeons, the Southern Medical Association, the American Academy of Orthopaedic Surgeons, and The Hughston Society.

He has served as team physician for Grambling State University in Grambling, Louisiana; Booker T. Washington High School in Shreveport, Louisiana; Huffman High School in Birmingham, Alabama; and the University of Virginia in Charlottesville, Virginia. He is currently team physician for Tuskegee University in Tuskegee, Alabama, and the Columbus Lady Blazers basketball team.

When Dr. Alexander opened his own practice for the diagnosis and treatment of orthopaedic problems in 1998, he had definite ideas about how patients would be treated. "When people come to my office, one of the things that is important to them is that they find this office as much of a refuge from pain as possible," Dr. Alexander said. "I want them to feel good about being here, about the experience, about being taken care of by their physician. My office reflects my appreciation of my patients. I feel strongly about how fortunate I am when patients come to my office. It shows that they have confidence in me. It's an honor for me to take care of them."

River City Orthopaedics and Spine Center keeps the "moral mission" of healing at the forefront of patient care by not only providing treatment for the affliction, but also by involving the patient in the healing process. "When patients come to

River City Orthopaedics

see me, those patients deserve as much time as it takes to educate them as well as try to determine what their problems are," he said. Even in the design and furnishings of his office, Dr. Alexander has the patients' physical and psychological needs in mind, with minimal effort examination beds, artwork that combines the artistic expression of anatomy of the musculoskeletal system with the aesthetics of human performance, as well as an uplifting and positive environment for healing. ➔

River City Orthopaedics and Spine Center was founded in January 1998 by Dr. Emory J. Alexander.

When the RiverCenter for the Performing Arts opens in the year 2001, its first production might suitably be a full orchestra rendition of the "Hallelujah Chorus." Indeed, this new diamond in a crown of downtown jewels has given Columbus

RiverCenter for the Performing Arts

several reasons to rejoice. It's classy. It's downtown. And it's the centerpiece of an unprecedented community-wide effort that raised $86 million to support arts and culture in the city.

The RiverCenter will be a class act, comparable to the best performing arts facilities in the country. People will be amazed at the high caliber of the facility. It's going to outshine most others around the country. It will be a first-class performing arts center that will be wonderful for Columbus's image.

Designed to blend in and complement other historic downtown structures, the 245,000-square-foot, $67-million performing arts center will include:
• The Bill Heard Theatre, named for Mr. and Mrs. Bill Heard Jr. This 2,000-seat performance hall will be the home of the Columbus Symphony Orchestra and will host performances of touring concert and

The RiverCenter, designed to blend in and complement other historic downtown structures, will be a class act, comparable to the best performing arts facilities in the country.

theatrical attractions that appeal to all kinds of audiences—everything from classics to country, ballet to Broadway, and opera to gospel.
• A 450-seat recital hall, featuring a $1-million organ donated by the Gunby Jordan family. This will be the performance home of the Schwob Department of Music of Columbus State University and community concert groups as well.
• A 165-seat Studio Theatre for Columbus State student ensembles and theatrical presentations. The theatre will also be available as a lecture hall and performance space for community organizations such as churches, civic clubs, and youth groups.
• A park for outdoor performances.
• An administration wing that will become home to six local arts groups, including the Columbus Symphony.

The performing arts center will also house Columbus State University's Schwob Department of Music in a 60,000-square-foot suite that includes classrooms, rehearsal rooms, an instrument shop, and faculty offices.

Located on a block historically known as Enterprise Square, RiverCenter is part of an exciting downtown area revitalization project that includes the Coca-Cola Space Science Center, the renovated Springer Opera House, the Riverwalk, the South Commons Sports Complex, the Columbus Civic Center, and a 46-acre Total System Services campus.

The *piéce de résistance,* however, is the public/private partnership that made it

The Bill Heard Theatre, named for Mr. and Mrs. Bill Heard Jr., will be the home of the Columbus Symphony Orchestra and will host performances of touring concert and theatrical attractions that appeal to all kinds of audiences.

happen. Once the idea took root in 1994, support for a performing arts center flourished. The state kicked in $17 million, the city of Columbus donated land valued at $1 million, and the citizens of Columbus generously responded to the Columbus Challenge, a fund-raising campaign for the arts that started with a $25-million dollar-for-dollar challenge grant from the Bradley-Turner Foundation. The $86 million raised by the Columbus Challenge, one of the largest fund-raising campaigns in the South and among the largest in the nation, will be used to help build the RiverCenter and to fund seven of the city's most important cultural organizations.

The RiverCenter, owned by the Georgia Department of Natural Resources, is expected to promote growth of restaurants and other entertainment businesses in the downtown area as well as serve as a recruiting tool for local companies. ❧

Photo by Jim Cawthorne.

Bibliography

AP National Telephone Poll, *Faith In The Second Coming Poll*, July 11-15, ICR of Media, Pa., Downloaded May 25, 1998.

Amalvi, Christian, *L'historographie francaise face · l'avÈnement d'Hugues Capet et aux terreurs de l'an Mil: 1800-1914*, Paris: Albin Michel, 1988, pp. 116-45.

Burr, George Lincoln, *"The Year 1000 and the Antecedents of the Crusades"*, American Historical Review, 6(1901), pp. 429-39.

Butler, Jonathan B. and Numbers, Ronald L. eds., *The Disappointed: Millerism and Millenarianism in the Nineteenth Century*, Indianapolis, Indiana, Indiana University Press 1987.

Callahan, Daniel, *"The Peace of God and the Cult of the Saints in Aquitaine in the Tenth and Eleventh Centuries"*, Historical Reflections/RÈflexions historiques, 14:3, pp. 445-66; *"The Peace of God, Apocalypticism, and the Council of Limoges of 1031"*, Revue bÈnÈdictine, 101 (1991), pp. 32-49.

Catholic Resource Network, The, Trinity Communications, *As the Third Millennium Draws near "Tertio Mellennio Adveniente"*, Apostolic Letter of Pope John Paul II, November 14, 1994.

Chase, David W., *The Averett Culture*, Coweta Memorial Association, Papers I, Columbus, Georgia, 1959.

Coca-Cola Space Science Center, Columbus, Georgia, 1998.

Columbus Ledger-Enquirer, *The Peace Society*, April 19, 1987; *Columbus' Last Battle*, Billy Winn, April 19, 1987; *Little Known Facts about City*, Billy Winn, November 30, 1993; *Civil War Wound Down In Battle for Columbus*, Sandra Backmon.

Columbus State University, *Focus on Columbus St. Univ.*, Vol. 3 No. 3, Summer 1997; *Focus on Columbus St. Univ.*, Vol. 4 No. 1, Fall 1997; The Archives, Simon Schwob Memorial Library, The Office of the Registrar, 1998.

Compton Encyclopedias.

Cotterill, Robert Spencer, *The Southern Indians: The Story of the Civilized Tribes Before Removal*, Norman: University of Oklahoma Press, 1954.

DePratter, Chester B., *The Archaic in Georgia*, Early Georgia 3: 1-16, 1976.

DeVorkin, David H., *"The A.D. 1006 Puzzle"*, The Astronomy Quarterly 5, 1985, pp. 71-86.

Duval, Frèdèric, *Les terreurs de l'An Mille*, Paris, 1908.

Fairbanks, Charles H., *Archaeology of the Eastern United States: Creek and Pre-Creek, pp. 285-300*, Chicago, IL., University of Chicago Press, 1952, Garrow, Patrick H.

Fields, Karen E., *Revival and Rebellion in Colonial Central Africa*, Princeton, N. J., Princeton University Press, 1985.

Gatch, Milton McC, *Preaching and Theology in Anloo-Saxon England: Aelfric and Wulfstan*, Toronto, U Press, 1977.

Georgia Trend, *Area Focus*, Ed Lightsey, June 1997.

Goldstein, Bernard, *"Evidence for a Supernova of A.D. 1006"*, The Astronomical Journal, 70:1, 1965, pp. 105-11.

Greater Columbus Chamber of Commerce, 1960-1998.

Gross, Terry, Host, Landes, Richard, Guest, *Fresh Air Radio Show, "Millennial Studies: Lunatics Waiting for the End. Again"*, December 16, 1997

Grosso, Michael, *Millennium Myth: Love and Death at the End of Time*, Wheaton, Idaho, The Theosophical Publishing House, 1995.

Handy, Bruce, *Turn-Off of the Century*, Time Magazine, Time Magazine On-line, May 5, 1997 Vol. 149 No. 18.

Hawkings, Benjamin, *A Historical Letter Written by Georgia Indian Agent...*, Atlanta, Georgia Department of Archives, 1813; http://members.surf-south.com/ ~ nifa/benhawk.html, *Lower Creek Towns of the Creek Confederacy, c. 1799*, World Wide Web http://members.surfsouth.com/ ~ nifa/creekhis.html.

Jennings, Jesse D., *Prehistory of North America*, New York, NY, McGraw-Hill, 1968.

Kane, Sharyn & Keeton, Richard, *Beneath These Waters*, Second Edition 1994, Library of Congress Number 94-142-455.

Kawada, Louise M. ed., *The Apocalypse Anthology*, Boston, Massachusetts, Rowan Tree Press, 1985.

Lopez, Robert Sabatino, *The tenth century; how dark the Dark Ages?*, New York, 1959.

Lupold, John S., *Chattahoochee Valley Sources & Resources: An Annotated Bibliography*, Thomson-Shore, Inc., 1988.

Mahan, Joseph B., *Columbus: Georgia's Fall Line "Trading Town"*, Windsor Publications, Inc., 1986.

Majtabai, A. G., *Blessed Assurance: At Home with the Bomb in Amarillo, Texas*, Boston, Massachusetts, Hughton Mifflin Co., 1986.

Mostert, Marco, *The Political Theology of Abbo of Fleury: A Study of the Ideas About Society and Law of the Tenth-century Monastic Reform Movement*, Middeleeuwse Studies en Bronnen, 2, Hiversum, Verloren Publishers, 1987.

Muscogee County School District, Columbus, Ga.

New South Associates, *Prehistory of the Middle Chattahoochee River Valley, Vol. 1&2*, Stone Mountain, Ga., New South Associates, 1989-90.

Rice, Edward, *John Frum He Come*, Garden City, N. Y., Doubleday & Co., Inc., 1974

Stevens, William Bacon, *A History of Georgia, Vol. II*, Savannah, Ga., The Beehive Press, 1972.

Stein, R. Conrad, *The Trail of Tears*, Chicago, IL., Children's Press,

Total System Services, Inc., *1997 Annual Report*, 1997.

University of Washington Office of News and Information, *Humans Have Feared Comets, Other Celestial Phenomena Through The Ages*, Downloaded May 25, 1998, http://www.jpl.nasa.gov/com-et/news59.html.

Van Biema, David, *Deciphering God's Plan*, Time Magazine, Time Magazine On-line, June 9, 1997 Vol. 149 No. 23.

W. C. Bradley Company, *The W. C. Bradley Co. Spectrum*, W. C. Bradley Company, Fourth Quarter 1997.

Winn, William W., *The Old Beloved Path: Daily Life Among the Indians of the Chattahoochee River Valley*, 1992.

Photos by Jim Cawthorne.

Enterprises Index

AFLAC Incorporated
1932 Wynnton Road
Columbus, GA 31999
Phone: 706-596-3493
Fax: 706-320-2288
E-Mail: mclayton@aflac.com
    kdyke@aflac.com
www.aflac.com

Beacon College
1622 13th Avenue
Columbus, GA 31901
Phone: 706-323-5364
Fax: 706-323-3236
E-Mail: beaconcollege2@mindspring.com
www.beacon.edu

Blue Cross and Blue Shield of Georgia
2357 Warm Springs Road
Columbus, GA 31904
901 Front Avenue, Suite 100
Columbus, GA 31901
Phone: 706-571-5371
Fax: 706-571-5487
www.bcbsga.com

Cessna Columbus
4800 Cargo Drive
Columbus, GA 31907
Phone: 706-569-2100
Fax: 706-569-2105
E-Mail: tlclark2@cessna.textron.com

Columbus Convention and Visitors Bureau
Post Office Box 2768
Columbus, GA 31902
Phone: 706-322-1613
Fax: 706-322-0701
E-Mail: ccvb@msn.com
www.columbusga.com/ccvb

Columbus Foundry
1600 Northside Ind.
Columbus, GA 31904-0201
Phone: 706-596-2222

Columbus Paper Company
807 Joy Street
Columbus, GA 31906
Phone: 706-389-1361
Fax: 706-689-1452

Columbus Regional Healthcare System
707 Center Street, Suite 400
Columbus, GA 31901
Phone: 706-660-6101
Fax: 706-660-6520
www.columbusregional.com

Columbus State University
4225 University Avenue
Columbus, GA 31907-5645
Phone: 706-568-2001
www.colstate.edu

Columbus Water Works
1421 Veterans Parkway
Columbus, GA 31901
Phone: 706-649-3400
Fax: 706-327-3845
E-Mail: mailbox@cwwga.org
www.cwwga.org

Commission on International Relations
and Cultural Liaison Encounters (CIRCLE)
Post Office Box 1340
Columbus, GA 31902-1340
Phone: 706-653-4712
Fax: 706-653-4970

David Rothschild Company, Inc.
512 12th Street
Columbus, GA 31901
Phone: 706-324-2411
Fax: 706-324-3947
E-Mail: drothco@gnat.net

Diaz-Verson Capital Investments, L.L.C.
1200 Brookstone Centre Parkway, Suite 105
Columbus, GA 31904
Phone: 706-660-1150
Fax: 706-660-1215

Dolly Madison-Interstate Baking Co.
1969 Victory Drive
Columbus, GA 31901
Phone: 706-324-6616
Fax: 706-322-3388

Dougherty McKinnon & Luby
1017 First Avenue
Columbus, GA 31902
Phone: 706-324-6213
Fax: 706-596-0528

Freeman & Associates, Inc.
1454 54th Street / Post Office Box 4318
Columbus, GA 31904
Phone: 706-324-4227
Fax: 706-324-3417
E-Mail: freemanassoc@compuserve.com

Georgia Power Company
1112 Veteran's Parkway
Post Office Box 1220
Columbus, GA 31902-1220
Phone: 706-321-3555
Fax: 706-321-3506
E-Mail: rjwatkin@southernco.com

Greater Columbus Chamber of Commerce
Post Office Box 1200
Columbus, GA 31902-1200
Phone: 706-327-1566
Fax: 706-327-7512

The Hardaway Company
945 Broadway /Post Office Box 1360
Columbus, GA 31902
Phone: 706-322-3274
Fax: 706-322-7856
E-Mail: mlampton2@standaedconcrete.org
www.hardawaycompany.com

Historic Columbus Hilton
800 Front Avenue
Columbus, GA 31905
Phone: 706-324-1800
Fax: 706-327-8042
E-Mail: csgchhf@aol.com

Holiday Inn Center City
1325 Veterans Parkway
Columbus, GA 31901
Phone: 706-322-2522, 706-327-9925
Fax: 706-322-9059
E-Mail: colhospit@mbusq.net
www.holiday-inn.com

The Hughston Clinic, P.C.
6262 Veterans Parkway
Post Office Box 9517
Columbus, GA 31908-9517
Phone: 706-324-6661
Fax: 706-576-3247
www.hughston.com

Hughston Sports Medicine Foundation, Inc.
6262 Veterans Parkway
Post Office Box 7457
Columbus, GA 31908-7457
Phone: 706-576-3380
Fax: 706-576-3379
www.hughston.com

Hughston Sports Medicine Hospital
100 First Court
Post Office Box 7188
Columbus, GA 31908-7188
Phone: 706-576-2100
Fax: 706-576-2130
www.hughstonsports.com

Industrial Metal Fabricators
7007 Flat Rock Road, P.O. Box 7066
Columbus, GA 31908
Phone: 706-561-1415
Fax: 706-561-4051
E-Mail: sales@industrialmetal.com
www.industrialmetal.com

Johnston Industries, Inc.
105 Thirteenth Street
Columbus, GA 31901
Phone: 706-641-3140
Fax: 706-641-3159
E-Mail: murrayjii@mindspring.com
www.johnstonind.com

The Jordan Company
6001 River Road, Suite 100
Columbus, GA 31904
Phone: 706-649-3000
Fax: 706-649-3017
www.prujordan.com

Kodak Polychrome Graphics
One Polychrome Park
Corporate Ridge Industrial Park
Phone: 706-568-8000
www.kpgraphics.com

Kysor//Warren
Plant #2
5201 Transport Boulevard
Columbus, GA 31907
Phone: 706-568-1514
Fax: 706-568-8990
Plant #4
#5 Mutec Drive
Columbus, GA 31907
Phone: 706-565-9113
Fax: 706-565-1723

Litho-Krome
1323 11th Avenue
Columbus, GA 31902-0988
Phone: 706-660-6700
Fax: 706-660-6725

Matsushita Battery Industrial Corp. of
    America
One Mutec Drive
Columbus, GA 31907
Phone: 706-561-0800

Meacham, Earley & Jones, P.C.
5704 Veterans Parkway
Columbus, GA 31904
Phone: 706-576-4064
Fax: 706-596-0621
E-Mail: meacham-earley@msn.com

Mead Coated Board
1000 Broad Street
Phenix City, AL 36867-5920
Phone: 334-448-6387
Fax: 334-448-6478

Miramar Securities, Inc.
1200 Brookstone Centre Parkway,
Suite 105
Columbus, GA 31904
Phone: 706-660-0064

Page, Scrantom, Sprouse, Tucker & Ford, P.C.
1043 Third Avenue
Columbus, GA 31901
Phone: 706-324-0251
Fax: 706-323-7519
E-Mail: psstf@psstf.com

The Pastoral Institute
2022 15th Avenue
Columbus, GA 31901
Phone: 706-649-6500
Fax: 706-649-6338
E-Mail: admin@pastorealinstitute.org
www.pastoralinstitute.org

Peachtree Mall
3131 Manchester Expressway, Suite 5
Columbus, GA 31909
Phone: 706-327-1578
Fax: 706-327-8715
E-Mail: peachtreemall@msn.com

Phillips Construction Company, Inc.
5201 Hamilton Road
Columbus, GA 31904
Phone: 706-324-7758
Fax: 706-327-5873
www.phillipsconstruction.com

Prudential Jordan Real Estate
6001 River Road
Columbus, GA 31904
Phone: 706-649-3006
Fax: 706-320-9085
www.prujordan.com

Reaves Wrecking Company, Inc.
701 10th Street
Phone: 706-322-8923
Fax: 706-322-1182
E-Mail: reaveswrecking@mindspring.com
www.reaveswrecking.com

Regions Bank
Post Office Box 1377
Columbus, GA 31901
Phone: 706-660-3778
Fax: 706-660-3791
www.regionsbank.com

Rehabilitation Services of Columbus, Inc.
6298 Veterans Parkway, Suite 5A
Post Office Box 8068
Columbus, GA 31908-8068
Phone:706-322-7762
1-888-343-2205
Fax: 706-327-6157
www.rsoc.com

RiverCenter for the Performing Arts
Post Office Box 2425
Columbus, GA 31902
Phone: 706-653-7993
Fax: 706-653-8664
E-Mail: jbaudoin@leo.infi.net
www.riverarts.net

River City Orthopaedics
1900 10th Avenue, Suite 320
Columbus, GA 31901
Phone: 706-653-6635
Fax: 706-653-8543

Robinson, Grimes & Company, P.C.
5637 Whitesville Road / Post Office Box 4299
Columbus, GA 31904
Phone: 706-324-5435
Fax: 706-324-1209
E-Mail: mail@robinsongrimes.com
www.robinsongrimes.com

Royal Crown Cola Company
1000 Tenth Avenue
Columbus, GA 31906
Phone: 706-571-6283
Fax: 706-571-6339

St. Francis Hospital
2122 Manchester Expressway
Columbus, GA 31904
Phone: 706-596-4000
Fax: 706-596-4017
www.sfhga.com
SouthTrust Bank
Post Office Box 9047
Columbus, GA 31908
Phone: 706-571-7300
Fax: 706-320-5425
www.southtrust.com

SunTrust Bank
1246 First Avenue
Columbus, GA 31901
Phone: 706-649-3600
Fax: 706-649-3757
www.suntrust.com

Swift Denim
Post Office Box 1400
Columbus, GA 31902
Phone: 706-324-3623
Fax: 706-571-7544

Synovus Financial Corp.
Post Office Box 120
Columbus, GA 31902
Phone: 706-649-2311
Fax: 706-641-6555
www.synovus.com

TIC Federal Credit Union
Post Office Box 52236
Fort Benning, GA 31995
Phone: 706-320-8500
Fax: 706-320-8540

Tom's Foods Inc.
900 8th Street
Columbus, GA 31902
Phone: 706-323-2721
Fax: 706-660-8248

West Chattahoochee Development Council
1107 Braod Street / Post Office Box 3631
Phone: 334-291-1270
Fax: 334-291-1154
E-Mail: phenixed@idi.net

Weyerhaeuser Containerboard Packaging
4847 Cargo Drive
Columbus, GA 31908
Phone: 706-568-0050
Fax: 706-569-7128

Willcox-Lumpkin Co.
200-13th Street
Columbus, GA 31901
Phone: 706-323-3613
Fax: 706-322-1650

J. H. Williams-A Division of Snap-On
6969 Jamesson Road
Columbus, GA 31906
Phone: 706-563-9590
Fax: 706-568-8178

Index

Abbo of Fleury, 156, 185

AFLAC Incorporated, 103, 124

Alabama Bar & Grill, 174

Allen, Mayor J. R., 104, 110

American Red Cross, 65, 73, 75

American Revolution, 33-34

Archaic Indians, 30, 32

Armstrong, Louis, 71

Ascot Ball, 112

Ashburn, George W., 42

Atlanta Committee for Olympic Games (ACOG), 159, 161

Bartran, William, 33

Beacon College, 178

Benning, Henry Lewis, 38, 68-69

Betjeman, John A., 65-66, 68

Black, Tom, 170

Blue Cross and Blue Shield of Georgia, 86-87

Booth, John Wilkes, 39

Boston Braves, 68

Bradley, W. C. Memorial Library, 75

Bradley, William Clark, 63

Bradley-Turner Foundation, 167, 182

Brown, Dr. Frank, 167

Browne, Rhodes, 63

Buick Challenge, 110-111

Bussey, Arthur, 68, 71

Cabrera, Governor Don Juan de, 32

Callaway Gardens, 79, 111-113

Callaway, Cab, 71

Camp Benning, 68-69

Cargill, J. Ralston, 66

Carnegie Library, 63, 165

Carolingian dynasty, 156

Cavazza, Carmen, 17

Cessna Columbus, 146

Chase Conservatory, 63

Chattahoochee River, 9, 14, 28, 32-33, 36, 38-39, 45, 62, 65, 96-97, 104, 154-155, 163-164, 171

Chesterfield's, 174

Chief Little Prince, 34

City Market, 63

City Mills, The 36, 39

Civic Center, 9, 13, 17, 147-148, 159, 165, 182

Civil War, 38-39, 44, 74, 104, 147-148, 170-171, 184

Coca-Cola Space Science Center, 17, 20, 38, 50, 138, 147-148, 170-171, 182, 184

Columbus Challenge, 167, 170, 182

Columbus College, 100, 138

Columbus Consolidated Government's Parks and Recreation Department, 161

Columbus Convention and Visitors Bureau, 14, 20, 147

Columbus Enquirer, 36-37

Columbus Foundry, 54

Columbus Georgia Chamber of Commerce, 50-51, 76

Columbus Iron Works, 54, 104, 147

Columbus Jazz Band, 112

Columbus Little Theatre, 100

Columbus Museum, 27-28, 30, 32, 64, 100, 127, 147, 167, 170, 172

Columbus Paper Company, 94

Columbus Regional Healthcare, 46

Columbus Regional Mathematics Collaborative, 17

Columbus Square, 98

Columbus State University, 9, 17, 20-21, 40-41, 138, 166, 169, 177, 182, 184

Columbus Symphony Orchestra, 100, 127, 166, 170-171, 182

Columbus Water Works, 80-81, 138, 163

Commission International Relations and Cultural Liaison Encounters, 9, 178-179

Company D, 64

Confederate Naval museum, 104

Confederate Naval Yard, 38

Conservation Kitchen, 65

Consolidated Government, 48, 82, 110, 161, 165, 167, 176-177

Cooper Creek Park, 17

Cottonmouth Hockey team, 17, 163

Coweta Falls Factory, 37

Crawford, Henry B., 66

Crawford, Martin J., 38

Creeks, 32-34, 37, 80

Cross Country Plaza, The 98

Daniel's, A.B., 63

Davis, Jefferson, 38

Dedwylder, Rozier, 167

Diaz Verson Capital Investments, Inc. 176

Dimon, J. Homer, 64-65

Dolly Madison-Interstate Baking Co., 139

Dougherty McKinnon & Luby, 182

Dowling, Ray, 106

Dreyspool's, Mrs., 63

Eagle Mill, 37, 40

Eames, Colonel Henry E., 66, 68

Earhart, Amelia, 69

Ellington, Duke, 71

ESPN, 162

Estates, The, 165

Federal Communications Commission (FCC), 74

First Baptist Church, 159

First Presbyterian Church, 160

Flournoy, Reynolds, 68

Floyd, General John, 33

Fort Mitchell, 32, 34

Fort Sill, 68

Fort, T. Hicks, 65

Fox Sports South, 162

Freeman & Associates, Inc., 149

Georgia Power Company, 58, 91, 165

Georgia Pride Women's Fast-Pitch softball team, 163

Glenn, Wilbur, 106

Godwin, John, 36-37

Golden Park, 147-148, 165

Gordon, Frederick B., 63
Great Depression, 69, 71
Greater Columbus Committee, 75
Green Island Invitational Tournament, 110
Gunby Jordan, 63, 65, 83, 106, 110, 182
Halley's Comet, 156
Hardaway Company, Inc., The, 58
Harrell, W. E., 106
Heard, Captain W. E., 65
Heritage Park, 38-39, 102, 171
Historic Columbus Foundation, 170-171
Historic Columbus Hilton, 148
Holiday Inn—Center City, 179
Holy Family Catholic Church, 160
Horne, Lena, 71
Howard Manufacturing Company, 37
Hughston Clinic, P.C., The, 120, 123
Hughston Sports Medicine Foundation, 120, 122-123
Hughston Sports Medicine Hospital, 122
Hydrick, Bobby D., 106
ICAPP, 17
Illges, A., 63
Illges, Captain John P., 65
Industrial High School, 63
Industrial Metal Fabricators, 136
Infantry School of Arms, 66
Intellectual Capital Partnership Program, 17, 138
Iron Works Trade and Convention Center, 110-111
Israel, 84, 158-159
Iverson, Alfred, 38
J. H. Williams-A division of Snap-on, 143
Jackson, M. F., 106
Jambon, Harold, 106
Johnston Industries, Inc., 128
Jones, Major J. Paul, 66
Jones, Seaborn, 36, 39
Jordan Company, The, 66, 82/Prudential Jordan Real Estate, 66, 82-83, 131
Jordan, G. Gunby, 63, 65, 83, 106
Key, James B., 65
Kitchen, Gordon H., 106
Knox, Wyck, 159
Kodak Polychrome Graphics, 50, 134-135, 165
Kunze, Albert F., 65
Kyle, James P., 63
Kysor/Warren, 150
Lafayette, Marquis de, 34
Lamar, Mirabeau Buonaparte, 36-37
Land, Bruce, 106
Layfield, Martelle, Jr., 106
Ledger-Enquirer, 11, 37, 71, 184
Lee, Ben, 63
Liberty Bond, 65
Liberty Theater, 71, 170-171
Litho-Krome, 93
Lower Creeks, 32
Lummus, Ezra Frank, 64
Lumpkin, Mrs. Frank G., 65

Martin, Mayor Frank, 159
Martin, Roy E., 71
Masters of the Renaissance, 14
Matheos, Lieutenant Antonio, 32-33
Matsushita Battery Industrial Corpl of America, 132-133
Mayer, Dr. E.H., 63
McClatchey, Homer R., 65
McKnight, Rick, 167
McLaughlin, Judge C. F., 65
Meachum, Early & Jones, P.C., 151
Mead Coated Board, 126-127, 130
Memorial Stadium, 74, 147, 165
Memorial Stadium, 74, 147, 165
Miller, Governor Zell, 166
Miller, J.T., 66
Miramar Securities, 175
Mitchell, Governor David, 33
Morton, Marshall, 65
Morton, Mrs. Marshall, 65
Moses, Raphael, 38
Mott House, 165
Mott, Colonel R.L., 38
Mound Builder civilization, 32
Municipal Airport, 69, 95
Murrah, Nolan, 106
Muscogee County Courthouse, 63-64
Muscogee County School District, 51, 106, 110, 165
Muscogee Salvage Committee, 73
Muskogean-speakers, 32
National Association of Intercollegiate Athletics (NAIA), 162
NCAA, 162
Nett, Colonel R., 163
New Deal, 72
Odum, George, 36
Oglethorpe, General James Edward, 33
Olympics, 125, 130-131, 161-162, 176
Otto III, 156
Owen-Brennan, 174
Oxbow Meadows Environmental Learning Center, 17, 21, 50, 138
Page, Scrantom, Sprouse, Tucker & Ford, P.C. 88,
Paleo Indians, 28
Pastoral Institute, The, 141
Patterson, Robert, 106
Payne, Billy, 159, 161
Peace Society, The, 39, 184
Peachtree Mall, 98, 116, 119, 142
Pemberton, John, 147, 171-172
Pershing, General John J., 66
Peters, Mayor Bobby, 9, 17, 167
Phillips Construction Company, Inc., 145
Pleistocene Epoch, 30
Ponce De Leon, 32
Pope Sylvester II, 156
Port Columbus National Museum of Civil War Naval History, 168-171
Professional Golf Association (PGA), 110
Profumo, F. X., 63
Prudential Jordan Real Estate, 83